Dynamics of Virtual Work

Series Editors
Ursula Huws
Hertfordshire Business School
University of Hertfordshire
Hatfield, UK

Rosalind Gill
Department of Sociology
City, University of London
London, UK

Technological change has transformed where people work, when and how. Digitisation of information has altered labour processes out of all recognition whilst telecommunications have enabled jobs to be relocated globally. ICTs have also enabled the creation of entirely new types of 'digital' or 'virtual' labour, both paid and unpaid, shifting the borderline between 'play' and 'work' and creating new types of unpaid labour connected with the consumption and co-creation of goods and services. This affects private life as well as transforming the nature of work and people experience the impacts differently depending on their gender, their age, where they live and what work they do. Aspects of these changes have been studied separately by many different academic experts however up till now a cohesive overarching analytical framework has been lacking. Drawing on a major, high-profile COST Action (European Cooperation in Science and Technology) Dynamics of Virtual Work, this series will bring together leading international experts from a wide range of disciplines including political economy, labour sociology, economic geography, communications studies, technology, gender studies, social psychology, organisation studies, industrial relations and development studies to explore the transformation of work and labour in the Internet Age. The series will allow researchers to speak across disciplinary boundaries, national borders, theoretical and political vocabularies, and different languages to understand and make sense of contemporary transformations in work and social life more broadly. The book series will build on and extend this, offering a new, important and intellectually exciting intervention into debates about work and labour, social theory, digital culture, gender, class, globalisation and economic, social and political change.

More information about this series at
http://www.palgrave.com/gp/series/14954

Sidonie Naulin • Anne Jourdain
Editors

The Social Meaning of Extra Money

Capitalism and the Commodification of Domestic and Leisure Activities

palgrave
macmillan

Editors
Sidonie Naulin
Université Grenoble Alpes, CNRS
Sciences Po Grenoble, PACTE
Grenoble, France

Anne Jourdain
Paris-Dauphine University
PSL Research University, CNRS, IRISSO
Paris, France

Dynamics of Virtual Work
ISBN 978-3-030-18296-0   ISBN 978-3-030-18297-7   (eBook)
https://doi.org/10.1007/978-3-030-18297-7

© The Editor(s) (if applicable) and The Author(s), under exclusive licence to Springer Nature Switzerland AG 2020

This work is subject to copyright. All rights are solely and exclusively licensed by the Publisher, whether the whole or part of the material is concerned, specifically the rights of translation, reprinting, reuse of illustrations, recitation, broadcasting, reproduction on microfilms or in any other physical way, and transmission or information storage and retrieval, electronic adaptation, computer software, or by similar or dissimilar methodology now known or hereafter developed.

The use of general descriptive names, registered names, trademarks, service marks, etc. in this publication does not imply, even in the absence of a specific statement, that such names are exempt from the relevant protective laws and regulations and therefore free for general use.

The publisher, the authors and the editors are safe to assume that the advice and information in this book are believed to be true and accurate at the date of publication. Neither the publisher nor the authors or the editors give a warranty, express or implied, with respect to the material contained herein or for any errors or omissions that may have been made. The publisher remains neutral with regard to jurisdictional claims in published maps and institutional affiliations.

Cover illustration: © Adrienne Bresnahan / Getty Images

This Palgrave Macmillan imprint is published by the registered company Springer Nature Switzerland AG
The registered company address is: Gewerbestrasse 11, 6330 Cham, Switzerland

Foreword

This ground-breaking book shines a welcome light on an issue that has up to now been very much neglected in sociological scholarship: the way in which everyday practices provide the raw material for new economic activities through commodification and marketization. In doing so it does not just open up for serious consideration economic activities that are often dismissed as trivial, but also illuminates the very dynamics of how capitalism develops: generating new forms of value from small, unobserved phenomena which, as time goes by, become the basis for important new occupations and industries.

These processes have begun to be theorized by feminist political economists, but this book goes beyond this: it actually observes them in a nuanced bottom-up way. In an approach that brings together both class and gender analysis, and hence draws both on mainstream sociological and feminist theory, the book goes beyond these theoretical insights, peering into the cracks between work and leisure through a qualitative lens.

In detailed ethnographic case studies, using examples as varied as selling personal belongings online, sexcamming, blogging, selling home-made food and craft objects and providing private tutoring, it explores the social meaning of the 'extra money' that is so generated. In doing so, it reveals major differences between people of different social classes, genders, and migration statuses.

While avoiding technological determinism, it highlights the role of digital technologies, and especially the Internet, in expanding and bringing to visibility these new forms of marketization and commodification. The book thus makes an important contribution to technology studies, in particular the expanding field of digital labour studies, as well as to sociological and feminist scholarship. It seems destined to become a classic that will be consulted for many years to come.

University of Hertfordshire, Hatfield, UK   Ursula Huws

Acknowledgements

The source of inspiration for this collection sprang from the editors' frequent discussions on the subject, starting back in 2015. The idea took shape at two annual conferences of the Society for the Advancement of Socio-Economics (SASE) in Berkeley (2016) and Lyon (2017), and at regular workshops with the contributors. We would like to thank all the participants in the Marketization of Everyday Life stream at the SASE conferences and especially those who have contributed to this book.

In addition to the book's contributors, we would like to acknowledge the support of a number of academic institutions. We thank the Independent Social Research Foundation; the French National Research Agency's "Investissements d'Avenir" program (ANR-15-IDEX-02) whose University Grenoble-Alpes Strategic Research Initiative (IRS 2017-MATRACA) and University Grenoble-Alpes Data Institute contributed to funding this research; the Maison des Sciences de l'Homme (MSH) Paris Nord; Paris-Dauphine University (IRISSO); and Sciences Po Grenoble (PACTE).

We would also like to convey our thanks to Diane Bertrand for her proof-reading of most of this book.

We are equally grateful to Ursula Huws and Rosalind Gill, the editors of the Dynamics of Virtual Work series in which this collection is published. Our thanks also go to the editorial team at Palgrave Macmillan.

Contents

1 Introduction: The Marketization of Everyday Life   1
Anne Jourdain and Sidonie Naulin

Part I   Pin Money   31

2 Commodifying Leisure and Improving Its Social Value: Knitters' Conspicuous Production on Ravelry.com   33
Vinciane Zabban

3 Making Money Out of Leisure: The Marketization of Handicrafts and Food Blogging   61
Anne Jourdain and Sidonie Naulin

4 Selling Second-Hand Items on the Web: New Skills for Everyone?   97
Adrien Bailly, Renaud Garcia-Bardidia, and Coralie Lallemand

Part II Savings 119

5 Comorian Women at Work: Juggling Insecure Jobs with the Transnational Suitcase Trade 121
Abdoul-Malik Ahmad

6 Domesticity as Value: The Commodification of Foodstuffs in Precarious Rural Russia 151
Glenn Mainguy

7 Nonstandard Working Hours and Economic Use of Free Time in the Upper Class: The Gender Gap 183
Anne Lambert

Part III Low Labor Income 209

8 Performing Amateurism: A Study of Camgirls' Work 211
Pierre Brasseur and Jean Finez

9 Making Money from TV Series: From Viewer to Webmaster with Financial Rewards 239
Anne-Sophie Béliard

Having or Blurring It All? Capitalism's Work at the Frontier 269

Index 275

Notes on Contributors

Abdoul-Malik Ahmad is a PhD student at Aix-Marseille University and at LEST (The Institute of Labour Economics and Industrial Sociology) (France). He is writing a dissertation entitled "Agency and strategies of 'the weakest': Comorian women in the suitcase trade". His research fields are economic sociology, the sociology of work and migration studies, with specific focuses on women agency.

Adrien Bailly teaches organizational theory at the Lorraine University (France) and is a PhD candidate at CEREFIGE (Centre Européen de Recherche en Economie Financière et en Gestion des Entreprises). He studies consumption and consumer resistance in the platform economy. He recently published "Renforcement et transgression du cadre de l'intermédiation numérique: le cas de l'accès de pair à pair" for the French interdisciplinary journal *Réseaux* (2018).

Anne-Sophie Béliard is Associate Professor in sociology at the University Grenoble-Alpes (France) and a researcher at PACTE (public policies, political action, territories). Her research fields are media sociology and web studies. She specializes in the study of TV series. Her current research topics cover digital practices, careers of amateurs and professionalization processes. She recently published *S'il-te-plaît, dessine-moi une série. Contributions en ligne et séries télévisées* (2016).

Pierre Brasseur is Research Associate at PACTE (public policies, political action, territories) (France). He co-chairs the Sexuality section of the French Sociological Association (AFS). His research interest lies at the intersection of disability studies, sociology of sexuality and sociology of work, with specific focus on sex work (sexual surrogates, sex camming and drag queens). He recently co-directed a special issue of the French revue *Genre, sexualité et société* about disability studies (2018).

Jean Finez is Associate Professor at the University Grenoble Alpes and a research fellow at PACTE (public policies, political action, territories) (France). His research fields are economic sociology, sociology of organizations and historical sociology. In 2015, he defended a PhD thesis on the evolution of the French railway market from the nineteenth century to today. He recently wrote "Ticket pricing by the French national railway company (SNCF), a historical sociology of tariff setting" (*Revue française de sociologie*—English edition, 2014). He is working in the online pornography industry.

Renaud Garcia-Bardidia is Professor at the University of Rouen Normandie (France) and a researcher at NIMEC (Normandie Innovation Marché Entreprise Consommation). He is a member of the "Sociology of Consumption and Digital Uses" of the AFS. His research fields are sociology of consumption with specific focus on internet uses and the way they transform cultural consumption.

Anne Jourdain is Associate Professor at the Paris-Dauphine University and a researcher at IRISSO (Interdisciplinary Research Institute in Social Sciences) (France). She co-chairs the "Digital Economy" network in the Society for the Advancement of Socio-Economics (SASE) and the "Economic Sociology" section of the AFS. Her research fields are economic sociology, sociology of work and sociology of art, with specific focuses on arts and crafts and on the digital platform Etsy. She recently wrote *Du Cœur à l'ouvrage. Les artisans d'art en France* (2014), and "Analysing the Symbolic Economy with Pierre Bourdieu: The World of Crafts" (*Forum for Social Economics*, 2015).

Coralie Lallemand is a PhD candidate at NIMEC (University of Rouen Normandy, France). She teaches marketing courses and studies consumption and gender through the lens of appropriation, exclusion and with relation to markets.

Anne Lambert is a researcher at the National Institute for Demographic Studies (INED, France) and co-chairs the "Mobility, Housing and Social Network" unit of research. Her research field includes non-standard work schedules, family organization and gender inequalities. Her previous work includes "Travail salarié, travail domestique, travail au noir: L'économie domestique à l'épreuve de l'accession à la propriété en lotissement périurbain" which received first prize from *Sociologie du travail* (2012).

Glenn Mainguy is Postdoctoral Researcher at Sciences Po Bordeaux (France) and research fellow at CED (Center Emile Durkheim). His research lies at the intersection of economic sociology, lower class sociology, sociology of work and rural sociology. He recently wrote "Figures du précariat rural. Support et capacités d'agir des individus précaires dans la société rurale russe" (*Nouvelles pratiques sociales*, 2018).

Sidonie Naulin is Associate Professor of Sociology at Sciences Po Grenoble (France) researcher at PACTE (public policies, political action, territories). She co-chairs the "Digital Economy" network of the SASE and the "Economic Sociology" section of the AFS. Her research interest lies at the intersection of economic sociology, digital sociology, media studies and food studies. She recently wrote *La Solidarité à distance. Quand le don passe par les organisations* (2016) with Philippe Steiner, and *Des mots à la bouche. Le journalisme gastronomique en France* (2017).

Vinciane Zabban is Associate Professor at Paris 13 University (France), and a research fellow at EXPERICE (Experience Cultural Resources Education) research centre. She co-chairs the "Consumption and Digital Sociology" section of the AFS. Her research interest lies at the intersection of science and technical studies, game and leisure studies and economic sociology. She is leading the research project TETRIS

(Territories and professional Trajectories in the French video game industry), funded by the LabEx ICCA (Artistic Creation and Cultural Industries).

List of Figures

Fig. 3.1	Cumulative distribution of sales among Etsy sellers	76
Fig. 3.2	Number of daily readers among food bloggers	77
Fig. 6.1	Коровник—*korovnik*—dairy cow barns, 24 April 2014, Совхоз Родина (*Sovkhoz Rodina*), Letunovo, Russia	157
Fig. 6.2	Part of Sacha and Marina's sheep, 26 April 2014, Astapovo, Russia	160
Fig. 6.3	Sacha and Marina's vegetable plot behind their house, 19 July 2014, Astapovo, Russia	160
Fig. 6.4	Babushka walking to a bus stop from the village of Tumenskoe to go shopping, because the village shop has closed down, February 2013, Tumenskoe, Russia	166
Fig. 6.5	Kolla and Natalia's house and wooden sign "Молоко Козье," 24 April 2014, Letunovo, Russia	167
Fig. 7.1	The new part-time work schedules	190

List of Tables

Table 2.1	The interviewees mentioned in the chapter	56
Table 3.1	The interviewees mentioned in the chapter	92
Table 4.1	The interviewees mentioned in the chapter	116
Table 5.1	The interviewees mentioned in the chapter	146
Table 6.1	The interviewees mentioned in the chapter	179
Table 7.1	Full- and part-time work by PNT (left) and PNC (right) in 2014 (%)	188
Table 7.2	The interviewees mentioned in the chapter	205
Table 8.1	The interviewees mentioned in the chapter	233
Table 9.1	The interviewees mentioned in the chapter	265

1

Introduction: The Marketization of Everyday Life

Anne Jourdain and Sidonie Naulin

1 Capitalism and the Commodification of Domestic and Leisure Activities

Thomas, a 25-year-old unemployed musician, buys and sells secondhand guitars locally on a web platform.[1] Elisabeth, aged 42, quit her job as an IT engineer to sell home-sewn items on her online Etsy shop and to take care of her young children. Delphine, a 30-year-old middle class civil servant earns freebies and money from advertising and partnerships with food brands thanks to her food blog. Deborah, aged 22, pays her rent from her paid activity as a camgirl performing erotic and pornographic online shows from home. Kolia, a 55-year-old intermittent low-skilled

A. Jourdain
Paris-Dauphine University, PSL Research University, CNRS, IRISSO, Paris, France
e-mail: Anne.jourdain@dauphine.psl.eu

S. Naulin (✉)
Université Grenoble Alpes, CNRS, Sciences Po Grenoble, PACTE, Grenoble, France
e-mail: Sidonie.naulin@iepg.fr

© The Author(s) 2020
S. Naulin, A. Jourdain (eds.), *The Social Meaning of Extra Money*, Dynamics of Virtual Work, https://doi.org/10.1007/978-3-030-18297-7_1

worker, and his 60-year-old pensioner wife Natalia sell their household-farm produce to supplement Natalia's pension.

All these individuals commodify their personal belongings or the products of their domestic and leisure activities. This book explores the marketization of practices previously considered to be recreational or domestic, such as blogging, cooking, craftwork, gardening, knitting, selling secondhand items, sexcamming, and, more generally, the economic use of free time.

Market expansion into areas not previously commodified is a long-standing phenomenon (Polanyi 1944) which creates new professions. For example, care workers are professionals who live off the commodification of traditionally free domestic activities. Similarly, artists and sportsmen make a living from the commodification of leisure activities. This book addresses the expansion of capitalism into domestic and leisure realms with a focus on the non-professional side of these markets.

Why are ordinary people who used to engage in domestic and leisure activities for free now trying to make a profit from them? How and why do people commodify their free time? Commodification and marketization are considered as synonymous here. These terms refer to taking an unpaid activity conducted in an individual's free time, and transforming it into a market product with a price tag. People who set out to make money from activities previously considered outside of the realm of paid work are not necessarily looking to "professionalize" their domestic or leisure activity or try to make a living from it. This then lends different meanings to the "extra money" generated by the commodification process.

"Extra money" can mean "pin money" to middle- and upper-class individuals with additional sources of income, who are just looking to finance the cost of their domestic or leisure activity. "Extra money" can also be seen as "savings" by people who commodify domestic and leisure activities as a form of "side job." This applies to people from the lower classes struggling to make ends meet, but also to middle- and upper-class workers anticipating a drop in income and wanting to maintain their social status by developing a side job. Lastly, "extra money" can also refer to the income from a main activity in the process of being professionalized. These distinct meanings of "extra money," which echo the "social meaning of money" depicted by V. Zelizer (1997), correspond to different amounts of money and different types of commitment to commodification. Meaning varies by the social class and gender of the people who commodify their domestic and leisure activities. The particular focus in this book is on gendered and/or popular domestic and leisure activities. There tends to be a lack of academic studies on these activities, which are seen as trivial and demeaning. Our aim is to show that commodification pervades even the most mundane social activities and that it takes on different meanings depending on the individuals' social characteristics and life histories.

1.1 Market Expansion

Two competing sets of theories analyze the overall social effect of commodification. On the one hand, some theories condemn the "moral contamination" of growing commodification in social relations. These belong to what V. Zelizer calls the "hostile worlds" theories based on the idea that "Such a profound contradiction exists between intimate social relations and monetary transfers that any contact between the two spheres inevitably leads to moral contamination and degradation" (Zelizer 2000: 817). This common assumption is shared by Marxist theory of "commodity fetishism" (Marx 1992), the Frankfurt School's criticism of the global commodification of culture (Horkheimer and Adorno 2002), anthropological thinking on commoditization versus singularization (Appadurai 1986; Kopytoff 1986), and even social theories observing a disconnect between profit-maximizing large-scale production and pure production based on the rejection of the economy (Bourdieu 1980, 1996). Applied to the case of the marketization of domestic and leisure activities, these theories see commodification as a form of "denaturing" everyday activities. Rather than conducting domestic and leisure activities for themselves, they are seen in an instrumental light as work to meet the needs of customers outside the domestic sphere. This consequently changes their meaning for the people conducting them. On the other hand, another body of theories points to the positive social impact of marketization. Economic theories see commodification as positive for consumers, since it helps consumers make choices by displaying prices that capture the quality of the goods

(Spence 1974). Commodification is also positive for producers. It can economically empower subordinate social groups, especially women, by means of the commodification of their activity. Feminist scholars have long argued that access to the labor market releases women from the household burden and their subaltern position (Delphy 1977). Putting a price on domestic work and traditional feminine leisure is said to secure social recognition of their "invisible work" (Kaplan Daniels 1987) and potentially access to welfare. It is also argued that it empowers women and low-skilled individuals by granting them access to their own earnings. From these angles, marketization is considered as a form of valuation, both for the products and the producers, and both economically and symbolically. This book draws on these different research fields to answer the empirical question of the economic and social effects of the marketization of everyday life.

Three factors can explain the current shift toward the marketization of domestic and leisure activities by ordinary people. First, the development of digital technologies has lowered the cost of access to markets. Virtually anybody with an Internet connection can now become a market supplier. Digitization of society can thus be considered as an enabling factor for the marketization of domestic and leisure activities. Second, the global economic crisis has driven a move to take advantage of every opportunity to make money, in particular among the job-insecure lower and middle classes. Third, the contemporary values of capitalism and neoliberalism in a post-Fordism era ("be an entrepreneur," "be creative," "be yourself," "achieve a work-life balance," etc.) can also explain the current importance of the marketization of everyday life, in particular among middle-class women. Conversely, it can also explain a growing demand for "homemade" products and services.

1.2 The Role of the Internet

The development of the Internet has made it easier for newcomers to commodify their domestic and leisure activities. Today, 87 percent of European households have an Internet connection.[2] The development of web platforms (Craigslist, eBay, Etsy, etc.) and social media networks

(Facebook, Instagram, Twitter, etc.) has further smoothed the commodification of personal belongings, products, and services. These platforms provide both easy access to virtual showcasing, including for people with relatively low information technology (IT) skills, and a large customer base due the visibility they offer. They reduce search costs and transaction costs, and their network effects are designed to make them profitable for both suppliers and consumers. Web platforms hence contribute to the marketization of domestic and leisure activities. There are two dominant theoretical schools of thought regarding the impact of digital capitalism on markets and labor. The optimistic view argues that the digital economy, more specifically the sharing economy, is empowering for workers (Botsman and Rogers 2011) that it creates new business opportunities and new jobs (especially in the form of self-employment) and consequently fosters economic growth. The pessimistic view, however, protests that the revolution is an illusion and stresses the negative effects of digital capitalism. Web platforms are accused of adding to the weight of financial and market centricity, acting as a new form of exploitation (Huws 2003; Scholz 2012), promoting poor-quality jobs (flexible, fragmented, and low paid) (Ravenelle 2017), sustaining and increasing inequalities between workers (Schor 2018; Casilli 2019), and undermining workers' collective social protection. The question could therefore be put as to how far the marketization of everyday life supports each of these views. Most of the case studies presented in this book concern Internet platforms. In some cases, the activity could not have been commodified without the Internet. Such is the case with the online camgirl shows and blogger activities. In other cases, the Internet acts merely as a facilitator, for example, for people selling their old belongings or homemade arts and crafts. In yet other cases, marketization is mostly independent of the Internet. Such is the case with rural couples who commodify their domestic food production from home. These different situations show that, although the development of information and communication technologies (ICTs) has clearly driven forward commodification, it was also around before the growth of the digital economy and still exists outside of it.

1.3 The Economic Context

Although the commodification of domestic and leisure activities can be explained in part by the new opportunities opened up by the development of ICTs, it can also be linked to the global economic situation. For a decade, the enduring economic crisis has driven a combination of high unemployment rates in Europe and deteriorating employment and working conditions, for low-skilled workers in particular (Méda and Vendramin 2017). This situation can prompt the lower classes to look to any means to try and earn extra income, including the commodification of domestic and leisure activities. Their profile is similar to that of "crowd workers" who "shift constantly between different forms of casual work regardless of whether it is digitally managed" (Huws et al. 2018: 158). Indeed, "Crowd work must […] be regarded as part of a broader spectrum of casual work, carried out, by and large, by the working poor, seeking any form of income they can find" (2018: 156). For people in a more secure situation, making money from their free time may be a way to forestall a future deterioration in their situation in a context where employment security and social protection are at risk. The need to work and earn money may also concern groups of people traditionally excluded from the job market. Students, retirees and stay-at-home mums are indeed encouraged to "be productive." As L. Adkins and M. Dever put it, there is the presumption in today's world that "all adults should be in the labor market or, if not in employment, should be seeking employment actively, indeed, they should be in a permanent state of 'work-readiness'" (Adkins and Dever 2014: 5). This situation might explain the marketization of domestic and leisure activities.

1.4 Commodification in Post-Fordist Societies

The commodification of domestic and leisure activities may finally be encouraged by the development of post-Fordist or neoliberal values such as the social upgrading of the figure of the entrepreneur in contemporary societies. As L. Adkins writes, breaking with the Fordist model of long-term employment, "the figures of the independent contractor and the entrepreneur have emerged as the ideal workers of post-Fordism" (Adkins 2016: 2). Those values would particularly concern the middle and upper class, but also extend to the lower class, as shown by the literature on "subsistence entrepreneurs" (Delacroix et al. 2018; Viswanathan et al. 2010). They are shared by some of our interviewees, especially those who consider commodification as a professional opportunity that gives rise to the creation of a micro-business, sometimes paired with an exit from inactivity, unemployment, or wage labor. From this point of view, commodification alters the forms of employment—and associated social protection—by fostering the development of self-employment. It contributes to the rise in own-account working (International Labour Organization 2015). Whether self-employed or not, commodifiers act as entrepreneurs when they set out to sell their products or services. In effect, they need to become salesmen and saleswomen working for the economic profit of their activity. The book hence explores the "entrepreneurialization" of society through the lens of commodification.

The rhetoric of entrepreneurship is increasingly associated with another narrative regarding creativity and passion, which also fosters the marketization of everyday life. The figures of maker and creative entrepreneur have become new ideals (Taylor and Luckman 2018), especially for women. Self-fulfilling creative jobs are often placed in contrast to "bullshit jobs" in the media (Graeber 2018). In keeping with these ideals, people are encouraged to earn money from their passion, and commodification is even supposed to intensify their passion. This type of rhetoric about passion is common in the art worlds, sports fields, and even political spheres (Le Roux and Loriol 2015). Many scholars have pointed out that it is usually used to justify insecure forms of work and employment (Banks et al. 2013; Mensitieri 2018; Simonet 2015). Insecurity is fostered in part by the associated "normalizing of connections between work and non-work, professional life and formerly personal aspects of people's lives" (Taylor and Luckman 2018: 4). Indeed, creative work consists mostly in emotional and affective labor (Conor et al. 2015; Gill and Pratt 2008; Gregg 2011; Hochschild 1983; Taylor and Luckman 2018), which is based on invisible gendered and domestic skills. For this latter reason—and in keeping with earlier feminist lessons on the invisibility of mostly feminine "domestic work" (Delphy and Leonard 1992; Kaplan Daniels

1987)—this labor has been conceptualized by post-feminist studies as "women's work" (Jarrett 2014) regardless of the worker's gender. The commodification of domestic and leisure activities relies on this emotional and affective labor since it is especially a "commodification of the relational" (Mirchandani 2010), as described in this book. In this sense, the development of commodification contributes to the general "feminization of work," which also comes with the "platformization" of work (Huws et al. 2017; van Doorn 2017): "the feminization of work thesis […] suggests that the working conditions historically experienced principally by women, and by formerly colonized and ethnic minority workers, [i.e. vulnerability, invisibility, availability, flexibility, low wage…] are increasingly representative of all workers' lives" (Webster and Michailidou 2018: 13). This book studies how and why people engage in the commodification of domestic and leisure activities, and hence in the economic recognition of their creative, emotional, and affective labor. Despite the general feminization of work, the social role assigned to women by today's capitalism still differs from that ascribed to men. That is why our examination also draws on the analysis of "the post-Fordist sexual contract" (Adkins and Dever 2016). With the end of Fordism (associated with the family model of the male breadwinner and dependent housewife), the social roles of men and women have been redefined and "middle-class women are now being directly interpellated as entrepreneurial subjects" (Luckman 2016: 91–92). The "post-Fordist sexual contract" (Adkins 2016: 2) has come to articulate new ideals for these women: "domesticity, familism, entrepreneurship, boundless love, heteronormative femininity and intimacy, excessive attachments to work, indebted citizenship and financial literacy" (Adkins 2016: 3). Many women see the commodification of domestic and leisure activities as a means to balance those ideals and gain social recognition. This book examines this aspiration to female empowerment and its social effects.

1.5 The Expansion of Labor

The commodification of domestic and leisure activities—whether on the Internet or elsewhere—contributes to the expansion of labor under today's capitalism. It blurs the boundaries between work and non-work (leisure, domesticity, and free time), leading us to reconsider the nature of work. In recent years, the development of web platforms has been the subject of many academic and media debates on the moving boundaries of work (Flichy 2017), many of them centering on the notion of "digital labor" (Cardon and Casilli 2015; Scholz 2012). Drawing on a Marxist reading grid, this notion defines the creation of digital content and data (on web platforms such as Facebook and Google) as labor since it generates economic value, even when the activity is individually perceived as recreational. Most of this economic value is appropriated by the digital platforms, hence the association of "digital labor" with "free labor" (Terranova 2000). Such debates are particularly stimulating, even though this book focuses mainly on people who are keen to monetize their activity and not on people who are totally unaware of the value they create. The commodification of leisure and domestic activities echoes more traditional debates on the boundaries of work. First, the boundary between amateurs and professionals has long been a point of discussion for the sociology of art and culture and sports sociology (Eitzen 1989; Moulin et al. 1985; Stebbins 2007; Weber and Lamy 1999). This literature is particularly useful to build typologies of commodification commitment, based on income level and the legal status of the activity. Second, the sociology of work has investigated the notions of "non-work" (Godechot et al. 1999; Parker 1965) and "side work" (Weber 1989), helping to conceptualize some logics of commodification and their connections with main occupations. Third, feminist gender studies have largely contributed to the question by labeling as "work" that which was not previously understood as work, that is, women's domestic activities. Referring to the notion of "domestic work," feminists criticized the invisibility and exploitation of women's actions in capitalist, patriarchal societies (Delphy and Leonard 1992; Kaplan Daniels 1987), much the way today's digital scholars view the notion of digital labor (Jarrett 2015; Simonet 2018). This feminist literature helps explore the porous boundary between work and leisure by conceptualizing it as a divide between production and social reproduction. Production work used to be masculine and social reproduction work feminine. The commodification of traditionally feminine and domestic activities such as knitting, crafts, and cookery helps turn reproductive work into productive work. As J. Webster and M. Michailidou put it, "the marketplace has entered traditional sites of reproductive labor, rendering them also arenas of value creation" (2018: 9). This book explores this movement and its social effects. In particular, it looks into the social upgrading that can be expected with the commodification of previously invisible and demeaned feminine activities. More generally, our book sets out to link these separate bodies of literature and the abovementioned socioeconomic literature, since the expansion of the market sphere is connected with the extension of the field of labor. In so doing, our purpose is to shape a fresh approach to the effects of commodification processes on women's and men's activities and lives in contemporary societies.

1.6 An Empirical Approach to the Marketization of Leisure and Domestic Activities

The ambition of this book is to address these theoretical questions by observing the social reality of commodification using sociological methods. Each contribution draws on an extensive field survey covering a number of years and generating rich, original, empirical results. Data are both qualitative and quantitative. They are based on ethnographic observations, semi-structured interviews, quantitative surveys, web scraping, and analysis of documentation and archives. We believe that empirical sociology is necessary to develop well-founded theories, but also to provide implications for public policymakers working on economic and labor regulation.

One of the strengths of this edited book is found in the social variations presented in its eight chapters. The first variation concerns the different kinds of activities that are commodified: knitting, crafts, cookery, blogging, selling personal items, gardening, writing about TV series, and sexcamming. These different activities involve different types of monetization in the form of direct monetary transactions and indirect economic returns generated by the audience secured by the activity (essentially on the Internet) by means of advertising, for example. Academic studies tend to be thin on the ground on many of these activities, seen as trivial and demeaning because they are feminine and/ or popular activities. Gender and social class are precisely two important social variations to an analysis of the different meanings of extra money today.[3] Women from the lower classes who engage in the marketization of their everyday lives are not working with the same logic as middle- and upper-class men who develop a side business. Even though some chapters are more focused on women and others on men, the general purpose is to compare the expectations and experiences of female and male commodification. In keeping with sociological work on digital media industries and platforms (Gill 2008; Gregg 2008), we draw particular attention to the persistence of gender inequalities, even when the commodified activities are traditionally seen as feminine. Moreover, class-related variations appear to be extremely important to understanding the social meanings of extra money. Our case studies are able to examine these variations—since they run the gamut of the lower, middle, and upper classes—and hence analyze the spread of the middle- and upper-class ideals of post-Fordist values—and their limitations—to the lower classes. One major question is whether the commodification of domestic and leisure activities has an empowering effect, or whether it sustains class and gender domination. Lastly, most of the data come from France, but two case studies concern the Comoros and Russia, taking the focus beyond Europe to help understand global capitalist transformations.

2 The Social Meanings of Extra Money

The collective research presents three main results regarding the commodification of domestic and leisure activities in contemporary societies. First, commodification generates small amounts of money which may be perceived as pin money, savings, or labor income. Second, the benefits of commodification are mainly non-economic. Third, commodification is work-intensive and time-consuming, which we propose to conceptualize as "extra work." We discuss these results and their social implications.

2.1 Pin Money, Savings, and Low Labor Income

The extra money generated by the commodification of domestic and leisure activities generally comes in small amounts. Although the media and occasionally academics highlight successful individuals who have managed to earn a living from commodification, especially in the digital economy, those cases represent the "happy few." Our statistical data find that the vast majority have to make do with modest economic benefits. This finding is consistent with other academic results on the gig economy (Huws et al. 2017). Our qualitative data show that the "happy few" are role models for some other committed commodifiers, explaining their commitment, and occasionally frustration, when they do not sell as much as they would have liked. Moreover, the economic profitability of commodification depends on social class and gender. According to quantitative results, the "happy few" are more educated than the rest of the population and, even in feminine activities such as handicrafts and food blogging, men are proportionally more successful than women (Jourdain and Naulin, Chap. 3). Gender analysis shows that women generally enjoy less free time than men because of domestic constraints, and they often choose to commodify less profitable activities (Lambert, Chap. 7). Moreover, this lower profitability of feminine commodified activities can be explained by gender itself: U. Huws shows that "skills that women exercise unpaid in the home […] tend to have a low value in the labour market" (Huws 2018: 3). As a consequence, the social meaning of extra money—no matter how small—differs by social class and gender. Three main commodification logics are differentiated, forming the book's three parts: extra money perceived as pin money, as savings, or as (temporarily low) professional earnings.

Pin money concerns mostly middle- and upper-class individuals who have other sources of income, and especially women in our book. Extra money is seen as a way to supplement income by knitters who spend leisure time on the Ravelry website (Zabban, Chap. 2), creative crafters who enjoy selling their bags, jewelry, and baby clothes on the Etsy web platform after their hours working for large companies, and food bloggers who monetize their audience and services (Jourdain and Naulin, Chap. 3). They do not need the money to live and, at best, reinvest it in their leisure activity, which can be quite expensive, in keeping with a traditional use of pin money (Zelizer 1997). In some cases, especially students with low incomes, this money might be a means to improve their everyday lives.

The lower classes, but also surprisingly middle- and upper-class individuals, may see extra money as economic savings intended to maintain or improve their social situation in a context of uncertainty. For people in insecure situations—unemployment, temporary employment, part-time employment, and, more generally, insecure jobs—the commodification of domestic and leisure activities is usually perceived as an essential "side job" that reduces their insecurity. This logic of commodification has developed with the economic crisis and growing global economic inequalities (Piketty 2014). It is particularly exemplified by the case of female Comorian migrants living in the South of France, in Abdoul-Malik Ahmad's chapter. For these women, trading clothes, shoes, and fashion accessories in their expatriate community is a way to save money in order to upgrade their social status in the long run. Members of the upper class display a similar logic of using commodification for social standing and economic purposes. Anne Lambert, in her chapter, shows how male pilots monetize their free time by means of tax planning and leisure activities that pay (e.g. as flying club instructors) in order to make extra money and to maintain their social status in the long run. She also analyzes the case of male flight attendants who resort to commodification in order to prepare a forthcoming career change, but also to improve their current working conditions by experimenting independence and productive work. More generally, her chapter reminds us that far from being marginal or new, these side job activities may be significant in terms of social and economic returns, and constitute the very essence and the core of the upper-class identity (Bourdieu 1989): "multi-positioning" is part of a dominant and male ethos.

The commodification of domestic and leisure activities can also be part of a professional logic, especially for the middle and upper classes. In this case, marketization is considered as a "main job," and the money earned—irrespective of amount—is seen as professional earnings. Many digital platforms encourage such professional logic: "the sharing or 'gig' economy claims to bring the romance of entrepreneurialism to the masses"

(Ravenelle 2017: 1), and many workers believe in this promise (Jourdain and Naulin, Chap. 3; Brasseur and Finez, Chap. 8). Even though professional commodifiers tend to earn more than others, most of them do not make a living from their activity. They have to rely on outside support such as their partner's wage, their own unemployment benefit or even a subsistence job, and consequently on the traditional labor and employment institutions (Abdelnour 2017). They may be women, like the "mumpreneurs" (Ekinsmyth 2011; Orgad 2019) who quit their salaried job in a large company to build a craft business on Etsy and improve their work-life balance (Jourdain and Naulin, Chap. 3). Or they might be camgirls who invest their time, body, and feelings to make a living from sexcamming (Brasseur and Finez, Chap. 8). They may also be men, such as website managers keen to transform their TV series viewing hobby into an occupation by monetizing their and other fans' passion (Béliard, Chap. 9). As Anne-Sophie Béliard's typology shows, the logics of professionalization differ in one and the same field of commodification (especially depending on the centrality of the passion). The chapters also show that they differ by gender: men and women are not committed to exactly the same values when they set up a business of their own. Female logics are driven much more by family and marital motives than male logics.

2.2 The Non-Economic Benefits of Commodification

Given that the commodification of domestic and leisure activities does not bring in a great deal of money, why do people commodify them instead of just doing them for themselves? The explanation lies in the non-economic benefits of commodification. Commodification rewards are often more symbolic than economic—a statement which is true even for people who rely on their small amounts of money to make ends meet.

Most of the time, the commodification of domestic or leisure activity starts during a hiatus in the work and/or family life cycle, associated with free time (Jourdain and Naulin, Chap. 3; Mainguy, Chap. 6; Brasseur and Finez, Chap. 8; Béliard, Chap. 9). Marketization is seen as a way to experiment a meaningful—at least self-financed—(side) activity. For male flight attendants, sideline activities represent a way to transcend the "superficiality" of their current well-paid job. It helps them endure the negative aspects of their main occupation (unrewarding, low-skilled, routine service job) and also (smooth the way to) prepare for future vocational retraining (Lambert, Chap. 7). In some cases, self-fulfillment goes hand in hand with the defense of values. For example, series viewers seeking to promote the fans' point of view on TV series, as opposed to the professionals' mainstream opinion, build for-profit web platforms for fans to express themselves in order to achieve their political goal (Béliard, Chap. 9). The commodification of a domestic or leisure activity is consequently not always oriented toward monetary gain, or, at least, it is not achieved "at any price." Sometimes, commodifiers prefer to give up a monetary gain when the expected paid work does not correspond to their vision of the domestic or leisure activity (Jourdain and Naulin, Chap. 3; Brasseur and Finez, Chap. 8; Béliard, Chap. 9).

The marketization of everyday life drives a more systematic organization of the domestic or leisure activity and an intensification of its practice. This "commitment" to the activity is reinforced by the emulation generated by market competition and crowd feedback. One of the unexpected rewards of commodification is therefore the development of skills and creativity, which are sometimes reinvested in a professional career (Béliard, Chap. 9). This side effect of commodification partly explains why people carry on with the activity (Jourdain and Naulin, Chap. 3).

More generally, people who commodify their domestic and leisure activities benefit from the pleasure of being part of a community of fellow amateurs (buyers, peers, audience, etc.). Their interactions—in the form of web forums, comments, and direct relationships—are not restricted to economic transactions. Commodification is a way to benefit from the social integration provided by work (Baudelot and Gollac 2003). This is all the more important for people who do not benefit from standard work assimilation (students, job seekers, housewives, sick or disabled persons, retirees, etc.) or whose passion is not shared by the rest of their household. Consequently, marketization fosters socialization.

Feedback and mutual support from the social worlds of commodification also have another implication: they contribute to the social recognition of the commodifiers. But there are other elements that contribute to the social recognition of individuals who commodify their domestic and leisure activities. First, the fact that someone is prepared to pay for their product is in itself a form of reward for their work and skills. Second, marketization gives public visibility to the product of a private activity. This is particularly true for people who digitally showcase their achievements. As Vinciane Zabban puts it, "by transforming and expanding knitting's social scene from the domestic to new areas, the Web and Ravelry platforms are changing the activity's symbolic value" (Chap. 3). Marketization is extending the scope of the activity beyond "intimate transactions" (Zelizer 2001). Digital platforms not only publicly showcase private production but also rank it using web metrics. Third, interactions with customers and peers place commodifying individuals in the rewarding position of an expert. All of this helps legitimize, both publicly and privately, a person who is used to doing an often disregarded domestic or leisure activity. People who commodify their domestic and leisure activities often refer to role models such as the figures of the "entrepreneur" (Jourdain and Naulin, Chap. 3), the "businesswoman" (Ahmad, Chap. 5), and the "manager" (Mainguy, Chap. 6). Commodification is thus often perceived as a form of empowerment. This is particularly true for the most economically and socially dominated. For example, migrant women who live in an economically insecure situation in their host country gain some forms of autonomy from their household on their international business trips (Ahmad, Chap. 5). Similarly, low-skilled unemployed males in post-communist Russia find a new social status and legitimacy in the domestic sphere by commodifying household-farm produce. To their families, even in the absence of formal labor, "They are no longer mere farm workers, but also traders, negotiators, and go-betweens with officials" (Mainguy, Chap. 6).

However, the quest for a better social status within the household by commodifying domestic and leisure activities is not friction free. Access to the symbolic rewards of marketization is often conditional on negotiation with family members (Jourdain and Naulin, Chap. 3). This is a particular problem for mothers whose commodifying activities are seen as an escape from their traditional family duties. Migrant women who go on trips to trade foreign goods in addition to working their main job in their host country find solutions in the form of preparing for their absence by finding people willing to take care of their children during their trip or preparing food in advance (Ahmad, Chap. 5). Marketization is therefore not necessarily a means of subversion of gendered roles. Quite the opposite sometimes occurs, such as when it actually reinforces the traditional gendered division of labor. And this can be the case for both men, like Russian men who can maintain their social role in the household in spite of the loss of formal job (Mainguy, Chap. 6), and women. Concerning women, E. Matchar (2013) has coined "new domesticity" as the current tendency to rebrand traditionally feminine roles as desirable, in particular through the marketization of domestic activities. "New domesticity" questions the coercive or empowering nature of the marketization of domestic activities: do women who engage in such marketization emancipate themselves or do they trap themselves in a traditional limited role? To a certain extent, this echoes the debate surrounding whether the marketization of a woman's body is coercive or empowering (Brasseur and Finez, Chap. 8).

2.3 From Extra Money to Extra Work

The commodification of domestic and leisure activities can be considered as "work." Like work, marketization requires time, economic resources, and skills. The one-time domestic and leisure activities need to be streamlined and disciplined. For example, bloggers plan their posts in advance (Mäkinen 2018; Jourdain and Naulin, Chap. 3), and knitters seeking to showcase their products (patterns) online have to translate them "in a standardized manner in order to fit the database" (Zabban, Chap. 2). In addition, work needs to be put into the context of the commercial aspect of the activity. Commercial work consists in defining market positioning, setting prices, building a "brand" by creating and maintaining a positive reputation, promoting the products, managing interactions with clients, knowing the trade legislation, and so forth. This represents "extra work" compared to the mere activity of producing something for oneself, family, and friends. An important part of this "extra work" in commodification is "digital labor." The case of taking photographs of the products to be sold is particularly significant. With the exception of two cases, all the commodifiers studied in this book need to showcase their products and services online. The ability to take pictures corresponding to the dominant aesthetic in the field would appear to be a powerful way to be ranked as a reliable and efficient seller. People consequently spend a great deal of time scrutinizing their competitors' photographs, taking their own photographs, learning how to take good photographs, purchasing good camera equipment, and so forth. Some respondents refer to their activity as a metaphorical "full-time job." Furthermore, the marketization of everyday life may be perceived by the administrative authorities as "undeclared work" (Bailly, Garcia-Bardidia and Lallemand, Chap. 4), while the work commitment demanded by this side-activity can sometimes transform it into a main occupation (Brasseur and Finez, Chap. 8).

Success in the commodification process appears to be closely associated with the ability to perform the "extra work" of commodification properly. This consequently often depends on having prior skills or on the possibility of relying on friends or family with specific skills. In some cases, marketization is directly related to the commodifiers' main occupation, enabling them to reinvest their professional skills in it. Such is the case with airplane pilots who become flying club instructors (Lambert, Chap. 7) and computer scientists who manage websites for TV series fans (Béliard, Chap. 9). More indirectly, language proficiency and legal knowledge are also enabling skills. In other cases, people who commodify their domestic or leisure activity have to "learn new roles and new practices previously performed by professionals" (Bailly, Garcia-Bardidia and Lallemand, Chap. 4). They may learn them on the job, from forum discussions, or from FAQs. Sometimes, skills are borrowed from the entourage. Family members and friends provide both practical help and moral support (Jourdain and Naulin, Chap. 3; Ahmad, Chap. 6). Yet given that commodification skills are unevenly distributed, marketization of domestic and leisure activities tends to reproduce social inequalities.

Reliance on others' skills highlights another form of "extra work": the management of others' work. Most commodifiers are unable to master the entire process of marketization alone: Etsy sellers sometimes outsource part of their production (Jourdain and Naulin, Chap. 3); migrant women doing transnational trade have to hire business intermediaries ("helpers") to purchase supplies in Middle Eastern countries (Ahmad, Chap. 5); pilots task tax consultants with part of their "work of capital"

(Herlin-Giret 2017) done in their free time (Lambert, Chap. 7), and so forth. All these situations call for management skills.

The commodification of domestic and leisure activities also includes specific "relational labor" (Baym 2014). The value of what is being sold is generally associated with its being handmade by an ordinary person. This is consistent with the current upscaling of traditional manual labor occupations (Ocejo 2017) and the authenticity of do-it-yourself "passion" work (Duffy and Hund 2015), and small-scale production. And it is placed in contrast to industrial, standardized, and professionally produced items. The specific value of "homemade" leads commodifiers of domestic and leisure activities to perform specific work consisting in marketing their products and personal identities as "authentic" and "ordinary" (Ashton and Patel 2018; Luckman 2015). Paradoxically, "amateur" branding calls for a particular labor of self-presentation (texts and pictures depicting the person and his or her domestic space) and availability for "private" interactions with buyers (chats, comments, emails, etc.). The commodification of domestic and leisure activities is often associated with a "commodification of the self" (Webster and Michailidou 2018), emotional labor (Hochschild 1983), and the development of interactional skills (Goffman 1978). This is particularly true of online marketization and feminine activities. For example, camgirls stage their performance in an apparently "natural" home setting and present themselves as spontaneous amateur "real people" who do the activity for fun in their leisure time. As Pierre Brasseur and Jean Finez (Chap. 8) put it, they commodify the so-called everyday life. Even in more traditional fields of activity, market players stage the "authenticity" and "homemade" nature of their products. Russian couples who sell domestic food products insist on the local, domestic, homemade nature of their products in order to convince their customers of their quality and distinctiveness (Mainguy, Chap. 6). This "extra work" conducted to lend value to the products and the producers is not always considered as "work" because it is generally "invisible work." This is all the more the case since marketization is conducted during free time and is meant to be a self-rewarding activity.

Indeed, the "extra work" induced by commodification is not always considered as a burden distracting from the core of the domestic or leisure activity. It is sometimes even perceived as a pleasant and rewarding experience. In many cases, people express intrinsic pleasure derived from "acting" as an entrepreneur or "playing" shopkeeper (Jourdain and Naulin, Chap. 3; Béliard, Chap. 9). This blurs the distinction between working, laboring, playing, and gaming (Lund 2014). Marketization of everyday life can be regarded as a form of "playbor," that is to say a "mix of fun (play) and productive work (labor)" (Citton 2013). Fun can be found in many aspects of marketization: the definition of a product and seller identity, the market transactions, and even economic performance. As Adrien Bailly, Renaud Garcia-Bardidia, and Coralie Lallemand put it, there can be a "playful relationship with economic performance," and the pleasure of seizing opportunities and the chance to "beat the market" as well as the conviviality generated by market exchanges can form a greater motivation than mere economic interest (Bailly, Garcia-Bardidia and Lallemand, Chap. 4).

Considering that extra work goes hand in hand with poor remuneration and non-economic benefits, our analysis leads us to regard extra work as free work. In keeping with T. Terranova, free labor has two meanings: firstly, it is "not compensated by great financial rewards (it [is] therefore 'free,' unpaid), but it [is] also willingly conceded in exchange for the pleasures of communication and exchange (it [is] therefore 'free', pleasurable, not imposed)" (Terranova 2000: 48). Some players, such as digital platforms and more traditional intermediaries, benefit from the economic value generated by the many commodifiers, just as the more recent literature on "digital labor" depicts it (Cardon and Casilli 2015; Scholz 2012). At the same time, commodifiers enjoy engaging in extra work that gives them pleasure, sociability, and new forms of social recognition. These two aspects of extra work go together and must be analyzed as two sides of the same coin.

3 Parts and Chapters

The analysis of the marketization of everyday life in contemporary societies by our collective research highlights three commodification logics and three forms of extra money: pin money associated with leisure, savings from side jobs, and professional earnings when the hobby is turned into a profession. This typology relates to different meanings of extra money depending on social class and gender. It structures the three parts of the book. In this general framework, the chapters are ordered according to the predominant logic of commodification in their investigated field, but different logics may be analyzed within one and the same chapter.

The chapters in Part I focus on commodification as a leisure activity, generating pin money. They specifically concern the middle and upper class and, in the first two chapters, women. In Chap. 2, "Commodifying Leisure and Improving Its Social Value: Knitters' Conspicuous Production on Ravelry.com," Vinciane Zabban explores the blurring boundaries between public and domestic spheres by studying knitting, an age-old, popular, female domestic practice. She focuses on the dedicated web platform Ravelry, which publishes and sells all users' patterns. Drawing on an online ethnography of the web platform and in-depth interviews with users, she reveals a major change within the practice driven by digital tools: the showcasing of personal production. In this field, the commodification of patterns, knitting kits, and knitting skills in the form of knitting lessons is scarce. It is an added extra to being part of a community and the social recognition sought from showcasing. Whether through commodification or not, knitters make many efforts to make personal achievement suitable for Ravelry's database. These efforts, accurately depicted in Vinciane Zabban's chapter, are consistent with the notion of extra work as free work.

In Chap. 3, "Making Money Out of Leisure: The Marketization of Handicrafts and Food Blogging," Anne Jourdain and Sidonie Naulin examine why female handicrafters and food bloggers engage in the marketization of their leisure activity. It appears all the more counterintuitive to do so, since those activities often bring in very small amounts of money. Drawing on interviews and surveys conducted of a population of French Etsy sellers and food bloggers, the authors show that marketization paradoxically brings more social than economic rewards. Most of the time, economic returns are seen as pin money that is reinvested to finance the continuation of the leisure activity. That does not prevent marketization from requiring a great deal of specific, but often invisible, work. The unequal distribution of the resources required to become a market player may explain income inequalities among commodifiers, but the pleasure taken in performing this work and acquiring new skills could well account for the continuation of what is apparently an unprofitable activity.

In Chap. 4, "Selling Second-Hand Items on the Web: New Skills for Everyone?" Adrien Bailly, Renaud Garcia-Bardidia, and Coralie Lallemand also describe forms of commodification that generate pin money, studying the French equivalent of Craiglist.com: Leboncoin.fr. Drawing on semi-structured interviews, participant observations, and an analysis of a set of e-mail exchanges between buyers and sellers, they scrutinize the non-professional selling practices on this well-known dedicated web platform for second-hand items. They analyze in particular the numerous skills required by commodification, and especially the promotional skills and interactional skills, that echo the feminine emotional and affective labor pointed by post-feminist studies. Extra work hinges on learning mechanisms. The chapter explains how these mechanisms work and shows the importance of the experience of commodification as a game in the process, as well as the centrality of conviviality. Again, pleasure appears to be a condition for extra work.

Part II highlights different forms of side jobs which provide economic savings for people from the lower classes, but also for members of the upper class. In both cases, individuals commodify leisure or domestic activities to maintain their social position following a change in their situation or because they expect a change.

In Chap. 5, "Comorian Women at Work: Juggling Insecure Jobs with the Transnational Suitcase Trade," Abdoul-Malik Ahmad writes about lower-class women in Marseille who have migrated from Comoros and found atypical employment in France. Those women engage in the transnational suitcase trade, buying manufactured products from different countries in Africa, the Middle East, and Asia, and selling them to Comorian customers in France. They often engage in such activities in order to finance the building of a family house in Comoros or a future family event (wedding, etc.). Drawing on biographical interviews and observations, Abdoul-Malik Ahmad shows how these practices of commodification in their free time help emancipate them from a class- and gender-subordinate position. The non-economic benefits of commodification (such as sociability and social recognition) appear to be important even for people who lack economic resources the most.

This result is in line with Glenn Mainguy's Chap. 6, "Domesticity as Value: The Commodification of Foodstuffs in Precarious Rural Russia." Based on a long-term ethnography in Russia's countryside and on recorded interviews, this chapter analyzes the commodification of domestic household-farm produce such as meat, vegetables, and honey by women and men living on the edge since the fall of the USSR in 1991. Here, extra work is engaged in to promote the domestic origin of the produce as a quality. Focusing on men, Glenn Mainguy shows that their legitimacy and social status has been undermined by unemployment and that commodification precisely helps them to restore this male legitimacy, within the society and their household. For people from the lower classes who especially suffer from the economic crisis, the marketization of everyday life appears to be the last resort to live a decent life.

Chapter 7, "Nonstandard Working Hours and Economic Use of Free Time in the Upper Middle Class," focuses on quite a different group of people. In this chapter, Anne Lambert presents the "sideline" activities of flight attendants and pilots working for a major airline in France. Drawing on interviews and quantitative data, she examines multiple jobholding by people from the middle and upper classes. These workers' particular working conditions (nonstandard working hours, stable employment contract, high level of income, and a huge amount of free time due to the profession's organization) give them leeway to develop sideline activities. It appears that these activities, their profitability, and their purpose differ, depending on social class and gender. One of the objectives is to develop—and sometimes prepare to make a professional transition to—a more meaningful activity, especially for flight attendants; another is to accumulate economic and symbolic capital in order to consolidate a social status, according to a dominant ethos.

The third part of the book focuses on people trying to transform their hobby into a profession. This situation is quite classic in the art and sports worlds, and examples of it can be found in much of the fieldwork examined in this book. The two cases presented in this part concern digital activities that are highly gendered.

In Chap. 8, "Performing Amateurism: A Study of Camgirls' Work," Pierre Brasseur and Jean Finez analyze the trajectories of women who start to perform amateur erotic and pornographic shows online from home in order to get money. Using interview material, they show the paradox of developing professional skills and transforming a "leisure" activity into a full-time job while the value of the shows rests in their "amateur" properties. The authors accurately describe the "extra work" of showcasing ordinariness (as clients imagine it to be) and constructing a public-private persona. This chapter provides insightful empirical elements regarding the online commodification of the female self in today's economies.

In Chap. 9, "Making Money from TV Series: From Viewer to Webmaster with Financial Rewards," Anne-Sophie Béliard draws on interviews with TV series viewers who have become webmasters of series fan websites to understand how passion and leisure are transformed into a monetized activity. She studies the social conditions that lead some male series fans to embark upon a professionalization pathway. It appears that the business model setup is associated with the type of commitment to the leisure activity and with the professional background and main occupation of the series viewers. Such differentiations are essential to understand how webmasters deal with either positive (because empowering) or negative (because denaturing) effects of money, and especially extra money.

Notes

1. This work is supported by the Independent Social Research Foundation; the French National Research Agency in the framework of the "Investissements d'Avenir" program (ANR-15-IDEX-02), University Grenoble-Alpes Strategic Research Initiative (IRS 2017-MATRACA), and University Grenoble-Alpes Data Institute; the Maison des Sciences de l'Homme (MSH) Paris Nord; Paris-Dauphine University (IRISSO); and Sciences Po Grenoble (PACTE).
2. https://ec.europa.eu/eurostat/statistics-explained/index.php?title=Digital_economy_and_society_statistics_-_households_and_individuals (Accessed 11 February 2019).
3. Race is not investigated in our book. As French sociologists living in France where ethnic statistics are proscribed, we (the editors) lack the data to engage in a race analysis.

References

Abdelnour, S. (2017). *Moi, petite entreprise. Les auto-entrepreneurs, de l'utopie à la réalité*. Paris: Presses universitaires de France.

Adkins, L. (2016). Contingent Labour and the Rewriting of the Sexual Contract. In L. Adkins & M. Dever (Eds.), *The Post-Fordist Sexual Contract: Working and Living in Contingency* (pp. 1–28). Basingstoke: Palgrave Macmillan.

Adkins, L., & Dever, M. (2014). Gender and Labour in New Times: An Introduction. *Australian Feminist Studies, 29*(79), 1–11.

Adkins, L., & Dever, M. (Eds.). (2016). *The Post-Fordist Sexual Contract: Working and Living in Contingency*. Basingstoke: Palgrave Macmillan.

Appadurai, A. (Ed.). (1986 [2009]). *The Social Life of Things: Commodities in Cultural Perspective*. Cambridge: Cambridge University Press.

Ashton, D., & Patel, K. (2018). Vlogging Careers: Everyday Expertise Collaboration and Authenticity. In S. Taylor & S. Luckman (Eds.), *The New Normal of Working Lives: Critical Studies in Contemporary Work and Employment* (pp. 147–168). Basingstoke: Palgrave Macmillan.

Banks, M., Gill, R., & Taylor, S. (Eds.). (2013). *Theorizing Cultural Work: Labour, Continuity and Change in the Cultural and Creative Industries*. Abingdon: Routledge.

Baudelot, C., & Gollac, M. (Eds.). (2003). *Travailler pour être heureux ?* Paris: Fayard.

Baym, N. (2014). Connect with Your Audience! The Relational Labor of Connection. *The Communication Review, 18*(1), 14–22.

Botsman, R., & Rogers, R. (2011). *What's Mine is Yours: How Collaborative Consumption is Changing the Way We Live*. London: HarperCollins Business.

Bourdieu, P. (1980). The Production of Belief. Contribution to an Economy of Symbolic Goods. *Media, Culture, and Society, 2*, 261–293.

Bourdieu, P. (1989). *La Noblesse d'État*. Paris: Éditions de minuit.

Bourdieu, P. (1996). *The Rules of Art: Genesis and Structure of the Literary Field*. Stanford: Stanford University Press.

Cardon, D., & Casilli, A. (2015). *Qu'est-ce que le Digital Labour?* Paris: INA.

Casilli, A. (2019). *En Attendant les robots: Enquête sur le travail du clic*. Paris: Seuil.

Citton, Y. (2013). Économie de l'attention et nouvelles exploitations numériques. *Multitudes, 3*(54), 163–175.

Conor, B., Gill, R., & Taylor, S. (2015). Gender and Creative Labour. *The Sociological Review, 63*(1), 1–22.

Delacroix, E., Parguel, B., & Benoit-Moreau, F. (2018). Digital Subsistence Entrepreneurs on Facebook. *Technological Forecasting and Social Change*, 1–13. http://sci-hub.tw/10.1016/j.techfore.2018.06.018.

Delphy, C. (1977). *The Main Enemy: A Materialist Analysis of Women's Oppression*. London: Women's Research and Resources Centre Publications.

Delphy, C., & Leonard, D. (1992). *Familiar Exploitation: A New Analysis of Marriage in Contemporary Western Societies*. Oxford: Polity Press.

Duffy, B., & Hund, E. (2015). "Having It All" on Social Media: Entrepreneurial Femininity and Self-Branding among Fashion Bloggers. *Social Media+Society, 1*(2), 1–11.

Eitzen, S. (1989). The Sociology of Amateur Sport: An Overview. *International Review for the Sociology of Sport, 24*(2), 95–105.

Ekinsmyth, C. (2011). Challenging the Boundaries of Entrepreneurship: The Spatialities and Practices of UK 'Mumpreneurs'. *Geoforum, 42*, 104–114.

Flichy, P. (2017). *Les Nouvelles Frontières du travail à l'ère numérique*. Paris: Le Seuil.

Gill, R. (2008). Culture and Subjectivity in Neoliberal and Postfeminist Times. *Subjectivity, 25*, 432–445.

Gill, R., & Pratt, A. (2008). In the Social Factory? Immaterial Labour, Precariousness and Cultural Work. *Theory, Culture & Society, 25*(7–8), 1–30.

Godechot, O., Lurol, M., & Méda, D. (1999). Les actifs à la recherche d'un nouvel équilibre entre travail et hors-travail. *Premières Synthèses*, Dares, 1–11.

Goffman, E. (1978). *The Presentation of Self in Everyday Life*. London: Harmondsworth.

Graeber, D. (2018). *Bullshit Jobs: A Theory*. New York: Simon & Schuster.

Gregg, M. (2008). The Normalisation of Flexible Female Labour in the Information Economy. *Feminist Media Studies, 8*(3), 285–299.

Gregg, M. (2011). *Work's Intimacy*. Cambridge: Polity Press.

Herlin-Giret, C. (2017). Quand les héritiers deviennent des « entrepreneurs » : les nouveaux appuis rhétoriques et pratiques de l'accumulation. *Revue de la regulation*, 22, https://journals.openedition.org/regulation/12388, Online 31 January 2018. Retrieved February 16, 2018.

Hochschild, A. (1983). *The Managed Heart*. Berkeley: University of California Press.

Horkheimer, M., & Adorno, T. (2002 [1947]). *Dialectic of Enlightenment: Philosophical Fragments*. Stanford: Stanford University Press.

Huws, U. (2003). *The Making of a Cybertariat: Virtual Work in a Real World*. New York: New York University Press.

Huws, U. (2018). Eating Us out of House and Home: The Dynamics of Commodification and Decommodification of Reproductive Labour in the Formation of Virtual Work. *International Journal of Media & Cultural Politics, 14*(1), 111–118.

Huws, U. Spencer, N., Syrdal, D., & Holts, K. (2017). *Work in the European Gig Economy: Research Results From the UK, Sweden, Germany, Austria, the Netherlands, Switzerland and Italy*. Brussels. Retrieved from http://www.feps-europe.eu/assets/9d13a6d2-5973-4131-b9c8-3ca5100f92d4/work-in-the-european-gig-full-report-pppdf.pdf

Huws, U., Spencer, N., Syrdal, D., & Holts, K. (2018). Working in the Gig Economy: Insights from Europe. In M. Neufeind, J. O'Reilly, & F. Ranft (Eds.), *Work in the Digital Age: Challenges of the Fourth Industrial Revolution* (pp. 153–162). London: Rowman & Littlefield International.

International Labour Organisation. (2015). *World Employment and Social Outlook: The Changing Nature of Jobs*. Geneva: International Labour Office, ILO Research Department.

Jarrett, K. (2014). The Relevance of "Women's Work": Social Reproduction and Immaterial Labor in Digital Media. *Television & New Media, 15*(1), 14–29.

Jarrett, K. (2015). *Feminism, Labor and Digital Media: The Digital Housewife*. New York: Routledge.

Kaplan Daniels, A. (1987). Invisible Work. *Social Problems, 34*(5), 403–415.

Kopytoff, I. (1986 [2009]). The Cultural Biography of Things: Commoditization in Process. In A. Appadurai (Ed.), *The Social Life of Things: Commodities in Cultural Perspective* (pp. 64–91). New York: Cambridge University Press.

Le Roux, N., & Loriol, M. (Eds.). (2015). *Le Travail passionné: L'engagement artistique, sportif ou politique*. Toulouse: Erès.

Luckman, S. (2015). *Craft and the Creative Economy*. Hampshire: Palgrave Macmillan.

Luckman, S. (2016). Micro-enterprise as Work–Life 'Magical Solution'. In L. Adkins & M. Dever (Eds.), *The Post-Fordist Sexual Contract: Working and Living in Contingency* (pp. 91–108). Basingstoke: Palgrave Macmillan.

Lund, A. (2014). Playing, Gaming, Working and Labouring: Framing the Concepts and Relations. *tripleC, 12*(2), 735–801.

Mäkinen, K. (2018). Negotiating the Intimate and the Professional in Mom Blogging. In S. Taylor & S. Luckman (Eds.), *The New Normal of Working Lives: Critical Studies in Contemporary Work and Employment* (pp. 129–146). Basingstoke: Palgrave Macmillan.

Marx, K. (1992 [1867]). *Capital: A Critique of Political Economy. Vol. 1*. New York: Penguin Classics.

Matchar, E. (2013). *Homeward Bound: Why Women are Embracing the New Domesticity*. New York: Simon & Schuster.

Méda, D., & Vendramin, P. (2017). *Reinventing Work in Europe: Value, Generations and Labour*. Basingstoke: Palgrave Macmillan.

Mensitieri, G. (2018). *Le Plus beau métier du monde. Dans les coulisses de l'industrie de la mode*. Paris: La Découverte.

Mirchandani, K. (2010). Gendered Hierarchies in Transnational Call Centres. In D. Howcroft & H. Richardson (Eds.), *Work and Life in the Global Economy: A Gendered Analysis of Service Work* (pp. 78–98). London: Palgrave Macmillan.

Moulin, R., Passeron, J.-C., Pasquier, D., & Porto-Vasquez, F. (1985). *Les Artistes. Essai de morphologie sociale*. Paris: La documentation Française.

Ocejo, R. (2017). *Masters of Craft. Old Jobs in the New Urban Economy*. Princeton: Princeton University Press.

Orgad, S. (2019). *Heading Home: Motherhood, Work and the Failed Promise of Equality*. New York: Columbia University Press.

Parker, S. (1965). Work and Non-Work in Three Occupations. *The Sociological Review, 13*, 65–75.

Piketty, T. (2014). *Capital in the Twenty-First Century*. Cambridge: Harvard University Press.

Polanyi, K. (2001 [1944]). *The Great Transformation: The Political and Economic Origins of our Time*. Boston: Beacon Press.

Ravenelle, A. (2017). Sharing Economy Workers: Selling, Not Sharing. *Cambridge Journal of Regions, Economy and Society*, 1–15. http://sci-hub.tw/10.1093/cjres/rsw043.

Scholz, T. (2012). *Digital Labor: The Internet as Playground and Factory*. New York: Routledge.

Schor, J. (2018). The Platform Economy: Consequences for Labour, Inequality and the Environment. In M. Neufeind, J. O'Reilly, & F. Ranft (Eds.), *Work in the Digital Age: Challenges of the Fourth Industrial Revolution* (pp. 163–174). London: Rowman & Littlefield International.

Simonet, M. (2015). La passion au travail, une ambivalence à ne pas dépasser. In N. Le Roux & M. Loriol (Eds.), *Le travail passionné: L'engagement artistique, sportif ou politique* (pp. 309–320). Toulouse: Erès.

Simonet, M. (2018). *Travail gratuit: la nouvelle exploitation?* Paris: Textuel.

Spence, M. (1974). *Market Signaling: Informational Transfer in Hiring and Related Screening Processes*. Cambridge: Harvard University Press.

Stebbins, R. (2007). *Serious Leisure: A Perspective for Our Time*. New Brunswick, NJ: Transaction Publishers.

Taylor, S., & Luckman, S. (Eds.). (2018). *The New Normal of Working Lives: Critical Studies in Contemporary Work and Employment*. Basingstoke: Palgrave Macmillan.

Terranova, T. (2000). Free Labor: Producing Culture for the Digital Economy. *Social Text, 63*(18-2), 33–58.

van Doorn, N. (2017). Platform Labor: On the Gendered and Racialized Exploitation of Low-Income Service Work in the 'On-Demand' Economy. *Information, Communication & Society, 20*(6), 898–914.

Viswanathan, M., Sridharan, S., & Ritchie, R. (2010). Understanding Consumption and Entrepreneurship in Subsistence Marketplaces. *Journal of Business Research, 63*, 570–581.

Weber, F. (1989). *Le Travail à côté. Étude d'ethnographie ouvrière*. Paris: EMESS and INRA.

Weber, F., & Lamy, Y. (1999). Amateurs et professionnels. *Genèses, 36*, 2–5.

Webster, J., & Michailidou, M. (2018). Building Gender Perspectives in the Analysis of Virtual Work. *International Journal of Media & Cultural Politics, 14*(1), 3–18.

Zelizer, V. (1997). *The Social Meaning of Money: Pin Money, Paychecks, Poor Relief, and Other Currencies*. Princeton: Princeton University Press.

Zelizer, V. (2000). The Purchase of Intimacy. *Law & Social Inquiry, 25*(3), 817–848.

Zelizer, V. (2001). Transactions intimes. *Genèses, 42*(1), 121–144.

Part I

Pin Money

2

Commodifying Leisure and Improving Its Social Value: Knitters' Conspicuous Production on Ravelry.com

Vinciane Zabban

> *Now, I can work while keeping my world in order.*
> *(Celia, 40 years old)*

1 Introduction

Needlework (sewing, knitting, quilting, weaving, crocheting, etc.) is part of the domestic economy, and has always held an ambiguous position from an economic point of view. As noted by Florence Weber when she studied gardening and other forms of do-it-yourself male domestic activities in a working-class setting, the domestic economy is hard to understand and analyze through the lens and terms of classical economics (Weber 1998). Knitting is similar in many ways to F. Weber's description and analysis of gardening, aside from the fact that it is practiced essentially by women. Long perceived as a female-oriented occupation, knitting has sometimes been considered as a money saver and has even been

V. Zabban (✉)
EXPERICE, Paris 13 University, Villetaneuse, France
e-mail: vinciane.zabban@gmail.com

practiced as a source of income (Coffin 1996). Yet this activity also bears a moral dimension and has been associated with *otium*, as a legitimate category of leisure activity. Knitting, then, has been seen as a relevant, decent task for women to prevent idleness, if not a productive activity in itself. In addition, knitted garments and knitting know-how and technique have long been almost exclusively the domain of local and family networks.

A 2008 survey found that 20% of the French population (mostly women) practiced needlework activity (Donnat 2009). In the United States, the Craft Yarn Council of America reported that 17% of North Americans were knitters in 2012. But what does it mean to be a knitter today? Why do people still spend time and money making their own clothes? We set out here to investigate this subject, taking a socioeconomic approach and contributions from the media, and scientific and technical studies. Considering the practice's contemporary digital expressions, we argue that studying contemporary approaches to knitting is a good way to help understand how digital systems are configuring "the new normal" of domestic activities (Taylor and Luckman 2018). We discuss, in particular, perceptions of the social value of women's activities in this context. In our modern societies, knitting is perceived mainly as a hobby, and knitwear is mostly intended as gifts and charity donations. That makes knitting a very good example of the social aspects involved in the valuation of goods, and what Viviana Zelizer calls intimate transactions (Zelizer 2002). As knitting is not seen today as a profitable activity, the value of knitwear lies essentially in the qualities attributed to the knitter and to the relationship between the knitter and the people who receive the gift. This value can be expressed in part by an assessment of the handicraft process itself: time spent, technical skills, and creativity. It is usually extremely hard to measure. Yet, the value of the resources needed for knitting is entirely measurable. Needles, knitting patterns, and yarns are goods with a price tag that circulate in profitable markets. Gary Alan Fine, in his study of leisure's subcultures, states that people do not choose leisure activities based mainly on personal preferences or on social characteristics to a lesser extent: leisure organizations need more importantly to provide relevant resources (material or otherwise) in order to attract and retain participants. "Leisure organizations have as their primary goal the provisioning of satisfaction, of fun" (Fine 1989). The current success of knitting is probably associated with the development and spread of new ways of providing fun to knitters, especially by using Internet tools to develop new information, as well as social and material resources. Our argument is that digital devices have accompanied social changes in knitting practices, and have contributed to the commodification of this activity on many levels. First, tools have been built that have transformed domestic knitwear into information products with characteristics that are measurable, shared online, and are contributing to the creation of significant value in an attention economy. These new features have an extremely important social impact by making domestic production public and monetized. Second, digital platforms develop third-party interaction and transaction spaces, which may or may not be monetized, and which are conducive to the formation of new relationships between production and consumption (Potts et al. 2008). Very few knitters actually embark on, or make a living from, a career in design or knitting, but many see it as an alternative enabling them to deal with contingencies (Adkins and Dever 2016), as a way to escape a dreary professional life and balance their work and family life.

We first outline the recent changes affecting the knitting sphere. We examine the role of Internet tools in those changes, especially Ravelry—a knitting and crochet website with both social network and database characteristics. We describe Ravelry's specific features and discuss its central role in establishing sociomaterial practices (Orlikowski and Scott 2015). Ravelry acts both as a data organizer for a broader informational infrastructure (Bowker et al. 2009) and as a social network structured as a database. This database structure is able to propose suitable content to a wide range of user profiles. The online platform hence offers a remarkable combination of social, commercial, and informational features.

Secondly, we detail how ordinary Ravelers contribute to the website, and especially to the pattern and yarn markets. We point to the ordinary, everyday nature of their contributions: using the website (production of metrics), but also, and chiefly, adding information content (projects). The website's project pages feed the database with a range of knitting experiences and achievements by identified users. They therefore appear more complex than the usual user reviews (Mellet et al. 2014). We argue that project pages are instrumental in how the Internet has revolutionized the knitters' lives. They provide access to others' practices and form "third places": neither public nor domestic. We contend that this new form of visibility and the extension of social spheres for knitters, in addition to new metrics and the complex intertwining of trading features, give these activities added social value. In that sense, we argue that by transforming and expanding knitting's social scene from the domestic to new areas, the web and the Ravelry platform are changing the activity's symbolic value. They are consequently transforming its social economy. The database's structure and dissemination of standard forms of measurement also mean that the project pages are making domestic and personal knitted production less ambivalent commodities.

Thirdly, we address the space created by Ravelry in which the boundaries between amateurs and professionals can appear blurred. Beyond mere hobby, succeeding in this environment calls for the right balance to be struck between important social media self-marketing and an expected professional quality of service. We take the example of interview respondents who have embarked on a professional approach to see how they deal with these constraints. These pathways reveal the continuity between use and design, and how boundaries are kept in place… in ways that are not always peaceful. However, such itineraries are also quite rare. Pattern designers account for a very small proportion of Ravelry users: 69,166 people are identified in the database as "designers"; that is, they have published at least one pattern (paid or free). They hence represent less than 1% of a total of more than 8 million user accounts. Nevertheless, this potential, which is constantly updated by the system, is an important factor for the users we met. The interviews highlight their interest in entering a market where entrepreneurship is ostensibly open to all, and where some imagine they can do business. Ravelry then appears as a hopeful tool in the process, described by Susan Luckman, of "micro-enterprise as a work-life 'magical solution'" (Luckman 2016).

Method

Our analysis is based on two main methods: an online autoethnography and in-depth interviews with Ravelry users ($n = 14$).

Autoethnography allows us to understand Ravelry's specific role in the complexity of knitting tools, resources, and activities. As Christine Hine points out, "An autoethnographic stance on ethnography for the Internet focuses on considering how connections present themselves and what choices are available for building meaning out of these diverse influences" (Hine 2015: 83). This approach also allows us to identify and mobilize data available on the site: number of elements that are available in the database (patterns, designers, project pages, etc.), content of project pages, and content of discussions on the forum.

The interviews make it possible to shift the focus by analyzing other modalities and trajectories of the practice. Most of the interviewees were identified through Ravelry's database ('people'), which allows users to be filtered according to a geographical area. They are all located in Paris or the Paris region. They were then contacted via the website's messaging system. The interviews were conducted, as much as possible, at the respondents' homes, and last between 2 and 3 hours. They include a biographical part; they question the material, technical, economic, and social dimension of knitting practice; and they include the role of digital technologies in it.

2 Ravelry: A Central Platform for the Knitting Social Network Market

2.1 Recent Social and Technical Changes in the Field of Knitting

In the face of the growth of ready-to-wear, and some feminist disapproval, knitting might have been expected to be on the decline. Yet, the activity endures and is enjoying a revival. Before discussing the innovations brought about by the Internet and the new kinds of exchanges made possible by platforms like Ravelry, we want to show that, although this growing resurgence is linked to the spread of the Internet, it is part of a longer historical trend.

The knitting market, especially in France, has long been monopolized by a handful of publishers (Phildar, Pingouin, and Bergère de France). These brands used to offer housewives a limited selection of "ready for use" patterns associated with low-quality threads for a reasonable price. As mentioned by one of the knitters we interviewed, the brands sold mainly sweater patterns, as it was not in their interest to sell patterns for a small amount of yarn (such as patterns for shawls or scarves). With little information on the types of yarn required for a given pattern, knitters were hard put to bypass the distribution model and find an alternative to this supply. Moreover, yarns and patterns were distributed mainly by franchised stores, placing another restriction on the knitter's choice. In the United States, this distribution model—subsequently described as "proprietary" (White 2007)—came under criticism back in the 1970s. Elizabeth Zimmermann, also known as "the opinionated knitter" (Zimmermann and Swansen 2011), emerged in "Do It Yourself" counterculture circles as a figure with a purpose to empower knitters. E. Zimmermann hosted a knitting program on public television, thereby contributing to the democratization of know-how through images and video, which is a cornerstone of technical learning on the Internet today. She advocated more creative, "intuitive" knitting, "rather than just being blind followers of the written word." Most importantly, she opposed the tied-selling of yarns and patterns, and called for them to be uncoupled in retail.

The uncoupling of yarns from patterns changed the production and distribution of knitting patterns and yarns. In particular, this enabled the yarn market to diversify, but it also meant that information on yarn characteristics and qualities (yardage, fiber type, weight, etc.) had to be developed and standardized. This in turn accentuated yarn quality differentiation and ranking, creating more interest in "noble yarns" among some new categories of knitters. In the late 1980s, some stores started specializing in "natural" yarns sold by the meter (e.g. *La Droguerie* in Paris). An iconic example of today's knitting market is found in the form of the new sock yarns dyed in fashionable natural colors, which appeared in the 2000s, often imported from South America. These light, fine yarns are sold in long-length yardage skeins (approx. 400 yards/100 g), which makes for an appreciable quantity of this quality yarn at a reasonable price. New kinds of patterns, shawls for instance, were then needed for this new type and quantity of yarn, as were new ways of promoting and distributing patterns.

This shows that changes in the market for knitting resources began before the spread of Internet platforms. It could even be said that the social environments where these new resources for knitting practices appeared were actually the very environments for the development of the Internet. However, recent information and communication technology developments have brought new information tools and new market forms, which have made a huge contribution to current knitting developments.

2.2 The Central Role of Ravelry's Database in the Online Knitting Information Infrastructure

Sewing, embroidery, and knitting handicrafters and communities engaged early on in boards, forums, websites, and blogs, although these female activities are strangely absent from existing research on the social and economic uses of the early and not-so-early Internet. Social networks such as Facebook are also an important medium for leisure circles today, and they are especially useful to newcomers who have difficulty navigating the supply of material and informational knitting resources. In effect, it is worth noting here that the Internet's impact on the knitting market does not only concern material resources. We agree with Gary Alan Fine that the distribution of leisure activity knowledge (e.g. learning resources), opportunities for sociability, and access to identity symbols are also crucial elements: "Although a bucket is sufficient for the collecting of mushrooms, it is not sufficient for 'mushrooming'" (Fine 1989: 323). As with other activities involving corporal skills development (DIY, music, cooking, face painting, and hairstyling), online video and picture exchange platforms (YouTube, Pinterest, Instagram, etc.) were also adopted very early on by knitters, as were online marketplaces (e.g. Etsy) dedicated to small handicrafts businesses (jewelry, sewing, handmade dyed yarns, etc.). In deference to Bowker et al. (2009), we choose to describe the variety of places dedicated to the business and culture of creative activities on the Internet as an informational infrastructure. Among them, Ravelry appears as a particular case because it acts as a central platform. A 2014 online survey conducted for the Craft Yarn Council with US crocheters and knitters (n = 3178)—49% of whom are over 55 years old—revealed Ravelry to be the number one popular social media site used for craft (71%), ahead of Facebook (61%) and YouTube (52%).[1]

Ravelry.com is a website dedicated to knitting and crochet. It was launched by a four-member team in 2007. It is partially closed, since the site's full content can only be accessed by connecting to a user account. Today, the site has 8.2 million user accounts, and has been described as "the best social network you've (probably) never heard of."[2] Ravelry offers extensive databases of free and paid knitting patterns and other resources (yarns, shops, and designers), but also offers personal spaces, groups, and forums. It can be described on the basis of three main functions:

- *As a project organizer for knitters* (said to be its original purpose): keeping track of yarn stash and project progress. Every user can create and share a project page (a total of 17,525,053 pages in November 2018), which can be associated with a specific pattern or personal creation. Photos of production can be uploaded and published, and personal notes or comments added;
- *As a knitting market*: as a resource for finding, choosing, and buying or selling patterns (804,584 patterns in November 2018, of which 27.5% are free) and yarns: Ravelry offers pro accounts to designers, yarn producers, and yarn shop owners. It provides an advertising service to publishers, yarn brands, shops, and designers. And most of all, it enables microtransactions to buy and sell patterns between user accounts via PayPal;
- *As a social network*: via groups (41,339) and discussion boards (748,400) whose topics are mostly yarn-related, but also prove to be places where people discuss about work, family, cooking, cultural consumption, and so forth.

Ravelry has been described by Sal Humphreys, in line with J. Potts et al., as an exemplary case of "social network markets" (Humphreys 2009; Potts et al. 2008). These authors put it that emerging social network markets "reorganize the processes of exchange and innovation, for the avenues they provide for creative endeavor, and the hybridity of the rewards that are derived from different stakeholders" (Humphreys 2009: 1). J. Potts et al. (2008) propose the concept of "social network markets" for analysis of the creative industries, as an alternative to the usual economic models that focus mainly on producer activity. In particular, they point up the challenge of considering the dynamics of interactions between agents, networks, and enterprise: "all are engaged in the mutual enterprise of creating values, both symbolic and economic" (p. 170). Social networks such as Ravelry, and Goodreads for instance, which focus on a specific, resource-dependent activity, actually seem able to weave an original and complex network of links, new interactions, and forms of transactions between participants that are heterogeneous in terms of practices, economic status, and social characteristics. Indeed, a long continuum of user profiles can be observed on the platform, ranging from designing and professional involvement to the simple consumption of patterns.

S. Humphreys, in her work, emphasizes how Ravelry intertwines social network features with trading facets (Humphreys 2009). We would like to add, from our point of interest, that its originality also lies in the combination of these features with a database structure. As has been observed in other fields such as science (Heaton and Millerand 2013), health (Dagiral and Peerbaye 2016), and online games (Zabban 2011), database structures enable heterogeneous user (or consumer) profiles to coexist and partake of the same space of practices and representations. At the same time, they provide fitting personalized access for individuals or groups with specific practices. They can then act as boundary objects between distinct social worlds, especially as regards the professional/amateur frontier (Star and Griesemer 1989).

Ravelry could therefore be seen as a market space where producers and consumers create new kinds of relationships, where there is no division in principle between them, and, in the words of Potts et al., as a central element in the ordering of a *social network market* where consumers' choices are particularly dependent on each other.

3 Building Measurability and Social Value for "Conspicuous Production"

Taking up the idea that the Internet is driving significant changes in the knitting economy, and that its spaces can be defined as "social network markets" as coined by Potts et al. (2008), what exactly justifies talking about market participation by ordinary knitters on Ravelry? What value do they create in this market? What value do they place on their involvement personally? What do they stand to gain from it? And what role do technological devices play in this respect?

We look here at the technical factors underlying the developments in knitters' production. Knitwear has been talked up in the media and transformed into intangible elements in that information about it (image and text) is produced, published, and shared online. This media buildup has been accompanied by the standardization and commensuration of these products brought about partly by Ravelry and its database format and partly by the requirements of online sales of raw materials. We identify this molding process for the online market and social networks, and highlight its social dimension based on the notion of "ostentatious production" developed by Florence Weber (1998). The term "ostentatious production," coined with reference to the concept of the leisure class's ostentatious consumption devised by Thorstein Veblen (2009), is also used in other more recent studies, including Elizabeth Currid-Halkett (2017), but in a different way. In her update of Veblen's analyses, E. Currid-Halkett uses the term to describe companies that produce goods of differing qualities and extensively supply and support the ostentatious consumption of the aspirational class today. Although E. Currid-Halkett's analysis is entirely relevant in this case, we have a different understanding of the term more in keeping with F. Weber who discusses the ostentatious production of ordinary productive practices, such as gardening, in the domestic economy without their being monetized or, in this case, marketed. This production is called ostentatious in that it is intended for display and a large part of its value is based on the social gratification (honor) it earns its producers (hobbyists or gardeners). We show here how these social rationales encounter a particular Ravelry exposure device, the project pages, which proves key to creating value in the online knitting market.

3.1 Ordinary Ravelers and Their Contributions to Pattern Value

Our interest here lies not only in the fact that knitting consumers have the potential to become designers and sellers via Ravelry. More generally, all kinds of user contributions and interactions constitute much-needed valuable information that contributes to the yarn and pattern markets.

Our interviews with Ravelers show how the website's uses can differ by social profile, even though our sample is biased as we recruited from the site with a geographical constraint. We wanted to conduct face-to-face interviews, wherever possible at respondents' homes, so the sample is mainly urban since they were recruited in and around Paris.

We met young educated women who were escaping their professional activity by taking up creative activities. They were also in search of a wider range of social opportunities: mothers quitting their job for a better work-life balance in a business that is more rewarding symbolically; knitting "veterans" such as Martine and Anne (both librarians, 51 and 48 years old) talking about their discovery of a good social window provided by the Internet, and some who were developing their professional use of Ravelry. Leslie (statistician, 30 years old) and Josephine (archivist, 39 years old), for instance, use Ravelry only to choose patterns, while Tina (office worker, 42 years old) is often on the discussion boards. Cecile and Celia (unemployed office workers, 43 and 40 years old) and Mathilde (a student in business school, 23 years old) use the site mainly for professional purposes, uploading their own patterns on Ravelry. Eric, the only man in our sample, is a yarn shop owner. As discussed in the third part of this paper, he owns designer account, and he also uses Ravelry for his commercial activity. Some of these individuals look through users' projects on the website in order to choose the right yarn for a given pattern, while others refuse to buy any yarn they cannot see and touch in a physical store. Some of them download only free patterns, while others are willing to pay for "professional designs." Some of them keep a sound, steady track of their knitting activity on Ravelry and socialize a great deal on the discussion boards, while others do not. But whatever kind of involvement they develop in their uses, each of their actions on the website constitutes a contribution to the yarn and pattern markets: they produce information and value even when they simply "favorite" or "queue" one pattern in order to keep track of it, or when they consult just one pattern page, because these actions show up in the site's popularity metrics.

There is therefore a wide variety of social profiles of users and roles (designer, trader, consumer), practices and activities: searching for a model, commenting on it and evaluating it, editing and selling it, updating a project page, selling a skein of surplus wool, discussing in forums and groups, and so forth. There is something for everyone. The tools proposed by Ravelry enable this heterogeneity to develop. As databases classically act as boundary objects (Star and Griesemer 1989), they allow each profile to develop individual and collective practices. At the same time, they are brought together and interconnected in a completely new and original way and on a completely new and original scale.

3.2 Project Pages: "The Sinews of War"

One of Ravelry's most interesting features for our purpose is the project page, because it forms a kind of "advanced" consumer review. At some 17.5 million project pages for more than 800,000 patterns and with an average of 23 project pages for one pattern, they probably represent the largest amount of data on the site. Of course, not all project pages are equally valued, and some patterns attract a huge number of projects (number one currently has 30,500 project pages), while others have none. The number of "projects" is a key factor in the pattern popularity metrics, alongside the number and value of ratings, favorites, and queues.[3] As a designer, Eric says in his interview that projects "*are the sinews of war.*"

Ravelry users can create "project" entries. Project pages may exist on their own: for instance, if someone creates an original knitwear garment without using a pattern, they can post a project page on it. Most of the time (86%), however, projects are related to existing patterns in the Ravelry database or elsewhere.

Although project pages are instrumental in pattern ranking on Ravelry, they are not strictly speaking evaluations of the patterns in the classic sense. When users create a project page, they do more than rate and advise, or even just keep track of their progress with the original pattern. They create new pieces of information and new relationships between these pieces of information. For instance, they may associate the original pattern with a new kind of yarn or different sizes of needles in Ravelry's database.

Moreover, they can contribute to the database with photos of their own achievements, and even add "Notes." In "Notes," they can give their assessment of pattern quality (in terms of how it knits up or is written) or relate the quality of the knitting experience: whether it is satisfying or frustrating; an "automatic pilot," demanding or headaches knit; rewarding or disappointing, and so forth. "Notes" can contain details of technical choices and the resolution of technical problems, as well as descriptions and explanations of changes that the knitter has made to the pattern, which may be very helpful to others. Some changes are minor (e.g. size adjustments, color or yarn changes), while others are substantial (e.g. turning a sweater into a zip-up cardigan or a sweater into a dress). Above all, project pages themselves can be searched, commented, shared, and faved.

Ravelry's projects are consequently similar to Florence Weber's gardens in that they allow production to be "visited" by strangers. They can be visited when looking for a specific pattern. Yet these pages can also be visited for other reasons—when looking for the uses of a specific yarn, for instance, and wondering what people might do with it. The possibility to view other knitters' work is, from many points of view, one of the key features of Ravelry. The Ravelers we interviewed stressed its usefulness, particularly in terms of the possibilities that the range of interpretations and adjustments opens up. Martine (librarian, 51 years old), for instance, who has been knitting since she was 12, told us that she thought it was impossible to alter a pattern until she saw that other knitters were doing it. Josephine raised the importance of having an idea of a knitted garment's fit on "real people," sometimes people with particular physical attributes that might require changes to the pattern.

3.3 Making Personal Achievement Suitable for a Database

Knitwear garments are handicrafts goods that generally exist and are exchanged off a market. As part of the domestic economy, they are in principle immeasurable, mainly due to a lack of standardized metrics:

which unit of measurement should be chosen to place a value on them? They can also be exchanged within a small network of relations. They are usually in this sense the objects and subjects of what Viviana Zelizer describes as intimate transactions (Zelizer 2002).

Yet when knitters put their "project" online in Ravelry's database and, to a lesser extent, on such media as their blogs and Instagram threads, they essentially create a new kind of outcome accessible to the widest audience. Project entries are indeed a mediatized form of the knitter's actual production: they can be considered then as constituting a distinct type of product, or "end result" of the knitting process. As Josephine (archivist, 39 years old) told us: "*It's a way to really end it.*" Granted, written records of knitting project processes (journals and records) existed before the Internet, and sometimes even included photos and leftover yarn, but they did not circulate widely, and it can be safely assumed that they were not central to the conspicuous dimension of production. Publishing and posting knitwear projects on the web therefore constitutes a major change in the practice. Project pages hence appear to emphasize the "conspicuous" dimension of knitting production, to take Florence Weber's analysis of the role of showcasing for the domestic gardening activity.

Although the project pages can be faved and commented on, project page owners do not have a clear idea of who their actual audience is. The knitters, however, at least direct their production at an audience of friends such as Ravelry friends, and at what Daniel Dayan describes as an "imagined audience" (Dayan 2005). Note that the most engaged knitters' frequent sharing of project photos on Instagram, Facebook, and other social networks diversifies their potential audience.

On Ravelry, this ostentatious dimension is reinforced by measurability in that projects have to be translated in a standardized manner in order to fit in the database. Indeed, the framework for the creation of individual project pages is quite restrictive, as Josephine also notes, when she says she feels helpless when she comes to the end of a sewing project, because "*there is no sewing category*" to publish it on Ravelry. It requires personal crafting to be translated into knitwear characteristics and, if possible, linked to existing information in the database: which pattern, how much yardage, which yarn properties, which special technique, and so forth.

Most importantly, it calls for photos to be provided that show the knitwear from different angles and often at different stages of the knitting process. Although not always the case, these photos should be both a true representation (they should give an accurate idea of the garment's color and shape, especially when worn) and comply with a codified aesthetic. Broadly speaking, the database structure provided by Ravelry brings more formalization and standardization to the practice of knitting, as designers tend to standardize pattern writing today, while previous editorial models allowed for variations in writing and coding by brands developing their own "style." Yet, in this way, Ravelers are more likely to compare their personal production.

Ravelry hence seems to bring new mediation and measurability to personal and "domestic" production. "Projects" mediated by Ravelry appear as intermediate products on the knitting market, in between pattern consumption and production. They can be referred to as commodities in that some users actually see them as a reward, especially for the use of free patterns: "*a way of giving back a little of what we have received*" (Celia, 40 years old).

4 Relationship Between Users and Designers: Bridges and Doors

On Ravelry, the divide between user status and designer status might appear blurred. In some ways, it is. The platform and new technologies in general are building new bridges and doors: they are creating new interactions, and opening up access to equipment and design techniques, and to distribution. However, as Georg Simmel notes, it is only possible to connect what has been, and is, maintained as separate (Simmel 1994), and that does not mean that every user is willing or able to become a designer, nor does it mean that there is no longer any effort made to lay down the lines to maintain the boundaries between hobbyists and professionals. Following this focus on Ravelers' most massive, everyday contributions, and their role in the broader evolution in the social significance of knitting, it appears important to examine the situations of those laying midway along the continuum.

4.1 From Knitting to Pattern Publishing and Monetizing: A Not-So-Obvious Pathway

Any Ravelry user can contribute to the database from his/her account with free or paid patterns. Ravelry's blog reports that 1,114,909 patterns were sold on Ravelry in 2012 for a total of $6,177,399.87 in sales.[4] The site takes a commission (3.5%) on the sale of patterns starting at $30 per month. Fees are reduced if users sell more than $1500 per month.

There is also the possibility for any user to create a "pro" account interface to manage pattern sales and Ravelry Ad services. This interface is intended for designers to manage their sales, local yarn shops to set up partnerships for the sale of in-store models, and various types of advertisers. Ravelry provides a range of targeted advertising services (e.g. a "*Buy this yarn*" button).

It is hard to estimate how many "pro" accounts there are on the site, but it is possible to find the number of users identified as current "designers." Designers are users identified in the database as creators of one pattern. The site has 69,166 active designer accounts representing just under 1% of its total number of Ravelry users. This small proportion points up that not all users aspire to become designers themselves.

Among the 11 knitters initially interviewed, not specifically as designers but merely as Ravelry users, four of them had already designed and published patterns on Ravelry. This overrepresentation probably has to do with our recruitment bias. We initially focused on the use of the website, and so we recruited via the site's messaging system: intensive users responded in the main. We then sought specifically to interview individuals involved in design, in some way, with a view to working on the commodification of a domestic and leisure activity. This gave us a collection of seven experiences of publishing models, displaying different degrees of commitment to production.

The designers we interviewed often describe themselves as very manual, DIY enthusiasts, or with a high level of skills and penchant for spatial representation, geometry, and math. Knitting is often not the only creative activity they practice, but it has many advantages for city dwellers lacking space. Their stories of how they began to create patterns are similar. In most cases, there is a defining moment when they suddenly felt the need to alter or adjust existing models. Some decided to publish these adaptations, considering that their contribution made them original creations. In this case, they publish for free most of the time. Sarah, for example, added a unicorn design to a basic baby blanket. As she herself designed this colored figure with tools she uses in her professional activity (she is an architect), she considers it an original creation, which entitles her to publish the pattern in her name. However, she does not wish to make it profitable.

In Celia's case, writing patterns for broad commercial circulation is quite a different process. Her Ravelry patterns are free so far, but she intends to charge for the next ones. She gives two reasons for this. Firstly, charged patterns actually seem to gain more credibility with Ravelers:

> *Because it's free, people won't fill their project pages and don't upload photos of their achievements. It's quite surprising. If you upload your pattern for free on Ravelry, you get hearts [fave], you get downloads. But if you upload your pattern for a fee, people will make it.*[5] (Celia, unemployed office worker, 40 years old)

Secondly, she says that charging for patterns shows her respect for professional skills: "*I have to fall into line. Because there's real work behind it. You can't pull the rug out from under the professionals' feet.*"

Only two of the knitters we interviewed actually present themselves as designers. Mathilde, who is 23 years old and is completing an MBA degree, decided early on to design her own sweaters. She then considered publishing patterns, but writing patterns for sweaters is quite a complex task, especially when different sizes need to be calculated. Passionate about knitting, she refused a six-month internship within a large firm and decided to try to build a professional career in knitting instead. She started out selling homemade dyed yarns on Etsy before moving on to the shawl patterns market. As noted earlier, shawls are an important category of knitwear on the Internet, with one of their key features being that one size fits all. She designed original shawl patterns using a cutting-edge technique, and decided to try to sell the patterns. She used the skills acquired in her studies to plan her business: she created an Instagram account and a dedicated podcast on YouTube, invested in a good camera to take pictures, and used professional pattern publishing tools. She also asked for volunteers to test the pattern. She then formed a partnership with a Parisian yarn shop, which sold her pattern in a kit. She told us that providing professional and original work was quite a challenge given her doubts about her legitimacy to do so.

Eric also has a problem with legitimacy, but in a different way. Already working in the wool trade as a yarn shop owner, his entry into the world of design may well appear to be illegitimate. Both have therefore put a great deal into bringing their patterns up to the standards they deem "professional." They have paid particular attention to pattern-writing quality and ensuring that there are no mistakes in the pattern, which has to comply with certain conventions. For Eric, for example, the fact that he is addressing a wide audience means that he has to stipulate certain details in the instructions that he thinks are obvious. Image is also essential. Both have been careful to take quality photos and use models.

4.2 "You Need People to Be Able to Make this a Career, Not a Hobby"

The blurring of the boundaries between producers and consumers is not without its problems. There are many debates regarding intellectual property, in particular, as shown by S. Humphreys (2008): at what point can it be said, for example, that enough changes have been made to a pattern to merit claiming rights?

Forums are a good indicator of the tensions generated by frictions between types of user. Non-professional patterns are frequently discussed: the posting of quality patterns for free or at slashed prices might be criticized as dumping, and as a threat to the professional community. Discussions on pricing are particularly indicative of these tensions. Pricing is a crucial point, because it raises the issue of the activity's value in a market "*flooded by freebies*" (designer quote on the forum). The price must be in line with those generally practiced, a subject often discussed by the platform's forums. Ravelry's team provides designers with a list of

2 Commodifying Leisure and Improving Its Social Value… 51

average prices by category.[6] Any higher price has to be justified by particular pattern complexity or originality.

> *Print costs aside, as wholesale is down the pan, I consider the value of the pattern—how much mileage the knitter might get out of it. And that means what they learn (I do consider patterns to be a solid teaching tool, I know others don't), how many times they'll knit it, how satisfied they are with the FO (Finished Object) and so on. It's also way easier to use a single price point when you design within a single item field.* ("Pattern Pricing," "Designers" discussion board on Ravelry, February 2018)

Pricing practices are also discussed on Ravelry's forum boards. Young designers may be expected to practice lower prices until they have built up their reputation, even though low pricing is generally controversial. Some discussions talk about the high cost of support implied by free and cheap patterns:

> *There's also the perspective that the cheaper the pattern, the more likely it'll need supporting—you only have to look over old discussions to see how disproportionately more pattern support is required for free/cheap patterns.*

More generally, discussions on the design forum boards, such as that below, tend to defend the value of design as an activity in the knitting field allegedly regularly threatened by voluntary contributions. Free pattern contributions are made essentially for social and symbolic rewards. A value is not put on the patterns in terms of the imperatives of professional production costs and materials. Although these patterns are often decried as unfair competition, there is no objective evidence that they really represent a threat. Existing research actually points to the positive aspects of online interactions between for-profit and not-for-profit actors (Beuscart 2004).

> *Knitting patterns are so undervalued as it is—tales of knitters willing to spend over $100 for yarn but flat out refusing to pay $5 for a pattern and expecting it to be free. In my opinion, we should raise our prices.*
>
> *You want to have really good designers? The kind of good that folks get after years and years of experience? Well, then you need an industry where people can*

support themselves well enough to make this their full-time job. And you need to pay the people who make it their full-time job well enough so that they can afford healthcare and can plan for retirement and can even afford a vacation from time to time. You need people to be able to make this a career, not a hobby. ("Pattern Pricing," "Designers" discussion board on Ravelry, February 2018)

Over and above the issue of pricing, we turn now to both the connection and the divide between ordinary Ravelers and "pros." Any user can post a pattern, but very few actually do, and becoming a "pro" is much more demanding than creating and uploading knitting instructions. Pattern entries in the database are controlled by volunteers, and inappropriate or incomplete contributions may be rejected. Ravelry offers professional status users easier access to socialization spaces (forum boards discuss intellectual property issues, as noted by S. Humphreys, in addition to pattern writing, etc.), but also a place for those in intermediate positions between consumers, producers, and sellers. Interviews and observations clearly show that this creates new types of relationships between these players. They also clearly show that it does not make relationships any more peaceful between users, hobbyists, and professionals.

4.3   Ravelry, a Valuable Social Space for Knitters

The project pages open a window for knitters to see what others have achieved. This view on the activity of others offers practical advantages, but also symbolic rewards. This applies to most of the social features offered by Ravelry and other online/offline spaces: "*It's not an old-fashioned thing I do on my own anymore, sometimes we even meet up in real life*" (Agnes, 48 years old). According to one of the creators of a French DIY exhibition, who had specialized in needlecraft, Internet tools are instrumental in knitters' "coming-out" process. She specifically quotes the international "Knit in Public Day," an event during which knitters post on the Internet photos and locations of them while knitting in public spaces. Other events, such as gatherings in knitting cafes and "yarn bombing" actions covering street furniture with knitwear, also incentivize knitters to "out" their craft in public. Referring again to F. Weber (1998), visibility plays an important role, especially in keeping this kind of activity in an intermediate position of conspicuous production: neither really a leisure nor a household chore.

All of the knitters we met said that the Internet and Ravelry raised their ability to develop their creativity through knitting. This often means liberating knitting from its exclusive family or care context. For years, Anne and Martine knitted knitwear only for the family's children and charity. So they were pleased to discover patterns and yarns to craft fashionable accessories that they were also willing to wear or to offer to friends. Younger knitters such as Leslie, Sarah, Josephine, and Nathalie all appreciate being able to share their creative experience—on top of their respective jobs—with a diverse audience. For their part, both Tina and Cecile intimately relate this creativity to their housewife status, even though Cecile—currently on a long-term medical leave of absence—also uploads patterns on Ravelry and has been giving knitting lessons for a long time. In a number of hiatuses in her professional career, she occasionally did piecework for Phildar, a French wool franchise.

Her profile is closer to Celia's (40 years old), which appears to be most illustrative of the intermediate economic place of knitting. Celia quit her job in welfare work eight months ago. She has two children (aged 5 and 8). Her husband is executive director in a leading French company and travels frequently, so she is mainly the one in charge of family care. She tells us that she did not like her previous job very much. She chose to work "*essentially to be self-sufficient.*" However, when combined with her domestic constraints, the job proved to be exhausting: "*I was struggling so much for a very, very low wage; it was totally ridiculous.*" Gifted in handicrafts, she has been knitting, blogging, and using Ravelry for a long time now. She uploads her own patterns and is trying to build a reputation on the network—she recently started participating in the discussion boards. She thinks it is quite impossible to make a living from selling patterns, but she would like to earn money by giving knitting lessons and selling knitting kits. The commodification of skills on courses and in workshops is often one of the major sources of income envisaged and taken up by "pro" and aspiring "pro" workers, especially since passing on knowledge and expertise remains a major line here in what can undoubtedly be described as a community of practice. Learning here is combined with forms of socialization and social participation (Lave and Wenger 1991).

However, as the work of Jean Lave and other researchers in the educational sciences points out, it is a big step to take from skills and formalization to knowledge transmission, which is not attainable by all individuals (Lave 1988). Celia appreciates the fact that these activities give her a better work-life balance. As she puts it: "*Now, I can work while keeping my world in order.*" The women we interviewed in the survey are quite well-educated, and have a good standard of living.

All the knitters we interviewed expressed a strong interest in the social aspect of their practices. Once again, the social value of domestic production such as knitting is not recent, but its resilience today may seem surprising, unless one agrees with Emily Matchar's theory of a return to domesticity (Matchar 2013). This new domesticity becomes ubiquitous as its spaces and audiences extend online well beyond the home. Digital mediation and social networks appear to very much amplify the social dimension of knitting. Although few people ultimately design new models, many benefit on Ravelry from the social value generated by their knitting practice.

5 Conclusion

In the light of the recent digitization of most aspects of everyday life, it is worth rethinking the current characteristics of the socioeconomics of ordinary "leisure" activities. In that respect, one of the major changes brought about by a specialized database-structured social network such as Ravelry may be its provision of new and intermediate places to a mostly female audience. These places, situated between the domestic, family sphere and the public sphere, enable the socialization of knitting practices to expand. Online tools therefore increase the visibility and hence the social value of activities usually suffering from a dual form of invisibility: as female domestic work and as female technical skills (Cockburn and Ormrod 1993; Gardey 2006; Wajcman 2000). An examination of contemporary knitting consequently frames the online reputation issue much more from the point of view of "honor" and social meaning (Beuscart et al. 2015) than a search for fame and "glory" (Cardon et al. 2011). By transforming both the material and informational infrastructure of knitting, and hence the configuration of the provisioning of this practice, new communication technologies have therefore had a strong impact on both the economic and social dimensions of knitting.

Ravelry's centrality appears to be a unique case in online leisure activity communities. This is probably due to certain characteristics intrinsic to knitting: the singularity of yarn as the raw material combined with the diversity of yarn characteristics and quality; the ease of handling combined with the hard-to-master nature of the practice; and, lastly, the ease of distribution of patterns (which are basically instructions and charts, which can be produced and circulated in A4 paper format). Those characteristics are consistent with the particular format of the database-structured social network market adopted by the website.

We have described a number of the effects of this particular arrangement. Firstly, in the continuity of the socio-technical changes preceding it, it makes for describable, measurable, comparable, and widely publishable local and domestic production. In this process, specific features such as project pages appear as new forms of conspicuous production within the practice and create visibility for others' work. This production, which feeds the network's database, and more common participation systems (ratings, comments, and favorites) enable users to make a highly significant contribution to the value and evolution of the goods traded on the social network. Secondly, it builds bridges and opens doors, creating new relationships and connections between producers and consumers. However, as we have seen, this does not prevent a significant separation of these roles, but the "amateur/professional" divide becomes less effective at describing them. Thirdly, and in relation to the previous points, sharing, production, and sales spaces such as Ravelry are seized on by a significant proportion of the women we met as alternative spaces, places for rewarding creative expression with attractive professional prospects. The survey also reveals the low proportion of professional pathways open to site users, and the difficulties they entail. In view of critical studies on the mediatization of post-feminist developments and the new forms of a gendered division of labor, it is worth considering here these projections of a female professional ideal combining entrepreneurship with domestic work (Adkins and Dever 2016; Duffy and Hund 2015). As these studies point out, these representations tend to make a significant workload and the associated contingency invisible.

Appendix

Table 2.1 The interviewees mentioned in the chapter

Pseudonym	Sex	Age	Occupation	Partner's occupation	Number of children (age)	On Ravelry since	Online patterns	Project pages
Martine	F	51	Librarian	Gardener	1 (26 years old)	2008		154
Eric	M	41	Yarn shop owner			2010	19 (2 free)	41
Mathilde	F	23	Student in business school	Engineer		2013	10	91
Leslie	F	30	Statistician	Game designer		2011		104
Celia	F	40	Unemployed office worker	Senior executive	2 (5 & 8 years old)	2008	4 (3 free)	157
Nathalie	F	32	Programmer	Web designer	1 (3 years old)	2010	2 (2 free)	23
Sarah	F	27	Architect	Teacher		2009	2 (2 free)	71
Tina	F	42	Office worker (training assistant)	Programmer	2 (11 & 14 years old)	2008		89
Cecile	F	43	Office worker (training assistant)	Manager in construction	2 (8 & 14 years old)	2012	8 (5 free)	164
Josephine	F	39	Archivist	Archivist	2 (10 months & 3 years old)	2009		134
Anne	F	48	Librarian	Cabinet maker		2008		402

Notes

1. Craft Yarn Council Website. https://www.craftyarncouncil.com/know.html. Accessed 10 February 2019.
2. Farhad Manjoo, "A Tight-Knit Community. Why Facebook can't match Ravelry, the social network for Knitters." July 6, 2011, *Slate*. http://www.slate.com/articles/technology/technology/2011/07/a_tightknit_community.html. Accessed 10 February 2019.
3. Note that Ravelers have to create a project page to be able to rate a pattern, but rating is not compulsory. The "most popular" is also "weighted to prefer recently popular things" as noted in a 2013 post from Ravelry's developer and owner Casey Forbes on the forum: https://www.ravelry.com/discuss/for-the-love-of-ravelry/2478208/1-25#2. Accessed 10 February 2019.
4. "2012, a Ravelry year in review!" January 2013. http://blog.ravelry.com/2013/01/11/2012-a-ravelry-year-in-review/. Accessed 10 February 2019.
5. This argument contradicts the views of many users we spoke to earlier, who said they reward free access to patterns by posting photos of the finished garment.
6. Ravelry's forums, "Sales by category, 2013–2015." https://www.ravelry.com/discuss/designers/3337981/1-25#21. Accessed 10 February 2019.

References

Adkins, L., & Dever, M. (2016). *The Post-Fordist Sexual Contract. Working and Living in Contingency*. Basingstoke: Palgrave Macmillan.

Beuscart, J.-S. (2004). Le devenir des innovations non marchandes sur l'Internet Une étude des modèles économiques des webradios. *Réseaux, 125*(3), 55–79.

Beuscart, J.-S., Chauvin, P.-M., Jourdain, A., & Naulin, S. (2015). La réputation et ses dispositifs. *Terrains and Travaux, 1*(26), 5–22.

Bowker, G. C., Baker, K., Millerand, F., & Ribes, D. (2009). Toward Information Infrastructure Studies: Ways of Knowing in a Networked Environment. In J. Hunsinger, L. Klastrup, & M. Allen (Eds.), *International Handbook of Internet Research* (pp. 97–117). Dordrecht: Springer Netherlands.

Cardon, D., Fouetillou, G., & Roth, C. (2011). Two Paths of Glory: Structural Positions and Trajectories of Websites within their Topical Territory. *ICWSM 5th AAAI Intl Conf on Weblogs and Social Media*, Barcelona, Spain.

Cockburn, C., & Ormrod, S. (1993). *Gender and Technology in the Making*. London: Thousand Oaks.

Coffin, J. G. (1996). *The Politics of Women's Work: The Paris Garment Trades, 1750–1915*. Princeton: Princeton University Press.

Currid-Halkett, E. (2017). *The Sum of Small Things: A Theory of the Aspirational Class*. Princeton: Princeton University Press.

Dagiral, E., & Peerbaye, A. (2016). Making Knowledge in Boundary Infrastructures: Inside and Beyond a Database for Rare Diseases. *Science and Technology Studies, 2*(29), 44–61.

Dayan, D. (2005). Paying Attention to Attention: Audiences, Publics, Thresholds and Genealogies. *Journal of Media Practice, 6*(1), 9–18.

Donnat, O. (2009). *Les Pratiques culturelles des Français à l'ère numérique enquête 2008*. Paris: La Découverte.

Duffy, B. E., & Hund, E. (2015). "Having it All" on Social Media: Entrepreneurial Femininity and Self-Branding Among Fashion Bloggers. *Social Media + Society, 1*(2), 1–11.

Fine, G. A. (1989). Mobilizing Fun: Provisioning Resources in Leisure Worlds. *Sociology of Sport Journal, 6*(4), 319–334.

Gardey, D. (2006). Culture of Gender, Culture of Technology: The Gendering of Things in France's Office Spaces between 1890 and 1930. In H. Novotny (Ed.), *Cultures of Technology* (pp. 73–94). New York: Berghahn Books.

Heaton, L., & Millerand, F. (2013). La mise en base de données de matériaux de recherche en botanique et en écologie. Spécimens, données, et métadonnées. *Revue d'Anthropologie des Connaissances, 7*(4), 885–913.

Hine, C. (2015). *Ethnography for the Internet: Embedded, Embodied and Everyday*. London: Bloomsbury Academic.

Humphreys, S. M. (2008). The Challenges of Intellectual Property for Users of Social Networking Sites: A Case Study of Ravelry. *Mind Trek Proceedings*, Tampere, Finland.

Humphreys, S. (2009). The Economies within an Online Social Network Market: A Case Study of Ravelry. *ANZCA 09 Annual Conference: Communication, Creativity and Global Citizenship*, Brisbane, Australia.

Lave, J. (1988). *Cognition in Practice: Mind, Mathematics and Culture in Everyday Life*. Cambridge: Cambridge University Press.

Lave, J., & Wenger, E. (1991). *Situated Learning: Legitimate Peripheral Participation*. Cambridge and New York: Cambridge University Press.

Luckman, S. (2016). Micro-enterprise as Work–Life 'Magical Solution'. In L. Adkins & M. Dever (Eds.), *The Post-Fordist Sexual Contract: Working and Living in Contingency* (pp. 91–108). Basingstoke: Palgrave Macmillan.

Matchar, E. (2013). *Homeward Bound: Why Women are Embracing the New Domesticity*. New York: Simon and Schuster.

Mellet, K., Beauvisage, T., Beuscart, J.-S., & Trespeuch, M. (2014). A "Democratization" of Markets? Online Consumer Reviews in the Restaurant Industry. *Valuation Studies, 2*(1), 125–146.

Orlikowski, W. J., & Scott, S. V. (2015). The Algorithm and the Crowd: Considering the Materiality of Service Innovation. *MIS Quarterly, 39*(1), 201–216.

Potts, J., Cunningham, S., Hartley, J., & Ormerod, P. (2008). Social Network Markets: A New Definition of the Creative Industries. *Journal of Cultural Economics, 32*(3), 167–185.

Simmel, G. (1994). Bridge and Door. *Theory, Culture and Society, 11*(1), 5–10.

Star, S. L., & Griesemer, J. R. (1989). Institutional Ecology, 'Translations' and Boundary Objects: Amateurs and Professionals in Berkeley's Museum of Vertebrate Zoology, 1907–39. *Social Studies of Science, 19*(3), 387–420.

Taylor, S., & Luckman, S. (Eds.). (2018). *The 'New Normal' of Working Lives. Critical Studies in Contemporary Work and Employment*. Palgrave Macmillan.

Veblen, T. (2009 [1899]). *The Theory of the Leisure Class*. Oxford: Oxford University Press.

Wajcman, J. (2000). Reflections on Gender and Technology Studies: In What State is the Art? *Social Studies of Science, 30*(3), 447–464.

Weber, F. (1998). *L'Honneur des jardiniers: les potagers dans la France du XXe siècle*. Paris: Belin.

White, R. (2007). The History of Guerilla Knitting. *24th Chaos Communication Congress*, December 27–30, Berlin. Retrieved February 17, 2019, from https://www.youtube.com/watch?v=owb1-E70R2s.

Zabban, V. (2011). Un monde en partage. La socialisation des espaces médiatiques du jeu en ligne, ou les reconfigurations sociotechniques du monde ludique. In C. Perraton, M. Fusaro, & M. Bonenfant (Eds.), *Socialisation et communication dans les jeux vidéo* (pp. 145–164). Montréal: Presses de l'Université de Montréal.

Zelizer, V. (2002). Intimate Transactions. In M. F. Guillén, R. Collins, P. England, & M. Meyer (Eds.), *New Economic Sociology: The Developments in an Emerging Field* (pp. 274–300). New York: Russell Sage Foundation.

Zimmermann, E., & Swansen, M. (2011). *The Opinionated Knitter. Elizabeth Zimmermann Newsletters 1958–1968*. Pittsville, WI: Schoolhouse Press.

3

Making Money Out of Leisure: The Marketization of Handicrafts and Food Blogging

Anne Jourdain and Sidonie Naulin

1 Introduction

Growing numbers of people are commodifying their leisure activities.[1] Today, 1.8 million handicrafters sell bags, clothes, and jewelry on Etsy, the leading web platform selling handmade items. Thousands of home cooks try to make money from their blogs and commodify their food services (homemade meals, cookery classes, cookbooks, press articles, etc.). This expanding marketization of everyday life is the result of two factors. First, there is the revival of arts and crafts and do-it-yourself (DIY) activities driven by dedicated TV shows (like "MasterChef"), the publication of books and magazines (such as "Mollie Makes"), and the

---

A. Jourdain (✉)
Paris-Dauphine University, PSL Research University, CNRS, IRISSO, Paris, France
e-mail: Anne.jourdain@dauphine.psl.eu

S. Naulin
Université Grenoble Alpes, CNRS, Sciences Po Grenoble, PACTE, Grenoble, France
e-mail: Sidonie.naulin@iepg.fr

© The Author(s) 2020
S. Naulin, A. Jourdain (eds.), *The Social Meaning of Extra Money*, Dynamics of Virtual Work, https://doi.org/10.1007/978-3-030-18297-7_3

emergence of specialist shops. The second factor is the enabling role of Internet technologies giving people a way to easily sell their products and services: "Digital communication [...] extends the possibilities for own-account working, for example, through the availability of online marketplaces and the possibility of using a digital shopfront instead of physical premises as the public face of a business" (Taylor 2018: 328).

Marketization takes different forms. Etsy sellers create their own virtual shop on the platform and sell craft products that they usually make at home. The platform makes a commission of approximately 3.5% on each transaction. In the case of food bloggers, marketization is an indirect output of the online publication of cookery recipes associated with blog audience figures. Given that food bloggers are seen as influencers in their community, food businesses contact them to pay them for advertising space and offer them free products to test along with sponsored posts. This commodification of relationships can become an incentive in itself.

Marketization generates variable and generally low income. Most sellers are hobbyists who work on another job which often has nothing to do with crafts or food. They regard the extra money they get from commodification as pin money. Only a minority seek to make a living from marketization, and only a handful of those succeed. Nevertheless, the media usually focuses on the latter and their "success stories."

The transformation of leisure into work and income-generating activities can be seen as a manifestation of the growing marketization of human activities. As shown by a number of studies, "Aspects of life are rendered highly organised and calculable, and monetised" (Mäkinen 2018: 142), and "Zones of private space and time that were once beyond the market are now being infiltrated by the requirements of paid work" (Webster and Michailidou 2018: 9). This meets "The post-Fordist expectation that all adults be engaged in paid work or, at least, be ready to do so, if unemployed" (Adkins 2016: 97). One consequence of these changes is the development of own-account working (ILO 2015), particularly among women. In France, our study location, women represented 21% of micro-enterprises in 1982 and 34% in 2012 (Abdelnour et al. 2017). Despite the growing number of women in business ownership, "Many [of them] do not readily identify with the label 'entrepreneur'" (Ekinsmyth 2011: 106). The rise of women's home-based crafts micro-enterprises and freelance work (Luckman 2015a) "challenges the assumed boundaries between paid work and leisure as well as between paid work and mothering" (Mäkinen 2018: 129). Selling homemade items on Etsy and food blogging are female activities that contribute to this phenomenon.

Generally speaking, marketization reshapes the boundaries between productive and reproductive work. The focus on success stories, and the dominant discourse of "leisure," "passion," "pleasure," and "choice," "obscures the additional labor that is involved alongside the creation of [the products]" (Ashton and Patel 2018: 148) and "hides the gendered nature of this work" (Rodney et al. 2017: 17). Journalist E. Matchar (2013) talks about "new domesticity" to describe this situation, and the expression has been taken up by critical academic literature (Luckman 2016). It describes the condition of white middle-class mothers in their 20s and 30s who escape traditional companies to work from home and balance work and family constraints. An empowering narrative runs through "new domesticity" in its suggestion that women can thrive on domestic work and motherhood. In this sense, marketization of female leisure activities is interpreted as a way for women who seek to balance work and family life to "have it all." By making money out of a leisure activity, they can both take care of their family and earn income. Although the implications of such a narrative have been scrutinized and criticized (Luckman 2016), there is a wide gap between rhetoric and reality that has not yet been entirely charted by social researchers. Empirical research is therefore needed to understand who these women marketizing their hobbies are, what their motivations are, what they gain from it, and how it changes their leisure activity itself.

What is the social significance of commodification by way of Etsy and food blogging? Why do middle- and upper-class women engage in such marketization? Why do they persist if the amount of money they make is modest and variable? And does the marketization of leisure activities have an empowering effect on women?

First, we map the emergence of the marketization of handicrafts and food blogging in women's trajectories. We then detail the economic and, more importantly, the non-economic gains of marketization to understand why women keep selling handmade items on Etsy and blogging about food—and thus keep doing the extra work required by commodification—even when they do not earn much money from it. Lastly, we conclude with a discussion of the empowering effects of marketization on women.

> **Method**
>
> Our two case studies—handicrafts and food blogging—are based on mixed-methods.
>
> First, we gathered statistical data on Etsy sellers and food bloggers. Using *web scraping*, we collected information on the 14,415 Etsy French shops in 2017, of which 88% were set up by women. We also sent a questionnaire to French food bloggers in 2011 (621 responses); 94% of respondents were women. Statistics pointed to huge inequalities between Etsy sellers and between food bloggers, shifting our focus away from solely the most visible, successful sellers.
>
> Second, we conducted semi-structured interviews with 17 Etsy sellers (14 women and 3 men) and 12 food bloggers (10 women and 2 men) between 2008 and 2018. We diversified the interviewees' profiles in terms of age, gender, location, visibility on the web, and type of handicrafts or cuisine. Particular attention was paid to the place of marketization in sellers' trajectories and everyday life.
>
> Third, we conducted ethnographic observations of crafts and food fairs such as Etsy Made in France and the Salon du Blog Culinaire in Paris and Soissons. We met and had informal discussions with many Etsy sellers and food bloggers at these fairs.

2 The Marketization of Leisure in Women's Trajectories

Typical trajectories can be drawn from our biographical interviews with Etsy sellers and food bloggers to explain why some women make the move to commodify their leisure activities. One of the main results of this biographical study is the particularly strong connection between professional career and life course. Marketization of a hobby often starts during a hiatus in the work and/or family life cycle. Marketization plays an offsetting role for women. Nevertheless, many social resources are required if commodification is to be possible.

2.1 Starting Marketization During a Hiatus

Many women in our qualitative sample started or developed their marketization of handicrafts or food blogging—if not the leisure activity itself—during a hiatus. Hiatuses are characterized by a lack of formal employment and/or forms of social isolation. Women on maternity, parental or sick leave, jobseekers, expatriates, pensioners, students, and so on, often present a combination of free time and forms of social isolation. During their hiatus, they become engrossed in a leisure activity at home such as cooking, crocheting, or sewing both to meet family needs and to cope with boredom. Many women learn handicrafts and cookery in the domestic sphere in childhood and adolescence from a relative, a mother, or a grandmother. Others learn those skills "on their own," from scratch, using web resources (blogs, forums, tutorials, etc.) and, in some cases, attending workshops and crafts or cookery courses. During the hiatus, these skills are (re)used to form both a leisure and a domestic activity. For example, Marjorie[2], a 25-year-old mother of one, who is employed in a polling organization and sells clothes on Etsy in her free time, learned how to sew from her aunt and her grandmother during school holidays. She has always sewn, but she really developed the activity during her parental leave. She looks up tutorials whenever she needs to find out how to make something. Vanessa's story is quite similar. Vanessa is a freelance journalist with two children. She has been running a food blog, attracting between 500 and 2000 visitors a day for some five years. She took up cooking when she was a student living on her own:

> *Funnily enough, I was interested in cooking even before I started a blog, back when I was a student ten years ago. Strangely, though, I don't remember ever cooking when I was a kid. My mother didn't like me being in the kitchen. She was afraid I would hurt myself. So I didn't even get to watch her cooking. However, I realized when I started cooking on my own in my student flat that I was recreating things that my mother and grandmother did. […] I got hold of a cookbook and there it was. I bought lots of food magazines at the time. […] The funny thing is that when I really started to cook, I would ask my mother for advice, and later the tables turned as she started asking me for advice!* (Vanessa, 37 years old)

The marketization of the hobby also often starts during a hiatus. In general, women knew Etsy and food blogs before they considered commodifying their leisure activity. Many Etsy sellers were Etsy buyers first and many food bloggers were food forum participants and food blog readers first. A total of 37% of food bloggers had already contributed to an Internet food forum, and half of them had done so before creating their own blog. Some 45% of the 14,415 French Etsy sellers use one and the same account to buy and to sell, while some may use two separate accounts. Although this figure says nothing about the timeline between buying and selling, it does show that the two activities are not exclusive for many Etsy sellers. Marketization is often the next step up from consumption. Immersion in their activity makes many women eager to share their passion with other like-minded people via online marketization in particular. Opening an Etsy shop or a food blog represents greater commitment to the activity and a will to convert a private domestic activity into a public, and, potentially, a profitable activity. It is also a way to join a social community and gain social recognition (see Part II). Vanessa explains why she created her blog:

> *I was very active on French online food forums. A dozen of us were very active contributors. Then we started to talk about blogs. I was a Pascale Weeks blog reader.*[3] *My daughter was born in 2004 so it would have been in 2004 that I started, because I was pregnant and I was on maternity leave and bored. And given that I'm a journalist by trade, I needed to write. So that's how it started. Because I was on leave throughout my entire pregnancy. I was stuck in bed with nothing else to do.* (Vanessa, 37 years old)

Maternity or parental leave is a typical catalyst for the commodification of women's leisure activities. Six of the 14 women in our qualitative sample of Etsy sellers started their activity while on maternity or parental leave, when they had the free time to develop a new activity at home. Like female entrepreneurs, their new activity is sometimes associated with motherhood (Harding 2006), such as making and selling baby clothes on Etsy. Marjorie opened her Etsy shop a year before she went on parental leave, but really developed her seamstress activity on leave. Her choice of clothing output also evolved with the birth of her daughter: "*I* used to only make clothes for myself. I made many things for myself. But I've made a lot of baby clothes since she was born." From here on, her Etsy shop displayed mainly babywear. Likewise, many food bloggers started blogging during parental leave, when having babies or infants at home raised the issue of "eating well" and better home cooking. For example, Delphine, a civil servant in her 30s, started cooking to cater for her son's food allergies and because she thought that homemade food was healthier for children. She created a blog to share her recipes with her friends, and now she has between 800 and 1300 readers a day.

Hiatuses can be seen as "turning points" (Hughes 1971) for leisure activities, since they alter women's trajectories and activities. At the end of the period, marketization can be continued, stopped, or raised to the level of a professional undertaking. Its importance in women's lives also depends on the extent of their dissatisfaction with their professional and domestic spheres.

2.2 Marketization as an Offsetting Activity for Women

Hiatuses, especially maternity leave, are often moments when working women reconsider their life priorities. Do-it-yourself activities, such as handicrafts and cookery, are domestic activities that can be conducted at home for the good of the family. They form part of the traditional reproductive activities, now rebranded as socially desirable (Matchar 2013). Marketization is initially often merely an extension of ordinary domestic activities. Most food bloggers explain that they do not cook specific dishes for the blog ("*it's everyday dishes*"), and half of the survey respondents spontaneously describe their blog recipes as "ordinary," "easy," and "quick." Marketization is a means to make domestic activities productive, streamlined, and potentially profitable. It can be seen as making reproductive work pay. The marketization of everyday life gives women a new possibility to balance parenthood with work by combining paid work with the achievement of their traditional reproductive work. For mothers, especially stay-at-home mothers, it is an opportunity to have their own space without having their entire life organized around their partner and children's needs. This trend is consistent with the individualization of society. For Marjorie, making and selling clothes on Etsy is a way to pass her time at home when her IT consultant husband plays guitar or video games:

> *He's happy to see I've got something I enjoy doing, but he's not interested in it. […] He plays music a lot. The living room is full of guitars. He also plays on the computer. He's a bit of a geek. So we each have our own activities. Every day, we spend an hour and a half doing our own thing in our own space. It's a balance, it's a good thing.* (Marjorie, 25 years old)

Likewise, food bloggers, even those without children, appreciate having their own creative space in the household. Audrey, a 24-year-old lab technician, and Charlotte, a 22-year-old student, who created their food blogs two years previously and have less than 250 readers a day, say of their blogs "*It's our private place*" (Audrey) and "*It's an outlet. […] Hands off*" (Charlotte).

Handicrafts and cookery are also valued because they provide an opportunity to master an entire production process and develop skills and creativity. Do-it-yourself activities have indeed become fulfilling activities for mostly middle-class women. Etsy sellers often talk in our interviews about the pleasure of doing things for themselves, from start to finish. Marjorie puts it this way:

> *I bought a sewing machine and it was the beginning of the end. I did nothing but sew. I've always loved making things. I've always been good with my hands. Sewing frees up my mind to think about other things. But there's also the preparation phase when I'm thinking about what I'm going to do, and that keeps my mind occupied. I like it. I spend hours looking at things I might like to buy on the Internet: fabric, buttons and all. I don't buy them, but I spend hours looking and it keeps my mind focused. I need it. I love this phase and the next phase, the actual making.* (Marjorie, 25 years old)

Creativity is particularly prized by Etsy sellers and food bloggers. It is generally driven by the practice itself: just 32% of the food bloggers say they started their blog to cultivate their creativity, but later on, more than 50% recognize that blogging has cultivated their creativity.

These aspects contrast with the experiences of some working women in their main occupation, which is why marketization is sometimes regarded as a way to offset discontent at work (boredom, adverse working conditions, frustration, stress, etc.). Diane, who works as a marketing manager for a start-up, created her shop on Etsy (selling textile jewelry) because she was bored with her previous job in a large company:

> *I worked for a British laboratory, which was taken over by an American lab. And I said to myself, 'A crushing office life is not for me'. And something was missing. I have desires, I felt I could do more enjoyable things. I didn't feel fulfilled. I loved sewing. […] And then, I thought, 'Take the plunge and create your own online shop'.* (Diane, 29 years old)

Like Diane with her Etsy shop, numerous food bloggers see blogging as a way to escape an unfulfilling job: "*I was a French teacher in Spain, [food blogging] was a way out*" (Laura), "*[I know a blogger who] is a doctor. For him, cooking is a way to relax and unwind from the stress*" (Robert), and "*I was bored. I was webmaster […] and I said to myself, 'Wow, why don't I create a blog?'*" (Soizic).

In most cases, the marketization of handicrafts and food blogging remains a rewarding sideline. Most Etsy sellers and food bloggers are hobbyists who do not intend to leave their main job in an occupation that often has nothing to do with crafts or food (clinicians, secretaries, survey managers, etc.), even if these jobs are less appealing than the commodified hobbies. In the case of the food bloggers, 76% intend to remain hobbyists, while 8% are already food professionals (cooks, food industry PR managers, cookbook writers, cookery teachers, food photographers, etc.) and 16% wish to become food professionals within two years. The intention to remain purely hobbyists is explained by the lack of constraints on leisure activities (most of them do not declare their activity as a business) and the risks associated with a career change. In addition, those amateurs are attached to "continuous, contractually formalised employment" (Huws 2013: 2), which gives them a regular wage and social protection (unemployment benefit, social security, and pension scheme). Yet they do have the option of embracing the post-Fordist ideal of entrepreneurship by trying hybrid models to combine their passion with security. Such is the case of Robert, whose blog (created a year ago) has stirred a desire to become a food professional:

> *I have two jobs. The first is my 'day job': I'm an IT project manager. That's what they call 'gainful' employment. And then I have set up a sideline business as a private chef.* (Robert, 45 years old)

In a few cases, often after a hiatus, the marketization of a leisure activity gradually comes to be seen as a way of changing profession, often to escape from an unsatisfactory situation. This is the case with Elisabeth, a mother of three, who quit her job as an IT engineer to make and sell textile goods (bags, blankets, etc.). During the interview, she was particularly critical of her working conditions in a large corporation. Her three-year break on parental leave made those working conditions even harder to bear:

> *I didn't like it anymore. I switched off. I didn't feel comfortable anymore. And it was complicated because there wasn't much of a future there. I always did the same work. Every higher position was already taken, so I didn't have many prospects. [...] I had seen other ways of working and it was difficult to come back to the 'every man for himself' method. [...] And it was complicated being a girl, as I often got put in charge of documentation 'because girls like documentation'.* (Elisabeth, 42 years old)

Elisabeth's case is representative of many women's occupational shift to crafts jobs. The individuals concerned are mainly educated women who work for large companies as consultants, human resources managers, engineers, sales representatives, and so on. Even though they have climbed the social ladder and earn a relatively comfortable income, these women can be highly critical of their occupation: they talk about a loss of interest in their work, mainly because they have no command of the entire production process and sometimes because they cannot bear the chain of command in their firm (Jourdain 2014). They often feel frustrated with their mundane jobs, especially when they have studied for years to get there. Their frustration is also due to the lack of career opportunities in their workplace. This is a gendered situation that is due partly to the glass ceiling and partly to the general deterioration in working conditions and terms of employment in contemporary societies (Méda and Vendramin 2017). Starting a crafts or food business is a way to avoid unsatisfactory working conditions, do a meaningful, rewarding job, and fulfill self-employment aspirations.

Etsy features a high number of women wanting to change career to become entrepreneurs in order to better manage the work-family balance. The platform specifically promotes home-based entrepreneurship with its motto, "Turn your Hobby into a Business on Etsy." This phenomenon appears to relate less to food blogging, which is less directly commodification oriented. Women who leave their job to become stay-at-home working mothers have been dubbed "mumpreneurs," a neologism coined from "mum" and "entrepreneur." C. Ekinsmyth defines them as "female entrepreneurs who operate at the interface between paid work and motherhood" (2011: 104). Even though she does not define herself as a "mumpreneur" (like other Etsy sellers do), Elisabeth has all the characteristics of one. She decided to quit her job to escape unsatisfactory working conditions, but also to take better care of her three children:

> *I said to myself, 'I'm going to do it differently.' I started sewing on parental leave so I thought, 'That's what I'll do.' I was a bit naïve. I didn't understand the implications of it all, 'It's going be great!! I'm going to work at home. That way, I'll have time for my children and I'll be able to work and sell and make money.'*
> (Elisabeth, 42 years old)

This interview extract is a perfect example of the "having it all" myth, which is particularly widespread among mumpreneurs and Etsy sellers who think they have found the ideal solution to balance work and family life (Luckman 2016). Elisabeth only works at her business during school hours, from 9 a.m. to 4 p.m. She is happy to spend a lot of time with her children, especially since their father gets home late at night. Besides, motherhood is particularly dominant in her business since many of the textile items she makes are designed for children, with her own children being the first to benefit from them. This situation seems to fit her "having it all" ideal, but the reality is actually far from that straightforward, as we will see in Part II.

Lastly, selling items on Etsy and blogging gives women the possibility to make their domestic activities profitable and publicly visible, and to achieve their potential by having a creative activity of their own. It can offer a positive social identity to women who lack recognition as workers or family members. These women see marketization as a form of empowerment. Nevertheless, commodification requires many social resources, which means it is not accessible for all.

2.3 Social Conditions Required for the Marketization of Leisure

Whereas there are few barriers to entry for leisure activities such as handicrafts and cooking, marketization of these hobbies requires many social resources. Marketization entry costs are low due to web platform accessibility, and there is no direct cost or need for sophisticated IT skills to create a blog or open an Etsy shop. However, and quite surprisingly at first glance, people who commodify their leisure are often more educated than the rest of the population. Most Etsy sellers are highly educated and hold or held high-level professional positions (consultants, teachers, lawyers, etc.) requiring intellectual skills (foreign language proficiency, communication skills, knowledge of accounting, etc.). Likewise, food bloggers have higher degrees than the rest of the female population, even though their occupations are diverse. The high level of education among women who commodify their leisure may be explained by the fact that cultural capital helps build formal reasoning. Cultural capital also fosters a feeling of legitimacy to speak publicly and defend an aesthetic conception of handicrafts or cookery, which is particularly specific to bloggers who commodify their activity (Naulin 2014; Cardon et al. 2014).

Educated women often commodify their leisure activity by reinvesting their professional skills in it since, despite the Internet-related availability of marketization, there are actually many skills required to become an economic player. Etsy sellers and food bloggers need to master online social networks such as Facebook, Twitter, Pinterest, and Instagram to be visible to potential customers. They must be aware of the other lifestyle blogs on the Internet. They also need to work on the presentation of their output and of themselves on the Internet and elsewhere (see Part II). Staging as a social skill (Goffman 1959), by means of pictures or the written word, is essential for marketization. That is why marketization is fostered by a high level of cultural capital associated with the use of acquired professional skills. Marketization itself is also a skill-building activity. Most food bloggers attest that their cookery, writing, photography, and information technology skills have seriously improved since the start of their activity.

When Etsy sellers or food bloggers do not have a command of the marketization skills they need, they sometimes rely on family or friends, even if they do not share their passion for crafts or food. Their son or daughter may create their online shop or their husband might take pictures of their dishes for their blog or help with the transportation of objects to physical crafts fairs. Vincent, a 40-year-old musician who has a two-year-old blog with some 200 readers a month, explains that his partner helped him with pastry-making at the start, *"because she is a food lover, in particular a pastry lover, so she is much more precise than [him]."* His brother, a sales representative for a food company, helped him set prices for the cookery classes he sold on his blog. Both continue to give him feedback on his undertaking.

Family is also a key resource for Etsy sellers and food bloggers when it comes to moral support. Commodifying a domestic activity implies negotiations with members of the household. The time spent on the leisure activity and its marketization is often seen as "deducted" from family time. Laetitia, a mother of two, who makes cushions and bags, and is particularly productive selling them online, explains how her family organization was affected by the marketization of her leisure activity while she was still working as an assistant for a large law firm:

> Did your husband support you in this activity?
>
> *Absolutely. Absolutely. And God knows how many sacrifices he made. Because our family life completely changed. [...] My husband is the one who cooks, shops and cleans. He's a cook himself, so as regards the cooking, it's great! He looks after the children, takes them to their sports, everywhere. [...] It's not been easy for our children. They're older now—twelve and sixteen years old—but when I started my son was seven. I can't tell you how many times he said, 'I know you prefer sewing to your children.' That's very hard to hear.* (Lactitia, 42 years old)

Similarly, Nathalie, a stay-at-home mother of three with a one-year-old blog, recounts her family's reaction to the time she spends cooking and blogging:

> My husband just says, 'I'm fed up with this. You're either in your kitchen or in front of your computer.' That's how he reacts [laughs]. My children say, 'Mom, can't you just get off your computer and come play with us?' (Nathalie, 33 years old)

Other food bloggers report criticism from their families that by the time the photos have been taken, the food is cold. However, all in all, family satisfaction (better meals and pride) appears to outweigh complaints. Many partners are not interested in the leisure activity itself, but they encourage it, especially as it is a domestic activity. Moral support from the family is particularly important to women who decide to try make a living from the marketization of their hobby. Such is the case with Fabienne, an IT executive for a major computer company who decided to take a sabbatical in 2004 when her children were one and three years old. She needed a break after an uninterrupted line of "study-employment-childbirth." During her sabbatical, she created her food blog. Her husband's support was crucial to her decision to try to make a living from the marketization of her blog and not go back to her previous job:

> I thought I would go back [to my former job] and I even did interviews. I knew what I would do [back in the company]. And then, a few days before going back, my husband said, 'Listen, if you want to go into that field [i.e. blog-related economic opportunities], go ahead, and resign.' Otherwise, I would have gone back because, on my own, I wouldn't have dared. I needed the support of my... his support is important to me. (Fabienne, 45 years old)

Family, and especially partners, also often provide financial support for the undertaking. In fact, most Etsy sellers and food bloggers do not make a living from the marketization of their leisure activity (see Part II). They consequently rely either on their own incomings (wages, welfare benefits, and family inheritance) or on their partner's (or their parents') incomes. When they quit their job to live off this activity, they generally rely on their partner, be it for moral support or income. Fabienne was able to keep going for four years between her resignation and the moment she started to make a living from her blog, which now has 7000 readers a day, thanks to the financial support from her husband who is a team manager for a computer firm. In the case of Etsy sellers, partners are also generally male executives earning relatively high steady incomes. Karine, a ceramist who launched a ceramic jewelry business on Etsy after quitting her salaried job as director of an art gallery, admitted during the interview that she did not earn enough from her new activity to pay the rent for her apartment:

> *My partner encourages me in everything I do.*
> *And the apartment?*
> *Yes, he pays. I don't have to pay the rent or charges for the apartment.*
> (Karine, 38 years old)

Lastly, despite its accessibility, marketization of leisure activities tends to be restricted to women with certain assets: a high level of education, acquired marketing skills, a supportive family, and alternative sources of income. That explains the middle- and upper-class profile of most of the Etsy sellers and food bloggers.

3 Why Sell $5 Handmade Rings on the Internet?

Marketization does not necessarily make the activity a money-spinner. Most Etsy sellers and food bloggers only really earn pin money on the Internet. They do not generally make a living from the marketization of their domestic and leisure activities. This then raises the question as to why thousands of women persevere with this unprofitable online marketization. In actual fact, their pin money is endowed with a social significance rooted in the many non-economic benefits of marketization.

3.1 The Modest Economic Profits of Marketization

The degree of marketization is found to be limited. The distribution of sales and incomes is particularly uneven on the Internet and often follows a "power law" (20% of sellers make 80% of sales). Our quantitative data confirm this: 10% of Etsy sellers make 88% of the platform's sales (Fig. 3.1). Only 1% of them earn the equivalent of the minimum wage. Most French Etsy sellers earn modest incomes from their online shops: their average monthly turnover is €91, and 50% of them earn less than €10 a month.

Similarly, only one-third of food bloggers earn any money from their activity, and most of them are paid in kind. Earnings are closely associated with audience figures and 20% of food bloggers attract 75% of the total food blog-watching audience (Fig. 3.2). There are different ways to make "something" out of a blog. The most frequent is advertising. Some 65% of food blogs host food brand advertisements, but there is very little to be earned from them unless the blog has a huge readership. Brands also send bloggers products (yogurts, rice cookers, cookbooks, etc.) for them to test and, if they like them, mention in their recipes. Half of all the food bloggers have already received such gifts. When it comes to actually making a profit, the number of bloggers concerned and the frequency of transactions decrease: only 8% of food bloggers have already been paid

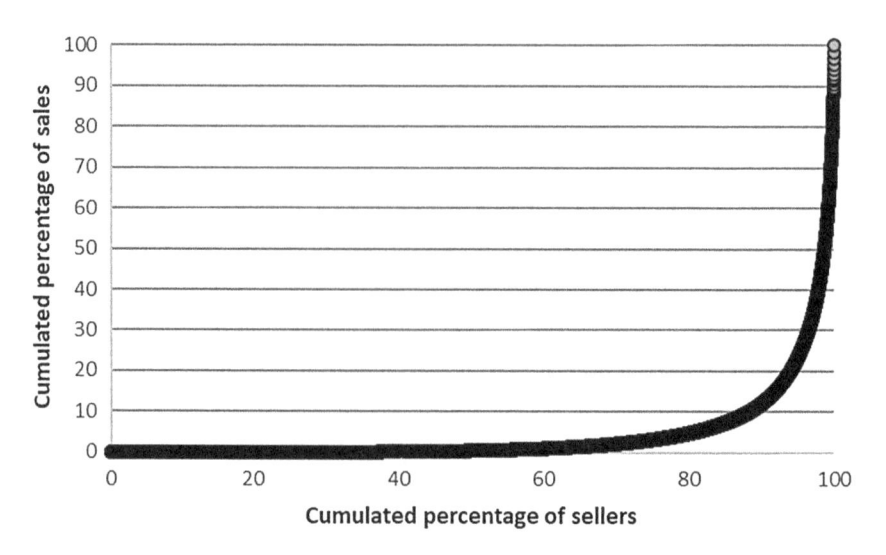

Fig. 3.1 Cumulative distribution of sales among Etsy sellers

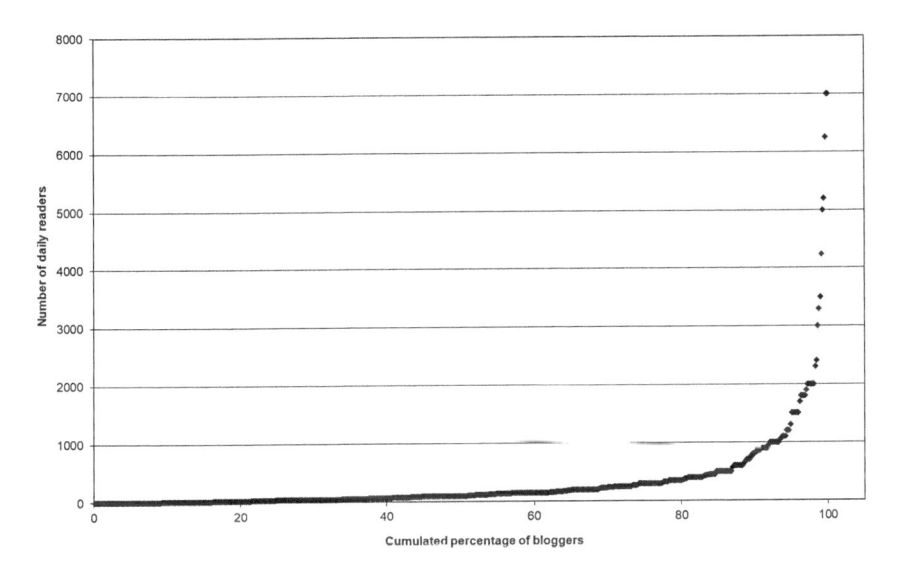

Fig. 3.2 Number of daily readers among food bloggers

(in money) to write a "sponsored post" for a brand, the same proportion has already collaborated more closely with a brand (e.g. being paid for providing a number of recipes to a brand website), and almost 6% have been paid for hosting a brand event (dinner, cookery class, trade fair, etc.). Among those bloggers who receive something, 75% earn less than €50 a month, be it in cash or in kind. All in all, there are direct food blogging profits to be made, but they are very modest and often paid in kind. Consequently, Etsy selling and food blogging are activities that cannot be seriously considered as profitable businesses.

Most Etsy sellers and food bloggers do not see their commodification activity as a true business. When food bloggers are asked about what their blog brings them, economic considerations rank last (2% money; 11% new professional opportunities; 28% possibility to test free products vs. 80% possibility to share one's passion; 75% personal satisfaction; 52% to develop one's creativity; and 50% entertainment). This ranking cannot only be interpreted in terms of "*amor fati*" (Bourdieu 2001) (because they do not earn money, they do not want to earn money). Indeed, for some of them, marketization happens without being sought, and for many of them, there is a will not to commodify their activity at any price. Half of the food bloggers say they have already refused brands' proposals to test products, and 40% have already refused advertising. Such is the case with Nathalie who created her food blog one year ago and has 65 readers a day. She turned down €50 vouchers because she did not want to put brands' web links on the front page of her blog (she has a dedicated page for that, which is far less visible), because "*it is not [her] image.*" She has also declined proposals to take part in a famous TV show for amateur cooks:

> *[The TV show], for example, has asked me to take part three times, and no, I don't want to. Because it doesn't showcase the cooking enough. I'm a bit of a purist [laughs]. Maybe there are not so many people like me, but there it is: on my blog, there are no advertisements flashing all over the place. I don't want to appear on TV just to appear on TV. I do things because they mean something, because it suits me. I don't want to lose what I'm all about. The blog is here for my pleasure and to impart things, to share. That's its function. […] I'm not trying to earn something from [my blog]. Making a name, a little pleasure, that's all. […] To me, it remains a hobby, a pleasure and, maybe in six months, I'll stop. I don't know. I don't want to become chained to it.* (Nathalie, 33 years old)

Etsy sellers and food bloggers thus often see themselves as amateurs, especially when they hold a salaried job in fields which have nothing to do with crafts or food. For example, Marjorie, who works for a polling organization, does not see herself as a real craftswoman or seamstress:

> *Craftsmen are much more professional people. They are more skilled. I'm self-taught. I've improved my skills, so now my finishes are good and all. But I would not talk about craftsmanship because, to me, craftsmanship is higher. It's haute couture.* (Marjorie, 25 years old)

Vanessa, a journalist who has been a food blogger for five years, talks about her leisure activity in the same kind of way, "*I do not pretend to master the fundamentals of cooking. I'm a long, long way away from that.*"

When actual money is earned from Etsy or blogging, the small amounts are usually reinvested in the activity (Zelizer 1994), especially by amateurs. Food bloggers use the money to finance the web platform hosting their blog when it is not free, to buy a camera to take better pictures of their dishes, or to invest in new cooking utensils. As Soizic, who created her blog four years ago, puts it:

> *For a long time, there were no [advertisements on my blog]. But recently, I gave in. I put up very discrete Google Ads to finance my web host. They bring in enough to pay for my web host by the end of the year. That's it. It's not income in itself.* (Soizic, 33 years old)

Likewise, Etsy sellers see the money as an opportunity to buy new raw materials (fabric, pearls, accessories, etc.), new tools, or a better camera. Marjorie, who sells the clothes she makes on Etsy, explains how what she perceives as "extra money" finances her hobby:

> *I say to myself, profits aside, if it pays for my fabric and the things I want to make for myself, if I can recoup the actual cost of what I buy to make my own clothes, then that's already a good thing. It means I can make myself lots of things for free, while having a great time making things for others.* (Marjorie, 25 years old)

For amateurs like Marjorie, commodification is not a profit-seeking activity, but serves rather to reduce the costs of an expensive hobby.[4]

Among the minority of amateurs who earn more money than their costs, some regard marketization as a means to improve their day-to-day life. This is especially the case with students whose income is particularly low. Charlotte, a 22-year-old food blogger and a master's student on an apprenticeship, living with her mother, confesses, "*I got two silicon steam cases. They cost €25 each. I would never have bought them by myself.*" Similarly, Carole, a 23-year-old who lives with her parents while studying international relations and management at university, sells clutch bags on Etsy in order to finance her trips to Turkey, Israel, and Lebanon where she gets the fabric and accessories for her items, "*To begin with, I only did it to be able to travel regularly. [...] People often ask me if I intend to set up a shop. Not at all, actually. My intention is to stay very mobile.*" In Carole's case, Etsy money is perceived as pin money and goes directly into her traveling expenses.

Some Etsy sellers and food bloggers set out to make a living from their activity. Unlike hobbyists, they often register as self-employed when developing a crafts or food business. Although they make more money on the whole than amateurs, they generally do not manage to earn a living from their online activity. They consequently seek to develop profitable side activities on the back of the popularity of their online showcase (DIY/crafts or cookery classes, consultancy, food photography, cookbooks, etc.) and, in the case of Etsy sellers, to diversify their points of sale (crafts fairs, decoration shops, etc.).

The modest amounts of money made from online marketization can generate frustration, particularly among aspiring professionals. In actual fact, the reality is a far cry from the success stories presented in the media and on platforms like Etsy, which promotes successful "featured shops" on its blog. At first, aspiring professionals regard the happy few who earn a wage from their online activity as proof that their professional dream can come true. As time passes, some of them start to feel bitter about their modest earnings: they had hoped they would sell more easily and make more money on the Internet. Their resentment sometimes targets the web platform that has not kept its marketization promise. For example, Elisabeth, who quit her job as an IT engineer to earn a living as a seamstress, has only sold a handful of her textile products on the Internet:

> *I've actually realized that if we don't help [the platform] make money, because we don't sell a lot or we don't attract new people to the platform or because we don't buy advertising, we get a poor ranking. It's a vicious circle. […] I'm disappointed with the platform. I find it hard. We're not helped, because we're completely invisible. And we don't make many sales.* (Elisabeth, 42 years old)

Over the years, those who persevere with their business ambitions despite low profits are those who can rely on other economic resources: a partner's substantial, steady income, family inheritance, a side job, and so on.

At the end of the day, only a small minority of Etsy sellers (about 1%) manage to earn a living from online marketization, and less than a dozen French food bloggers potentially earn the equivalent of the minimum wage from their blogs. Other bloggers, however, use their blogs to get a job in the food industry in an indirect form of blog marketization. The happy few who manage to make a living from online DIY or food activities receive a great deal of media coverage and academic attention. Despite their very small numbers, they represent an ideal for many aspiring professionals who hope to live off their crafts and cooking skills. Compared to other Etsy sellers and food bloggers, the fortunate few have a different social profile: more masculine, more educated, more urban and richer for food bloggers, and more masculine and child-free on Etsy. Some of them see themselves as entrepreneurs working full-time to make a name for their brand, particularly on Etsy where business is more central to the activity.

> **How about the men?**
> Men are often overlooked in the literature on leisure marketization. As partners, they often support their wife's activity, especially when it is a domestic activity. As sellers, however, they differ from the women. Our statistical data show that they represent 12% of Etsy sellers and 6% of food bloggers. Their average monthly turnover on Etsy is €150, compared with €84 for the women. Even in a female field, men are more successful than women and gender inequalities develop. In the case of the Etsy sellers, the interviews with the men ($n = 3$) suggest that they take a different angle to the marketization of leisure activities than the women. The commodification of their activity is more frequently driven by professional ambition. Unlike the women, the men are quick to alter their goods and services to make them more profitable. For example, Jonathan, a 41-year-old artist living with his wife and daughter, developed mini-design collections on Etsy alongside his one-off contemporary works of art, because they "*need to eat too.*" Moreover, men's careers are less influenced by their family trajectories. In the case of food bloggers, we also find a statistical overrepresentation of men among the most successful bloggers (in terms of readership and economic output) (Naulin 2014). The interviews ($n = 2$) suggest that family life and making money are secondary in their motivation to blog. The relative success of men in the marketization of female leisure activities can be explained by traditional gender inequalities in the professional fields associated with handicrafts and food blogging, that is, arts and crafts (Jourdain 2014) and catering (Naulin 2017). It may also be tie in with persistent gender stereotypes that associate men with art and talent, while women are relegated to domesticity and "inconsequential" activities.

3.2 The Non-economic Profits of Marketization

Given that the marketization of amateur output is not generally an income-generating activity, why bother to try making money out of it at all? Why do Etsy sellers and food bloggers insist on commodifying their skills and items when they could do crafts and cook for free, for themselves and for friends and family? This question is all the more challenging that the market, from a "hostile worlds" angle, is frequently seen as a corruption of the spirit of art and leisure, which is meant to be free (Zelizer 2011). An empirical study of people who commodify their leisure activity is needed to address this issue.

Amateurs who commodify their activity actually justify doing so in terms of the small economic profits they make and other kinds of benefits. First of all, they consider marketization as a means to extend the scope of their activity. For Etsy sellers who used to give their handmade items as gifts or sell them to close relatives, and for food bloggers who used to pass their recipes to family and friends, online commodification represents an extension of the scope of their activity beyond "intimate transactions" (Zelizer 2001). Elisabeth typically started to sew for her three children before considering selling her items online and, later, trying to earn a living:

> *I began making bags. They were gifts, gifts for the teachers. And tee-shirts on which I flocked prints. For example, my youngest son, at school, his teacher organized massage sessions, so they massaged each other, so they needed blankets, so I made a blanket with a dinosaur and a name. I customized a lot. And later, when I came back off maternity leave, I thought, 'Why not sell?'* (Elisabeth, 42 years old)

Marketization also represents a challenge that forces Etsy sellers and food bloggers to step outside of their comfort zone by publicly displaying their achievements and setting them up to be compared with others. Comparison and social interaction foster emulation. Many food bloggers report that taking part in contests organized by brands (e.g. to create a recipe using one of the brand's products) is a means for them to invent new recipes, cook unusual products, and stimulate their creativity. Etsy sellers report the same phenomenon in their interactions with potential clients who ask them to make slightly different objects than those displayed in their Etsy shop.

Marketization also fosters socialization. Social interactions are developed with clients and readers. On business platforms such as Etsy, sellers and buyers are connected by means of a specific messenger. Some Etsy sellers—particularly amateurs who sell just a few items—appreciate being able to talk to their customers: they feel they are not engaged solely in anonymous market transactions. Likewise, food bloggers particularly appreciate comments from readers who have tried their recipes. Robert, a food blogger for one year with 65 readers a day, says:

> *There are two ways of sharing: one is sharing by letting people taste my recipes, and the other is sharing with people who read and round out my recipes. It is a more extensive type of sharing. […] When I cook one of my recipes again, I pick up the recipe on my blog and read the comments: this person told me to do this and so on. So I get better, I evolve, I don't get stuck.* (Robert, 45 years old)

This feedback, which is sometimes all the feedback they get when they live in an environment where people do not really share their passion (as is the case with one in three food bloggers), is often mentioned as the main motive for carrying on with the activity. Nathalie, a food blogger who is a stay-at-home mother of three, says:

> *It's an incentive to say to yourself, 'I've got a comment. That means it interests someone, so I'll carry on.' There are days when you lose the will. […] There are moments when you feel trapped. […] I've made many recipes where I haven't had the courage to take pictures [for the blog], because it was late, […] I was tired, the kids were screaming, they were hungry. If a comment pops up at these moments saying, 'Look, it's great, I love your blog, etc.', well, okay then, I need to carry on.* (Nathalie, 33 years old)

Socialization generated by marketization also remains in the peer community (Cox and Blake 2011). Before the advent of blogs came cookery forums (Marmiton, Supertoinette, etc.), which built a community of food lovers. Blogs have brought a new dimension to the exchanges, and the very dense interactions they have fostered have created a "virtual community" (Rheingold 1993). Many food bloggers post comments on other blogs, and the community fabric is strengthened by a convention of mutual support (answer comments, visit commentators' blogs, swap blog links, etc.). These forms of exchange not only obey Internet socialization norms but also assist players' profile-raising strategies (Dupuy-Salle 2014): two out of three bloggers leave comments on blogs in order to promote their own and tend to target high-traffic blogs. On Etsy, the same mutual back-scratching convention exists for the same reasons (e.g. exchange of "favorite shops" to improve their ranking by the Etsy algorithm). Online interactions between peers occur mainly on the Etsy website forums. These forums address specific business questions (e.g. "Buyer sent wrong address") and unrelated discussions (e.g. "Answer the question with a song"). The most highly organized forums use "teams" created by "leaders" who select the team members, moderate discussions, and sometimes organize events (16,220 teams were listed in July 2018). Many women speak highly of participation in Etsy forums and blogosphere exchanges, especially since these conversations are very encouraging and positive about their achievements, and because they make them feel less isolated. These discussions allow them to share their problems with people who understand them, since they have the same life experience (see Part I). In addition, discussions sometimes extend beyond crafts, cooking, and business to motherhood and domestic issues. This type of online socialization concerns specifically middle-class women who master the social codes required in such spaces (no spelling mistakes, politeness, introducing oneself, etc.). Such socialization also requires time. That is why the most committed Etsy sellers (particularly the team leaders) are keenly aspiring professionals with a mumpreneur profile, that is, stay-at-home mothers who can rely on their partner's income and do not need to earn money by themselves.

Online socialization regularly gives rise to physical meetings for both Etsy sellers and food bloggers. Team leaders on Etsy organize meetings and exhibitions, such as the biannual Etsy Made in France fair, in cities around France. Food bloggers also organize private meetings on a local basis and try to meet up at food events. For many years, the Salon du Blog Culinaire, the French equivalent of the International Food Blogger Conference in the USA, was held on a national basis. Consequently, almost half of the French food bloggers have already met some of their peers face-to-face. Contrary to the classic picture of anonymous market transactions, especially on the Internet, marketization actually fosters social interactions among women seeking to socialize.

Thirdly, marketization provides visibility and a new form of social recognition. Etsy shops and food blogs showcase sellers and their work. This can attract media coverage. One in three food bloggers has already been featured in one type of media (23% on an online-only news site, 22.5% in the national or regional press, and 12% on national or regional radio or television). Many Etsy sellers also seek to place their products on decoration and fashion blogs, and sometimes in the traditional media. It is also gratifying when the activity is recognized by fellow hobbyists, customers, and brands. Many food bloggers relate how "proud" their circle is (parents, partner, children, friends, colleagues, etc.) when they are mentioned in the media. Some of them also remark on a change in their relationships with the people around them. Laura, a 29-year-old food blogger with 1500 readers a day, has grown closer to her grandmother as a result of coverage on her blog. One of the rewards of marketization is therefore the positive image that can be relayed to a person's entourage. Most of Marjorie's buyers are actual friends who she regularly asks to look at her Etsy shop whenever she posts a photograph of a new piece of clothing. The case of Martine (whose blogger's name is Grannyta), a retired housewife married to a vet (Yves), is also a good example of this phenomenon. She has had a blog for five years, with between 2800 and 9000 readers a day. She told us:

> *The blog gave me things to tell my husband. I can tell him things that I did without him: cookery workshops and so on. Before [the blog], I was 'Yves' wife'. Now, I have become 'Grannyta' and he has become 'Mr. Grannyta'.* (Martine, 60 years old)

The success of Martine's food blog, and the connections and opportunities it generates, has given Martine a sphere of activity of her own and a new social identity outside and also in her household. More generally, the marketization of leisure activities is a self-confidence booster. Fabienne, a former IT engineer who has had a food blog for six years, intimates:

> *The blog ultimately made me realize that I really could write. Everybody says… [my relatives] in hysterics, they tell me, 'You have a Master's degree, you've written ten eight books, and one day, you read your name in a newspaper, and you say to yourself, 'Well, look at that, I like to write.'* (Fabienne, 45 years old)

Marketization is consequently experienced by many as a form of empowerment with respect to partners, parents, colleagues, friends, and so on. As K. Jarrett writes, a "use-value persists even within the broader context of commodified exchange" (2014: 25). Moreover, by publicly showcasing homemade items, be it clothes, jewelry, or home-cooked food, weblogs and online shops elevate these activities traditionally demeaned for their female attributes. Do-it-yourself (DIY) activities tend to be trendy and to legitimize and aestheticize the domestic sphere, making easier to take up doing them. However, this social upgrading is particularly ambiguous when it still carries the negative image of massively female activities unable to provide stable income.

3.3 From Leisure to Extra Work?

As with many activities, resources are needed to marketize a hobby: time (which is why many Etsy sellers and food bloggers start commodifying during a hiatus), economic resources (crafts materials and kitchenware, computer, camera, etc.), and skills (personal and relational). It can therefore be termed "serious leisure" (Stebbins 2007). The difference between marketization and mere leisure activities is found in the rational organization that commodification entails. For example, the visibility of Etsy sellers on the platform and blogger audience numbers are associated with the frequency and regularity of their online publication of new items and posts. For the sake of efficiency, many bloggers choose to plan their posts in advance (Mäkinen 2018). They need to frontload and discipline their leisure activity, which is particularly time consuming. Some 18% of food bloggers spend more than an hour a day maintaining their blog (taking, uploading, and editing photos; writing copy; answering comments and emails; negotiating commercial campaigns; checking other blogs; etc.). Consequently, many food bloggers and Etsy sellers use work-related terminology when depicting their activity. Delphine, a food blogger who is a full-time civil servant with two children, says her blog is "*a full-time job.*" Laura, a food blogger for two and a half years who is preparing for a competitive civil service examination, talks in a similar manner about sponsored posts:

> *I find it great in the sense that you discover products and create things and, at the same time, deliver real work.* (Laura, 29 years old)

Other food bloggers even use a language of constraint. Nathalie, for example, says, "*It forces me into a certain regularity,*" and Charlotte that, "*You also have to discipline yourself to make recipes every week.*" Consequently, compared to the mere leisure activity, commodification generates extra work. This extra work takes different forms.

Marketization implies commercial work with customers for Etsy sellers, and with brands for food bloggers. They need to learn how to manage interactions, how to set prices, how to read a business contract, and even possibly how to respond in the event of a dispute. Peer discussions and forums are the main sources of information for those who do not already have such skills. Business and management activities are sometimes seen as one of the purposes of the activity. Tue-Minh, an Etsy seller who makes paper sculptures, told us that she enjoyed playing shopkeeper outside of her job as a hospital pediatrician:

> *Actually, what I like about it is that sort of business game. Because it's not my educational background, it's not my thing, and I think I wouldn't have been good at it. I never saw myself doing marketing or business studies, things like that. But to gradually discover those things, that's like a game for me. And, since there is no real financial stake for me, I play shopkeeper, I play business strategy.* (Tue-Minh, 41 years old)

Keeping shop is not seen as degrading work, but as a stimulating game.[5] Lucrative online activities actually tend to blur the conceptual distinction between "playing," "gaming," "working," and "labouring" (Lund 2014).

In addition, like entrepreneurs, Etsy sellers and food bloggers have to define their market positioning (a brand for the former and an editorial line for the latter). Food blogs can take different lines for different audiences, as Fabienne, a food blogger who now makes a living from this activity, explains:

> *As I see it, blogs need to reflect something: either a personality or creative flair. You need to sense the person behind it. It has to express something. a lifestyle, a personality, an artistic side. Some blogs concentrate more on copy […], others on pictures […], others on techniques […]. Personally, I'm more "let's get cooking", but there are women who are more dream world, like a fashion magazine.* (Fabienne, 45 years old)

Once Etsy sellers and food bloggers have chosen their market positioning, they need to engage in intense "digital labor" (Scholz 2012) to create and sustain a positive online reputation for their personal brand. Communication skills are therefore required "to engage in unpaid social labor" (Baym 2014: 2). N. Baym defines this "relational labor" as "regular, ongoing communication with audiences over time to build social relationships that foster paid work" (2014: 4). For Etsy sellers and food bloggers, relational labor consists in presenting themselves, selling their work, signaling their expertise, and interacting with others on different social media (Facebook, Instagram, Pinterest, and Twitter) and in blogs and forums in order to build their audience and develop loyalty (Ashton and Patel 2018). In the case of bloggers, it also consists in registering the blog on web-indexing platforms, writing comments to prominent food bloggers, and soliciting brands to build partnerships that will make the blog active, visible, and profitable. The fact that many food bloggers have blog business cards, as we saw at the Salon du Blog Culinaire, demonstrates the growing professionalization of food blogger communication and the importance of their networking. Online visibility is also highly dependent on platform and search engine algorithms. Good ranking and visibility call for Etsy sellers and food bloggers to carefully tag their designs, recipes, pictures, and so forth. Karine, a professional ceramist, spends a great deal of time trying to improve her Etsy shop's online ranking:

> *Etsy uses incredibly sophisticated algorithms. You need keywords. It took time to learn that. It's not obvious. The more effective your keywords, the higher you appear in the search results. [...] So by doing that, I gradually worked my way up the rankings. It's quite hard work. For example, for Mother's Day, you have to add in the keyword 'Mother's Day'. For each season, the front image has to match the season. It's digital work I love to do, but it has to be done. At the start, my products got completely lost. I had two visits a month for a product. I didn't understand why. I took the time to read Etsy's online training information and I understood where the problem was. It took me months to get there.* (Karine, 38 years old)

Professionals are the most involved in such activities, but even hobbyists may spend a few hours a week managing their online shop or blog.

Communication is not just for the shops or blogs; it also concerns Etsy sellers and food bloggers themselves. The value of homemade output and audience size are closely associated with the person behind the shop or blog. "The public performance of the crafts producer's personal identity as part and parcel of the consumer value of their products—and as a proof of the stripped-back value chain of buying 'direct' from the maker—has become an essential part of the home-based maker's online marketing identity" (Luckman 2015b: 148). Food bloggers explain their success by the fact that readers can identify with them. As "ordinary" women (by middle-class standards), they cook for their family using non-professional utensils and affordable ingredients. They also have to combine paid job with family demands and sometimes constraints (food allergies, diabetes, veganism, etc.). Much like a neighbor or relative, they give cooking advice and can be directly contacted by means of comments (71% of food bloggers "often" or "systematically" answer their blog comments). "Proximity" and "ordinariness" explain why brands perceive food bloggers as consumer influencers. However, the Etsy seller or food blogger's online persona is more often than not a controlled, selective, and sometimes glamorized version of their "true" self, and it is one that needs working on. Specific self-presentation work is required to produce this online marketable "authentic" self (Goffman 1959). For example, Marjorie opens the "About" section of her Etsy shop with:

> *I've always enjoyed sewing, from wedding dresses for my Barbie dolls through dozens of shelved projects to my first skirt ... [...] My shop contains all the little sewing projects I'm so passionate about. I love making and perfecting them.* (Marjorie, 25 years old)

Marjorie took time to write this introduction when she created her shop on Etsy. She likes to fine-tune her presentation and the presentation of her clothes on her webpages, and she spends a great deal of time on it. As with many other sellers, she considers a project is finished not when she finishes sewing a piece of clothing, but when she has photographed the piece and put it on her Etsy shop with a brief description.

Narratives often speak of passion, authenticity, and creativity, just like the fashion bloggers (Duffy and Hund 2015) and vloggers (Ashton and Patel 2018). Etsy sellers and food bloggers often use words such as "passion," "research," "aesthetic," "original," "invent," "imagine," and "create" when talking about how they view handicrafts and cooking. They carefully consider whether to publish pictures of themselves, disclose their job or city of family residence, and talk about children and private family events (weddings, divorce, illness, etc.). Half of all food bloggers talk about their personal and professional life sometimes in their blog, transforming "the unpaid labor of social reproduction […] into online value creation" (Webster and Michailidou 2018: 11). The human face and "authenticity" of women who commodify their hobbies are actually products of time-consuming staging (interacting with clients and readers, taking pictures, and writing copy), narrative skills, and ethical choices.

The Etsy sellers' and food bloggers' commitment to make their leisure practice profitable—streamlining of their hobby, definition of their market positioning, communication work—make their activities look like entrepreneurship. Although food bloggers almost never define themselves as "entrepreneurs," Etsy sellers embrace this rhetoric typical of the post-Fordist era of platform capitalism much more easily (Adkins and Dever 2016). Sometimes the very creation of an Etsy shop is itself driven by the aspiration to become an entrepreneur with her own business. Beate, who quit her job as a consultant in a large corporation and who now identifies herself as a "mumpreneur" with two children, is particularly clear about her initiative to start a crocheted baby clothes business on Etsy:

> *Crochet was not really… to tell you the truth… I know I write on my shop that it's always been my passion, but that's not true. That was driven by the need to find an idea. […] I wanted to launch my own business.* (Beate, 46 years old)

Like Beate, some Etsy sellers without crafts skills taught themselves to make jewelry and bags, mainly from web tutorials, just to be able to open a shop on Etsy. The "business orientation" of some aspiring professionals has also led some of them to completely drop the production part of their activity, outsourcing it so that they can focus exclusively on the commercial aspects of their business. These profiles are overrepresented among the lucky few who are financially successful on Etsy, even though they do depart from the platform's DIY philosophy.

4 Conclusion

The new ideal of domesticity suggests that the marketization of leisure activities empowers women in modern capitalist societies by giving them the opportunity to combine work and family tasks for a fulfilling life. Such typically commodified female activities are the sale of handmade items on Etsy and food and cookery blogging. Our research into these two fields confirms, as have other studies (Adkins and Dever 2016), that female micro-entrepreneurial homeworking is actually no work-life "magical solution" (Luckman 2016: 91) to the situation of women on the labor market. Yet our study also complicates the picture: female micro-entrepreneurial homeworking concerns just a tiny minority of the women who commodify their hobby. On the whole, women who commodify their leisure activities are not looking for an occupation. Even though they may see marketization as an offsetting activity to cope with boredom or adverse working conditions in their main job, the women are aware that Etsy and food blogging are not serious ways to earn income and become economically independent. New domesticity is ultimately nothing more than a glamorous fairytale encouraging a minority of women who want to earn a living from handicrafts or food blogging, to stay at home and take care of unpaid domestic tasks, which therefore remain "invisible work." (Kaplan Daniels 1987). As we have shown, certain social conditions—such as a gainfully employed partner—are required for the dream to come true. Marketization of leisure activities ultimately has the capacity to empower hobbyists more—in terms of self-esteem—than aspiring professionals who find that financial independence is rarely forthcoming. In both cases, only a particular kind of work, associated with the properties of the online medium of marketization, can make the activity pay. This intensive extra work of commodification can be analyzed as a form of "free labor." In keeping with T. Terranova, free labor has two meanings: "free" means "unpaid," but also "pleasurable, not imposed" (Terranova 2000: 48). The extra work provided by Etsy sellers and food bloggers mostly benefit the digital platforms and companies, and is therefore partly an unpaid work (Simonet 2018). At the same time, it provides pleasure, sociability, and social recognition to Etsy sellers and food bloggers. Such ambivalence reinforces the difficulty to tackle the issue of the empowering effects of the marketization of domestic and leisure activities.

Appendix

Table 3.1 The interviewees mentioned in the chapter

Pseudonym	Marketization field	Sex	Age	Occupation	Number of children	Maturity of online activity	Number of readers per day or number of sales
Audrey	Food blog	F	24	Lab technician	0	2 years	30 readers
Beate	Etsy shop	F	46	(Former consultant) Creative entrepreneur	2	3 years	40 sales
Carole	Etsy shop	F	23	Student	0	2 years	119 sales
Charlotte	Food blog	F	22	Student	0	2 years	150 readers
Delphine	Food blog	F	30	Civil servant	2	3.5 years	800–1300 readers
Diane	Etsy shop	F	29	Marketing manager for a start-up	0	1 year	3 sales
Elisabeth	Etsy shop	F	42	(Former IT engineer)Seamstress	3	1 year	15 sales
Fabienne	Food blog	F	45	IT executive in a computer company	2	6 years	7000 readers
Jonathan	Etsy shop	M	41	Artist	1	A few months	3 sales
Karine	Etsy shop	F	38	(Former director of an art gallery)Ceramist	0	1 year	626 sales
Laetitia	Etsy shop	F	42	Assistant in a law firm	2	5 years	604 sales
Laura	Food blog	F	29	Preparing for a competitive civil service examination	2	2.5 years	1500 readers
Marjorie	Etsy shop	F	25	Survey manager for a polling organization	1	1 year	4 sales
Martine	Food blog	F	60	Retired	2	5 years	2800–9000 readers
Nathalie	Food blog	F	33	Stay-at-home mother	3	1 year	50–80 readers
Robert	Food blog	M	45	IT project manager	3	1 year	25 readers
Soizic	Food blog	F	33	Food writer	1	4 years	–
Tue-Minh	Etsy shop	F	41	Salaried pediatrician	0	5 years	41 sales
Vanessa	Food blog	F	37	Freelance journalist	2	5 years	500–2000 readers
Vincent	Food blog	M	40	Musician	1	2 years	150 readers

Notes

1. This work is supported by the Independent Social Research Foundation; the French National Research Agency in the framework of the "Investissements d'Avenir" program (ANR-15-IDEX-02), University Grenoble-Alpes Strategic Research Initiative (IRS 2017-MATRACA), and University Grenoble-Alpes Data Institute; the Maison des Sciences de l'Homme (MSH) Paris Nord; Paris-Dauphine University (IRISSO); and Sciences Po Grenoble (PACTE).
2. All names have been changed.
3. Pascale Weeks is a French food blog pioneer. She created her food blog in 2004.
4. The fact that most of these earnings are not declared is largely due to the nature of the income from marketization, its low amount, its reinvestment to finance the activity itself, and ignorance of the law. A gray economy consequently emerges, which might be seen as unfair competition by professional sellers.
5. This contrasts with professional artists-craftsmen (ceramists, cabinetmakers, glass-blowers, etc.) who see the commercial and business aspects of their trade as "dirty work" (Hughes 1962; Jourdain 2014).

References

Abdelnour, S., Bernard, S., & Gros, J. (2017). Genre et travail indépendant: Divisions sexuées et place des femmes dans le non-salariat. *Travail et Emploi, 150*, 5–23.

Adkins, L. (2016). Contingent Labour and the Rewriting of the Sexual Contract. In L. Adkins & M. Dever (Eds.), *The Post-Fordist Sexual Contract: Working and Living in Contingency* (pp. 1–28). Basingstoke: Palgrave Macmillan.

Adkins, L., & Dever, M. (2016). *The Post-Fordist Sexual Contract: Working and Living in Contingency*. Basingstoke: Palgrave Macmillan.

Ashton, D., & Patel, K. (2018). Vlogging Careers: Everyday Expertise Collaboration and Authenticity. In S. Taylor & S. Luckman (Eds.), *The New Normal of Working Lives: Critical Studies in Contemporary Work and Employment* (pp. 147–168). Basingstoke: Palgrave Macmillan.

Baym, N. (2014). Connect with your Audience! The Relational Labor of Connection. *The Communication Review, 18*(1), 14–22.

Bourdieu, P. (2001). *Masculine Domination*. Stanford: Stanford University Press.
Cardon, D., Fouetillou, G., & Roth, C. (2014). Topographie de la renommée en ligne. Un modèle structurel des communautés thématiques du web français et allemand. *Réseaux, 188*, 85–120.
Cox, A., & Blake, M. (2011). Information and Food Blogging as Serious Leisure. *Aslib Proceedings, 63*(2/3), 204–220.
Duffy, B., & Hund, E. (2015). 'Having It All' on Social Media: Entrepreneurial Femininity and Self-Branding among Fashion Bloggers. *Social Media + Society, 1*(2), 1–11.
Dupuy-Salle, M. (2014). Les cinéphiles-blogueurs amateurs face aux stratégies de capitation professionnelles: entre dépendance et indépendance. *Réseaux, 183*, 65–91.
Ekinsmyth, C. (2011). Challenging the Boundaries of Entrepreneurship: The Spatialities and Practices of UK 'Mumpreneurs'. *Geoforum, 42*, 104–114.
Goffman, E. (1959). *The Presentation of Self in Everyday Life*. New York: Anchor Books.
Harding, R. (2006). *GEM Full Report*. London Business School, London.
Hughes, E. (1962). Good People and Dirty Work. *Social Problems, 10*(1), 3–11.
Hughes, E. ([1971] 1984). *The Sociological Eye: Selected Papers*. New Brunswick: Transaction Books.
Huws, U. (2013). Working Online, Living Offline: Labour in the Internet Age. *Work Organisation, Labour and Globalisation, 7*(1), 1–11.
International Labour Organisation. (2015). *World Employment and Social Outlook: The Changing Nature of Jobs*. Geneva: International Labour Office, ILO Research Department.
Jarrett, K. (2014). The Relevance of "Women's Work": Social Reproduction and Immaterial Labor in Digital Media. *Television & New Media, 15*(1), 14–29.
Jourdain, A. (2014). *Du cœur à l'ouvrage. Les artisans d'art en France*. Paris: Belin.
Kaplan Daniels, A. (1987). Invisible Work. *Social Problems, 34*(5), 403–415.
Luckman, S. (2015a). *Craft and the Creative Economy*. London: Palgrave Macmillan.
Luckman, S. (2015b). Women's Micro-Entrepreneurial Homeworking. *Australian Feminist Studies, 30*(84), 146–160.
Luckman, S. (2016). Micro-Enterprise as Work–Life 'Magical Solution'. In L. Adkins & M. Dever (Eds.), *The Post-Fordist Sexual Contract: Working and Living in Contingency* (pp. 91–108). Basingstoke: Palgrave Macmillan.

Lund, A. (2014). Playing, Gaming, Working and Labouring: Framing the Concepts and Relations. *tripleC, 12*(2), 735–801.

Mäkinen, K. (2018). Negotiating the Intimate and the Professional in Mom Blogging. In S. Taylor & S. Luckman (Eds.), *The New Normal of Working Lives: Critical Studies in Contemporary Work and Employment* (pp. 129–146). Basingstoke: Palgrave Macmillan.

Matchar, E. (2013). *Homeward Bound: Why Women are Embracing the New Domesticity*. New York: Simon & Schuster.

Méda, D., & Vendramin, P. (2017). *Reinventing Work in Europe: Value, Generations and Labour*. Basingstoke: Palgrave Macmillan.

Naulin, S. (2014). La blogosphère culinaire. Cartographie d'un espace d'évaluation amateur. *Réseaux, 183*, 31–62.

Naulin, S. (2017). *Des mots à la bouche. Le journalisme gastronomique en France*. Rennes: Presses Universitaires de Rennes.

Rheingold, H. (1993). *The Virtual Community in Cyberspace*. Reading: Addison-Wesley Publishing.

Rodney, A., Cappeliez, S., Oleschuk, M., & Johnston, J. (2017). The Online Domestic Goddess: An Analysis of Food Blog Femininities. *Food, Culture & Society, 20*(4), 685–707.

Scholz, T. (2012). *Digital Labor: The Internet as Playground and Factory*. New York: Routledge.

Simonet, M. (2018). *Travail gratuit: la nouvelle exploitation?*. Paris: Textuel.

Stebbins, R. (2007). *Serious Leisure: A Perspective for Our Time*. New Brunswick, NJ: Transaction Publishers.

Taylor, S. (2018). Beyond Work? New Expectations and Aspirations. In S. Taylor & S. Luckman (Eds.), *The New Normal of Working Lives: Critical Studies in Contemporary Work and Employment* (pp. 327–345). Basingstoke: Palgrave Macmillan.

Terranova, T. (2000). Free Labor: Producing Culture for the Digital Economy. *Social Text, 63*(18-2), 33–58.

Webster, J., & Michailidou, M. (2018). Building Gender Perspectives in the Analysis of Virtual Work. *International Journal of Media & Cultural Politics, 14*(1), 3–18.

Zelizer, V. (1994). *The Social Meaning of Money: Pin Money, Paychecks, Poor Relief, and Other Currencies*. Princeton: Princeton University Press.

Zelizer, V. (2001). Transactions intimes. *Genèses, 42*(1), 121–144.

Zelizer, V. (2011). *Economic Lives: How Culture Shapes the Economy*. Princeton and Oxford: Princeton University Press.

4

Selling Second-Hand Items on the Web: New Skills for Everyone?

Adrien Bailly, Renaud Garcia-Bardidia, and Coralie Lallemand

1   Introduction

In recent years, digital platforms that enable non-professional users to buy and sell second-hand items have developed rapidly. In France, the main actor of this market—*Leboncoin.fr*—boasts impressive figures: 28 million single visitors (meaning more than one French person in two visits this website on a monthly basis), more than 29 million advertisements available, and 7 billion pages viewed each month (Médiamétrie 2018).[1] This platform and more specialized ones such as videdressing. com, for instance, are participating in the renewal and expansion of more traditional forms of second-hand selling, like open-air jumble sales and garage sales.

A. Bailly
Lorraine University, Metz, France
e-mail: Adrien.bailly@univ-lorraine.fr

R. Garcia-Bardidia (✉) • C. Lallemand
University of Rouen Normandie, Rouen, France
e-mail: renaud.garcia-bardidia@univ-rouen.fr; coralie.lallemand@orange.fr

© The Author(s) 2020
S. Naulin, A. Jourdain (eds.), *The Social Meaning of Extra Money*, Dynamics of Virtual Work, https://doi.org/10.1007/978-3-030-18297-7_4

These practices of buying and selling second-hand goods open up new opportunities for non-professional users to acquire extra money. The massive development of such practices has led the French government to tackle these new forms of undeclared work. A law promulgated on 23 October 2018 states that the frequency and regularity of these activities lend them a professional character. Consequently, this law obliges digital platforms in the collaborative economy to cooperate with the French state to avoid committing tax fraud. These sales also have non-economic benefits for the users of these platforms. Indeed, many actors, including users themselves, often associate these "new" ways of consuming with representations revolving around sharing, solidarity, ecology, alter-globalization or resistance, and so forth. According to Botsman and Roger (2011), collaborative consumption is indeed *"a force for change that could have a real impact in terms of sustainable development as well as in terms of restoring the social bond."*[2] For his part, A. Caillé emphasizes that this way of consuming *"recreates the social bond of proximity on the Internet, and constitutes a space for reconstitution of national solidarity."*[3]

In fact, these practices clearly echo longer-standing customs. The resale of second-hand products has indeed been largely documented in the case of flea markets (e.g. Roux 2005). This research stream has shown that such practices require considerable interaction skills from non-professional sellers, particularly to prove the value of their goods. In addition to product-related expertise, sellers therefore need to master skills related to persuasion and customer relationship management. Outside the well-defined contexts of the flea market, non-professional selling practices today rely heavily on digital environments. Everything suggests that this digital dimension adds at least three difficulties to these resale practices. First, mastering the digital tool itself requires complex skills that are often unevenly distributed. These seem to be becoming more crucial as the presence of digital technology increases in all social spheres. Furthermore, these skills are not purely technical. They are also social. For example, it is now understood that digital technology is fundamentally transforming the imperatives of the presentation of self (Schau and Gilly 2003). But Internet uses and the skills they require are unequally distributed in societies, and this inequality is not diminishing with increasing Internet penetration (DiMaggio and Hargittai 2001). Secondly, online sales involve many interactive skills that are often overlooked by researchers (Abdul-Ghani et al. 2011). However, these skills play an important role in how users build up the trust needed to achieve their sales. This is especially true when buyers and sellers are non-professionals, when they probably will not meet again, and when the platform does not provide any devices to ensure that the transaction will be harmless for both parties. Finally, the meaning of these sales is likely to differ between users, as in other forms of collaborative consumption. More precisely, sales between private individuals are subject to a recurrent tug of war between, on the one hand, an attitude of giving and building social ties and, on the other hand, a utilitarian dimension (Borel et al. 2016).

These points suggest that the specific contexts that enable non-professional users to sell to other ordinary users require complex and specific skills, particularly regarding sales performance. As in other situations, amateurs may have taken the Internet as an opportunity to learn new roles and new practices that were previously performed by professionals. For these reasons, it seems interesting to analyze how they mobilize their skills to do business, and to look at the learning mechanisms specific to online intermediated private sales. To do this, we carried out an empirical study of how of the website *leboncoin.fr* is used.

2   *Leboncoin.fr*: A Field for a Better Understanding of Online Sales between Private Individuals

In order to better understand the various skills, learning processes, and performances required by online sales between private individuals, we conducted empirical work with users of *leboncoin.fr*. This website seems suitable for understanding the specific issues we highlighted in the previous section.

With nearly 28 million classified advertisements currently online and a turnover that reached 214 million euro in 2016, *leboncoin.fr* is now the fourth most visited website in France. It is the leader of the free online advertisement market and receives 800,000 new advertisements a day.

Leboncoin, which is the French version of the first Swedish personal advertisement site, blocket.se, is an Internet platform often presented as the digital evolution of garage sales or flea markets. Advertisements on the website are broken down into nine categories: employment, vehicles, real estate, holidays, multimedia, home, leisure, professional equipment, and services.

The website is in some aspects analogous to its competitor, ebay.fr, although sales cannot be made through an auction system and users are not evaluated. Its business model is based on advertising banners, while advertisements submitted by its users are published free of charge (with the exception of some options). When taking part in the website, users can take on several roles (buyers, sellers, renters *leboncoin.fr*, bargain hunters, curious strollers, scammers, etc.). The online interface is designed to be very simple, and sellers and buyers are left to their own devices to conduct transactions. As in many exchanges between non-professional people, trust is an essential condition to the success of deals. Its importance is also reinforced by the newsworthy figure of the scammer, which is often relayed on the Internet or through traditional media. The evaluation processes of other users are informal and numerous and often rely on social representations.

Although sale offers are submitted via the interface of *leboncoin.fr*, the first contact is made by e-mail or telephone. In both cases, remote negotiations may be necessary and may give rise to many exchanges. Products can be sent by post, but the overwhelming majority of exchanges are face-to-face. This contextual diversity is likely to generate numerous interactions and very varied performances on the part of selling consumers.

From the point of view of users, this context is both extremely complex and poorly defined. Each transaction takes place according to unique procedures that depend on the interaction between users. Consequently, one might think that sellers have to mobilize very specific and versatile skills in order to prove the value of their offers, play a credible seller role, and smooth the course of interaction with the buyer. In other words, the minimal framework provided by *leboncoin.fr* seems to provide a good opportunity, even a borderline case, to understand the specificity of the skills and learning required from non-professional sellers.

Method

In order to study the social relations, representations, and hierarchies underlying the matching process on *leboncoin.fr*, we undertook comprehensive interviews and used interaction as a unit of analysis. We tried to understand the skills required by non-professional sellers in order to build their advertisements and stage their seller role. We also focused on how they could acquire these skills if necessary.

In order to explore these mechanisms, we rely on 28 semi-directive interviews carried out between 2013 and 2016. Informants were selected to maximize a diversity of practices, both in terms of type (e.g. buyers, sellers), duration, and frequency, and in terms of categories of purchased and sold products. This variety aims to obtain sufficient saturation of the information collected. The 28 users were interviewed in their homes when possible in order to facilitate free speech but also to make additional observations (objects used, storage places, computer practices, etc.). By interviewing users who buy, sell, or both via *leboncoin.fr*, we were able to outline the expectations corresponding to each status. This diversity also allowed us to better understand learning trajectories, notably regarding the importance of navigating between the roles of buyer and seller. On the basis of various exploratory observations, we developed an interview grid around five themes: (1) description of the concrete conduct of transactions; (2) problems encountered and methods used to solve them (notably with regard to trust); (3) evolution of the practice, especially with regard to the skills and techniques used to do business; (4) representations associated with consumer-to-consumer platforms and their users; and (5) previous experiences in other consumer-to-consumer markets (e.g. garage sales). These themes allowed us to understand how vendors showcase theirs offers. By focusing on their difficulties, we were able to isolate the different skills they need as well as the learning processes that compensate for any shortcomings. Finally, questions about the transaction process as well as consumer representations allowed us to identify the most valued sales performances and the variety of buyers' expectations regarding them.

A first open Intra-interview coding was carried out in order to identify the emerging themes concerning the concrete practices of the users. Inter-Interview analysis then revealed the thematic regularities of the emerging categories, which were gradually compared with the theoretical frameworks we used. At the end of the research, a second axial coding was carried out in order to check and consolidate results.

Based on this work, we were able to better describe how skills are mobilized and acquired via *leboncoin.fr*. This research provides us with an understanding of some issues that are specific to the work of non-professional sellers. Our fieldwork identifies that selling consumers need to master a variety of promotional skills. It seems that this consumption context is particularly favorable to acquiring such skills on the spot. Nevertheless, it also gives rise to very varied selling performances that are likely to generate tensions between participants. Here we attempt to trace the origins of these tensions.

3 The Promotional and Interactional Skills of Second-Hand Selling

The practices we studied involve many skills. Nevertheless, we note that they tend to be considered trivial by those who master them. Sellers often describe them as common sense. Thomas, an unemployed musician who frequently uses the platform to buy and sell guitars and related products, told us:

> *I wouldn't go so far as to call it marketing, but you have to promote the product you sell. There are a lot of things that can give you an advantage over other sellers and that can ensure that your ad will reach more viewers than other ads. But then again, I think it's mostly common sense. I'm not… I'm not a sales person, I've never learnt sales techniques or anything. I mean, this is not my job. Then again, there's nothing difficult about selling a product that you know well.* (Thomas, 25 years old)

The common idea that everyone uses *leboncoin.fr* implies strong expectations about other users: everyone is gifted enough to use the platform properly. In other words, consumers who do not have the necessary skills to do business by themselves are often perceived by their peers as lacking a basic education. Georges, a 34-year-old clerk who has been using *leboncoin.fr* for years, sums up that feeling:

> *I don't think you need to pay for a matchmaker, a go-between, when you're dealing with civilized people.* (Georges, 34 years old)

Thus, a meritocratic logic often prevents any form of empathy toward less competent users, despite the fact that it involves assimilating the many skills that competent users had to acquire in order to use the website and successfully sell goods. Two kinds of skill seem to be particularly important: marketing skills and interactional ones.

3.1 The Marketing Skills of the Second-Hand Seller

The first set of skills required to sell between lay persons consists in marketing skills needed to commodify second-hand products. Notably, such operations imply the ability to determine a price that stands the test of the market. Assessing the value of the goods is a complex task, especially when it comes to second-hand products (Geertz 1978; Sciardet 2003). In order to set a price, sellers must take into account the market prices on the website, the condition of the product, its relative obsolescence, and competition from other consumer-to-consumer websites and professionals (online or brick-and-mortar sellers). The most competent sellers go as far as to incorporate trading tactics into their pricing, by which the price evolves according to negotiations with buyers. Price is therefore a composite construct produced by many quantitative and qualitative factors. To maximize the price without compromising selling opportunities requires significant skills. This is all the more true given that prices charged on this website do not correspond to those of new products or to those on competing websites such as *ebay.com*. As expressed by Laurent, a 21-year-old student who buys and sells on the platform in various product categories on a regular basis:

> *[The pricing depends on] how you used your product… If you didn't use it a lot and it was expensive, you can hope to sell it for a good price. But you have to keep in mind the market prices. Phones are a bit like cars, their prices drop every year. Plus, a lot of discount stores now sell cheap products, so you can't sell expensive stuff anymore. It's what you'd call obsolescence. […] You always have to try to pump up the initial price because people love to haggle and feel like they made a bargain. That's important.* (Laurent, 21 years old)

The ability to sell products via *leboncoin.fr* also relies on the promotional skills of sellers. Depending on the product category, sellers may have to acquire very specific knowledge in order to promote their products. Sellers also need to build appealing advertisements by mastering the website's interface and conforming to the numerous constraints of this medium. For example, buyers expect the sellers to write qualitative descriptions of their products and to publish informative and aesthetic pictures. This process depends on market knowledge but also on a social reflexivity often called "empathy." Sellers must indeed praise the qualities of their products but also be transparent about the signs of deterioration that are characteristic of second-hand goods. Resolving this tension is essential to generate interest while maintaining trust, as explained by Thomas, who buys and sells guitars on the platform:

> *[When selling something,] it is important to make a short description, a fairly accurate one. As an example, when I sell a guitar, I like … you have to follow some basic rules. You have to describe the wood it's made from, etc. A little bit… Even the dimensions, stuff like that. It definitely means something for buyers. The size of the guitar neck, stuff like that… […] Then again, when you add these kinds of details, it helps people make the final decision. And it makes your product stand out. […] [Describing his advertisement] So, there's a general picture which is rather beautiful. We can also see the leather strap which is included. You can see that this is in good condition just by the look of it. It's shiny and everything. And there, extremely important for this kind of guitar, we can see the serial number, made in USA, 2009, just behind the head of the guitar. […] Then, I add something about the way it looks, in order to let people know that the bridge is a little worn and… […] So that's it. Also it as to be relatively well written, with spaces, line breaks, not a big… awful… block of text.* (Thomas, 25 years old)

A successful sale not only requires producing a quality advertisement, it also involves putting forward the merits of the offer in various contexts. Sellers must be able to continue to promote products in electronic and face-to-face exchanges. In the latter case, the work can resemble that of a professional salesperson. Sometimes, it may even result in swindling buyers, as illustrated by Lucile, a 59-year-old restaurant owner, who is a beginner user of *leboncoin.fr* but an experienced businessman:

> *I was driving the car and [the buyer] started to look worried because the clutch was giving me some trouble. The car stopped. So I made him drive. I stayed in*

> *the car, otherwise he would have disappeared with it [laughing]! He also challenged me because the air-conditioning didn't work! I was aware of that, I'd tried to get it fixed by professionals a few times, but they couldn't do it. Anyway I told him that I'd disabled the air-conditioning due to some health condition. [...] After the ride, we went back to my restaurant. There was some kind of puddle on the floor under the car... I said to myself: 'Damn, I'm in trouble!' ... So I told him: 'Listen, just come home with me! You'll see: there is not a single stain! No water or oil: my garage is spotless!' And it worked [he bought it].* (Lucile, 59 years old)

Although most exchanges are not of this nature, this transcript illustrates the performance needed to defend the value of the goods and close the sale.

3.2 Interactional Skills

The study of transactions in this consumption context shows that the commercial skills needed to successfully sell second-hand goods go beyond simply promoting products. Indeed, participants tend to perceive poor-quality advertisements as a signal of a likely lack of involvement in forthcoming interactions, quite similarly as motivation is inferred from educational information in job markets (Spence 1973). For this reason, buyers may avoid bad-quality advertisements despite sufficient informative content and attractive prices, as expressed by Benoit, an 18-year-old student who has used *leboncoin.fr* to find and resell video games since he was a child:

> *Who knows, it might have been the best deal ever... But when it's so badly written, you don't give it a try. [...] I just didn't feel like dealing with him. I didn't want to... to sell to people who... When you sell something, you do it right. [...] I think that, when you put an ad online, if it's riddled with spelling mistakes... You don't respect the buyer either. In any case... you have to try to make something which is at least presentable. To my mind, he doesn't respect me. He doesn't respect the buyer because he... he's botched his ad. You already have... I mean, you can only expect that he won't respect you either if you buy the thing he's selling.* (Benoit, 18 years old)

Moreover, this kind of expectation seems related to Goffman's interaction rules (1959). During interactions initiated via *leboncoin.fr*, it indeed seems crucial to respect rules whose scope is strictly ceremonial, that is, rituals. Our empirical material repeatedly illustrates how failure to meet this kind of expectation can undermine transactions nevertheless perceived as advantageous by both parties from a strictly economic point of view. Similar to product promotion competences, we note that this type of commercial skill is all the more complex since it must be mobilized in various contexts. Charlotte, a 32-year-old PhD student in management science who used to hold a leading position in an employers' union, thus indicates how specific online rules of politeness, in other words digital literacy, frame buying and selling interactions initiated on *leboncoin.fr*:

> *Yes, I think I [have already blamed people for the way they talked to me], but not in an aggressive way. I mean, for instance, if someone contacts me and doesn't say 'Hello', doesn't use capital letters, talks like trailer trash, and speaks to me in a familiar way… For sure it won't go smoothly. You can be sure I will hassle him right away and I even, in fact, emphasize my message and the politeness of my message by saying: 'Good afternoon, Sir, looking forward to reading you', etc. Basically, being over formal with him to show him that he's a misfit.* (Charlotte, 32 years old)

These comments illustrate how the ability to embody a credible persona in various contexts is one of the most essential skills when selling goods via *leboncoin.fr*. Depending on their ability to meet these interactional expectations, sellers will indeed be associated with positive or negative social stereotypes.

4   Becoming a Competent Second-Hand Seller

Sellers thus must master numerous promotional and interactional skills within the various contexts of the practice. In order to do so, they can import competences from other social spheres, or try to acquire them based on the specific characteristics of the medium they use.

4.1 Importing Skills and Tools from Work and Home

Mobilizing skills related to one's professional activity is common among users of *leboncoin.fr*. For example, some of our informants are salespeople. As a result, they can easily import skills acquired in their professional environment and use them in this specific context. These sellers also use tools imported from their workplace to carry out their transactions. The example of Mathieu, a 30-year-old salesperson, who sells a large amount of video games on *leboncoin.fr*, illustrates this overlap between professional and personal spheres:

> *Well, I had some information [about the buyer]. I knew where to find him in the event of a problem. We have a bank verification system at work. The first thing I did was to verify the cheque he gave me. […] With this system, we can verify if the bank account is red or if the cheque is stolen.* (Mathieu, 30 years old)

When second-hand sellers cannot import professional skills, a lack of product knowledge or selling skills can be compensated by resorting to outsiders, usually friends or relatives. We note numerous frequent intergenerational exchanges that mostly depend on the type of skill involved. For example, young users often call on their elders to take advantage of their knowledge of cars or real estate. On the contrary, we identify frequent reverse socialization phenomena with regards to digital technologies and the use of the website itself. The interview of Chloé, a 23-year-old logistics executive, and a skilled user of *leboncoin.fr* but a car novice, illustrates the reciprocity of intergenerational knowledge exchanges as well as the way users who master second-hand selling techniques can acquire some sort of expert status:

> *The problem is that buying a car from a private individual when you know nothing about mechanics isn't very easy. I was lucky my uncle was there to help me … […] A lot of people are starting to ask me to publish their ads. Some people call me in to do their ads. People also ask me advice about goods they're buying. It's because I regularly use this website. So I publish their ads and make contact with buyers. Then, I let them manage the situation.* (Chloé, 23 years old)

4.2 Building Skills on the Job

As a medium, *leboncoin.fr*'s website itself provides many ways to progressively acquire the aforementioned necessary skills. While some users claim to have used the tips provided in the FAQ section of *leboncoin.fr*, most seem to have developed their skills on the job. This phenomenon can be explained by several reasons. First, the website allows its users to view and post advertisements for free via their personal computer or smartphone. This free, remote service allows users to explore the rules of the practice with no social or economic risk. Thus, *leboncoin.fr* promotes an easy entry into the practice that then leads users to build their skills through other types of mediation that we identify. It seems to allow learning by trial and error. Vicarious learning also plays an important role in acquiring selling skills. Its helps users develop their pricing techniques. Indeed, millions of advertisements are published via the website in various product categories. In most cases, a beginner can roughly align his price with that of the market if he does not have the necessary skills for shrewder pricing. With time and practice, sellers should be able to fix prices with more efficiency. The way that sellers learn to build their advertisements is subject to a similar phenomenon. By consulting the advertisements published by their competitors, beginners can identify relevant elements to be included in their own advertisements as well as the best way to highlight them.

Most users made their first contact with *leboncoin.fr* as buyers. This is an important part of the learning process that allows them to become competent sellers. Indeed, the buyer status seems to act as an intermediate step toward the status of seller. In other words, users tend to project their previous experience as a buyer to identify what is expected from them as a seller. By allowing cheap purchases, the website promotes an alternation between these two statuses, making this phenomenon an extremely efficient way of learning how to sell products, as explained by Thomas:

> *[The first time I used this website], it was to get a foot switch [musical equipment]. [...] Stuff like that, nothing fancy. So, I started to use the website to buy things. Well, at the beginning… I didn't have a lot of things. I think that*

now… I have second-hand stuff all over the place so… So I have a lot of stuff to sell. When I started… I guess I could say that I didn't know a lot about this kind of equipment. The fact is that buying so much second-hand stuff… Since you can get really cheap products, you can afford to buy things just to try them out (laughing). That's how I came to sell things. You buy something, you think, 'Ah, that's nice'… and then you figure out that there's something else that you want more, so you sell stuff on… That's how I came to sell things.

So, your perspective as a buyer can also help you to sell things?

Yes, definitely! I saw a ton of bad ads which helped me understand what a good ad is [laughing]. (Thomas, 25 years old)

4.3 Getting Caught Up in the Game

Our data allow us to understand the mechanisms that help users to learn selling skills on the job. The in-depth interviews we have conducted also show how users may strengthen these mechanisms, thanks to some specific features of the user experience offered by *leboncoin.fr*.

First, most users told us that they consult advertisements on this website even when they are not considering any purchases. This type of playful practice can sometimes lead users to develop a strong interest in product categories that they do not intend to buy or simply cannot afford. Some people also visit recently published advertisements without any kind of criterion, thus showing more general curiosity. When these wandering practices develop into an intrinsic interest for users, market monitoring may settle into a daily routine and sometimes even into some kind of entertainment that replaces television shows, as Léonie, a 51-year-old business agent told us:

> Even when I don't need anything, I go on this website to look around and discover things I might need. I look at so many things that I don't need: I just wander! It's more amusing that the reality shows [that my wife watches]! I do it every day, in the morning and after meals. It's like having a coffee for me. (Léonie, 51 years old)

We identify a second type of mediation that may accelerate the learning mechanisms associated to selling on *leboncoin.fr*. It is related to the increased consumption desire documented by J. Denegri-Knott and M. Molesworth (2010). Like other second-hand shopping websites, *leboncoin.fr* allows its users to speed up the consumption cycle of products by (re-)selling them after use. With this opportunity to quickly sell on their goods, consumers tend to act on their desires more impulsively. J. Denegri-Knott and M. Molesworth (2010) help us understand that this process not only satisfies desires but also renews them quicker. Through this process, the marketplace therefore leads users to buy and sell their products at a faster pace, which has the effect of drastically accelerating skills building by the mediation of buyer status and by vicarious learning in general. Chloé, a 23-year-old logistics executive, thus uses *leboncoin.fr* to play video games virtually for free:

> My sister has done a lot of deals on leboncoin.fr. She buys things, and if she doesn't like them, she sells them on, even for a higher price sometimes. She uses things twice and then sells them to get something better. She always tries to get better products. I do the same. Every time I want to buy a video game, I finish it then sell it for the same price. We can afford it because we know we'll manage to sell it. (Chloé, 23 years old)

Users might also get caught up in the game by developing a playful relationship with economic performance, in other words by playing shopkeeper through their use of *leboncoin.fr*. When this happens, they tend to chase bargains not only for their economic value but also for the satisfaction of seizing these rare opportunities. This combination of economic and playful interest may lead users to monitor the website in order to "beat the market," which can help them to quickly strengthen their selling skills. The accelerating effect of this phenomenon is similar to the one mentioned above. It differs from wandering practices because it leads to actual transactions and may lead to additional revenue, as in the case of Thomas:

> Of course, if I can earn some money, it's nice. I don't think I'll get a lot of money for this guitar, but it's worth trying. That's why I always look for bargains. If I find a really good deal, even if I don't want it, I can… I might buy it just to instantly sell it and make some quick cash. […] So, you have to watch the website to find this kind of bargain. You also need some cash to be able to make quick purchases and wait until you sell them. (Thomas, 25 years old)

In addition to, or in the absence of, this type of phenomena, users can get hooked on the practice by the frequently convivial experiences it generates, as indicated by Mathieu, a 30-year-old salesperson, here talking about a furniture purchase. Once again, the interest for the website goes beyond its simple economic dimension even though it may include economic efficiency. In this case, this process does not speed up the aforementioned learning mechanisms, but reinforces the desire to resort to the website. Conviviality helps to sustain the practice long enough to acquire the selling skills needed to publish efficient advertisements. Thus, potentially pleasurable interactions between buyers and sellers should not be underestimated. They may encourage beginner users to make the significant time investment required to become a proficient second-hand seller:

> *This lady and I had a really good feeling about each other, it was so good I stayed with her for two hours, drinking coffee in the afternoon even though I didn't pay for the goods or take them. I had to come a second time because I forgot to pay when I left. […] We had a really nice time.* (Mathieu, 30 years old)

Our empirical data show that the skills needed to sell via *leboncoin.fr* can be imported from other contexts or built on the job because the technical environment fosters specific learning mechanisms. The success of the website is also due to its ability to provide non-economic benefits that will act as mediation toward selling skills. The value derived from the practice may indeed go beyond a pure economic interest when users develop a playful relationship with the market, or when they appreciate the convivial interactions sometimes generated by second-hand peer-to-peer shopping. These non-economic interests significantly boost acquisition of skills. Individual interactions also determine how sellers will play their role during transactions.

5 Performing the Role of the Salesperson

A study of the learning processes needed to successfully sell via *leboncoin. fr* reveals not only that this practice is based on a variety of skills, but also that the role of the seller can be performed in varied ways. We question the origin of this diversity of selling performances and bring to light the tensions that may result from it.

5.1 The Various Roles of Non-professional Sellers on *leboncoin.fr*

As we have seen, users have many ways to acquire the skills they need to sell products on *leboncoin.fr*. Our fieldwork allows us to hypothesize that, depending on the dominating process that allowed them to build these skills, users develop and adopt different seller roles. For example, we observe that users who have acquired their sales skills by developing a playful relationship with economic performance tend to establish some form of friendly power play in order to negotiate prices. Users whose skills are mainly rooted in professional spheres are more likely to play their part in the interaction by mimicking the behavior of sales professionals. The opinion stated by Charlotte, a 32-year-old PhD student in management science who considers professionalism as an important value and works as a mystery shopper in her free time, illustrates this point. Indeed, she is used to business circles, thanks to her former professional activity. She explains how she tries to increase the chances of success of her offers by reproducing the attitude of a professional seller:

> *[When I use the website to rent a flat] I write e-mails in a very, very professional way. First of all, my ad is written in very professionally. I actually base my ads on professional ones. The second point is that I answer e-mails in a very professional way. The third point is that each and every criterion I use to select the person I deal with is a professional one, or at least is really similar to professional criteria. Fourth, I act… I behave like a real estate agent. I try to mimic them in order to rent the flat. I turn myself into a real estate agent, it's a game. Then, I conduct the visit of the apartment like an authentic real estate professional.* (Charlotte, 32 years old)

On the opposite end of the scale, users who have developed their interest in the practice, thanks to the convivial dimension of interactions, are more likely to perform a role based on a hospitality principle. In doing so, they tend to mitigate the transactional dimension of the meeting between buyers and sellers. In this case, the "at home market" is the meeting place of supply and demand but also of people sharing common interests, as explained by Denis, a 61-year-old pensioner who regularly sells and spends time chatting with buyers:

> *[My wife and I] tend to invite people into our home, even to offer them a coffee or something friendly. [...] We feel the need to establish a friendly relationship with people.* (Denis, 61 years old)

Of course, the behavior of people selling goods via *leboncoin.fr* cannot be reduced to strictly mechanical effects. It seems, however, that each mediation that fosters the acquisition of selling skills plays a non-negligible part in the type of role that sellers will perform. In a sense, we can spread these roles into a spectrum whose extremities would be conviviality and professionalism. Each of these roles can be performed with interactional skills and therefore commercial success.

5.2 When Interactional Expectations Differ

The diversity seems to have the advantage of allowing users with different dispositions to develop their selling practices in different ways. Indeed, users get caught up in the game through mediations that please them, and can do their selling work in a way they feel comfortable according to the situation. However, we note that these varied performances must, to a certain extent, meet the expectations of equally varied buyers. Thus, tensions can emerge from the fact that buyers and sellers can occupy very different positions within the hospitality-professionalism spectrum of expectations.

As we have seen, some users appreciate the friendly dimension that can occur during a transaction. For example, they may enjoy discussing common interests made obvious by the object of the deal. However, some users do not like, and sometimes loathe, this kind of conversation and prefer to limit interactions to their transactional dimension. These discrepancies in terms of expectations may produce significant mismatches between participants and thus render their interactional skills inoperative.

In that sense, Benoit, an 18-year-old student who buys and sells video games, expresses the way he wants the transaction to proceed:

> [When I buy something] I want it to play out like in a retail store. When it's time for the transaction, I know what I'm buying, I know what it's like, and I pay for it. [...] [When I sell something], I just say: 'Hello, this is what I'm selling' and that's it. I won't say: 'Hello, how are you? Name your price. I bought this product in order to do this...' No. (Benoit, 18 years old)

Conversely, considerable tensions may appear when a buyer expects a somewhat welcoming encounter and meets a seller who completely excludes the hospitality dimension from his or her performance. In the specific case of the following transcript of Charlotte's statement, the buyer blames this incompatibility on the social status of the seller, thus sanctioning it with social stigma:

> Some girl wanted to buy some DVDs from us, so... since [my husband and I] were close to her home, we set up a meeting by the building she lives in. She was a weirdo. So we met, and then... Since she was a weirdo, she didn't let us in. So you just end up in the middle of the street, selling DVDs from your trunk as if you were selling pot. I really felt it that way. (Charlotte, 32 years old)

6 Conclusion

Our fieldwork allows us to draw several conclusions regarding the skills needed to sell second-hand products via *leboncoin.fr*. We first show that these skills take two main forms: product promotion and interaction management. We then show that, despite their complexity, users benefit from a variety of mediations that allow them to acquire these selling skills on the job. Notably, the extreme simplicity of the website's interface, the ways in which the market device allows lurking, and the possible asynchronous communication modes (e.g. e-mails) offer multiple technical mediations. They allow users to explore the practice (notably by mimicry). In the event that the future seller is not comfortable enough to undertake this exploration process alone, the recurring recourse to peers acts as a social mediation that secures the first phases of the practices. Finally, desire-related mediations (Boullier 2001) also encourage the acquisition of skills through an increased desire to consume, through the satisfaction to "play the shopkeeper game" properly, or through convivial interactions between buyers and sellers. Through these different learning processes, users may develop different ways of performing their role while selling goods.

Our work shows that, thanks to the various ways of learning and selling allowed by the context we studied, acquiring skills may not be one of the main difficulties of this practice. The main difficulty may rather be matching users sharing the same interactional expectations. Ultimately, it does not seem absurd to deduce that the least risky way to sell second-hand products between consumers is to perform an intermediate role within the conviviality-economy spectrum. In the case of sales between private individuals, this is particularly so. Our empirical material shows that the differences in expectations inherent to these contexts can significantly affect the course of interaction. Impression management (Goffman 1959) is a fundamentally contextual practice that requires some adaptation on the part of participants. For this reason, the ambiguities we identify make this work extremely uncertain for non-professional sellers. What attitudes, words, and accessories should be adopted when situations are so changeable? What role should be played when the public may expect a convivial performance as well as a strictly economic one? This is a crucial issue since the reception of these Goffmanian performances makes it possible to illustrate the common definition of a social situation and thus to produce trust (Misztal 2001), which is so decisive in a peer-to-peer economy. It should be noted, however, that these tensions are relatively unlikely to concern contexts such as anonymous marketplaces (e.g. ebay. com) where expectations in terms of social bonding are relatively low and shared. Finally, our work shows that, thanks to the various ways of learning and selling allowed by the context we studied, acquiring skills may not be one of the main difficulties of this practice. The main difficulty may rather be matching users sharing the same interactional expectations while allowing for a diversity of selling performances (Trespeuch et al. 2018).

Appendix

Table 4.1 The interviewees mentioned in the chapter

Pseudonym	Sex	Age	Occupation
Thomas	M	25	Unemployed
Chloé	M	23	Logistics executive
Georges	M	34	Clerk
Lucile	M	59	Restaurant owner
Léonie	M	51	Business agent
Laurent	M	21	Student
Denis	M	61	Retired
Mathieu	M	30	Salesperson
Charlotte	F	32	PhD student
Benoit	M	18	Student

Notes

1. Source: https://corporate.leboncoin.fr/leboncoin-fr-aujourdhui-cest/ (Accessed 6 February 2019).
2. Source: http://appli6.hec.fr/amo/Public/Files/Docs/241_fr.pdf (Accessed 6 February 2019).
3. Source: https://fr.wikipedia.org/wiki/Leboncoin.fr (Accessed 6 February 2019), translation by the authors.

References

Abdul-Ghani, E., Hyde, K., & Marshall, R. (2011). Emic and Etic Interpretations of Engagement with a Consumer-to-Consumer Online Auction Site. *Journal of Business Research, 22*(3), 1060–1066.

Borel, S., Guillard, V., & Roux, D. (2016). Ce qui circule entre nous en ligne. *Revue du MAUSS permanente*, November 1, 2016. Retrieved February 17, 2019, from http://www.journaldumauss.net/?Ce-qui-circule-entre-nous-en-ligne.

Botsman, R., & Roger, R. (2011). *What's Mine is Yours: How Collaborative Consumption is Changing the Way We Live*. London: Collins.

Boullier, D. (2001). Les conventions pour une appropriation durable des TIC: utiliser un ordinateur et conduire une voiture. *Sociologie du travail, 43*(3), 369–387.

Denegri-Knott, J., & Molesworth, M. (2010). 'Love It. Buy It. Sell It': Consumer Desire and the Social Drama of EBay. *Journal of Consumer Culture, 10*(1), 56–79.

DiMaggio, P., & Hargittai, E. (2001). From the 'Digital Divide' to 'Digital Inequality': Studying Internet Use as Penetration Increases. *Princeton University Center for Arts and Cultural Policy Studies, Working Paper Series Number 15*. Retrieved February 17, 2019, from https://pdfs.semanticscholar.org/4843/610b79d670136e3cdd12311f91f5cc98d2ee.pdf.

Geertz, C. (1978). The Bazaar Economy: Information and Search in Peasant Marketing. *The American Economic Review, 68*(2), 28–32.

Goffman, E. (1959). *The Presentation of Self in Everyday Life*. London: Harmondsworth.

Misztal, B. A. (2001). Normality and Trust in Goffman's Theory of Interaction Order. *Sociological Theory, 19*(3), 312–324.

Roux, D. (2005). Les brocantes: ré-enchantement ou piraterie des systèmes marchands. *Revue Française du Marketing, 201*, 63–84.

Schau, H., & Gilly, M. C. (2003). We are What We Post? Self-Presentation in Personal Web Space. *Journal of Consumer Research, 30*(3), 385–404.

Sciardet, H. (2003). *Les Marchands de l'aube: ethnographie et théorie du commerce aux Puces de Saint-Ouen*. Paris: Economica.

Spence, M. (1973). Job Market Signaling. *The Quarterly Journal of Economics, 87*(3), 355–374.

Trespeuch, L., Robinot, É., & Valette-Florence, P. (2018). Quelles sont les caractéristiques des crowdfunders dans le secteur du luxe? L'apport de la théorie de la diffusion des innovations. *Innovations, 56*(2), 67–88.

Part II

Savings

5

Comorian Women at Work: Juggling Insecure Jobs with the Transnational Suitcase Trade

Abdoul-Malik Ahmad

1 Introduction

Many women from Africa, Asia, and Latin America take to the roads every year, traveling thousands of kilometers with goods and manufactured items (clothes, shoes, fashion accessories, etc.).[1] They carry them as baggage or wear them disguised as personal effects to avoid declaring their commercial purpose and having to pay customs duties. Studies on the transnational "suitcase trade" and female *trabendo*[2] (Peraldi 2001; Sandoval 2012; Schmoll 2005; Lesourd 2014; Barreau 2016) often focus mainly on the female traffic traveling back and forth between home country and the transborder, transnational places where they stock up. Very few studies appear to address the case of migrant women living in a host country and plying the transnational suitcase trade between their place of residence, different marketplaces, and their country of origin. We therefore felt it important to explore the stories of migrant Comorian

---

A.-M. Ahmad (✉)
Aix-Marseille University, CNRS, LEST, Aix-en-provence, France
e-mail: ahmad.abdoul-malik@univ-amu.fr

© The Author(s) 2020
S. Naulin, A. Jourdain (eds.), *The Social Meaning of Extra Money*, Dynamics of Virtual Work, https://doi.org/10.1007/978-3-030-18297-7_5

women living in Marseille, now a trading platform in recession (Tarrius 1992; Peraldi 2001), since the late 1970s.

These women are from Comoros, a nation made up of four islands (Grande Comore, Mohéli, Anjouan, and Mayotte) in the Mozambique Channel, between Madagascar and the East African coast. France colonized the archipelago of Comoros in the nineteenth century and, in 1974, agreed with Comoros to hold a referendum on independence. The French referendum imposed a count per island, which would see Mayotte remaining under French administration as a TOM (Overseas Territory) until its recent departmentalization in 2011, disputed by the Comorian government. In 1975, Comoros, with the exception of Mayotte, declared unilateral independence. However, the islands were soon embroiled in repeated political crises,[3] which would eventually destabilize the country's economy and trigger the first emigration flows to France, the former colonial power. Ethnologist A. Barbey (2008) finds there is a Comorian preference for the city of Marseille. About one-third of Comorian migrants in France live there, while those who live in other French cities have generally visited Marseille on vacation or for a special occasion (wedding, funeral, or associative meeting). The women in the study ply their transnational trade between Euro-Mediterranean (Ventimiglia and Istanbul), Asian (Dubai and China), and African (Kenya, Tanzania and Madagascar) marketplaces. They take advantage of their vacations to buy and sell manufactured products (clothes, shoes, fashion accessories, etc.) and gold for weddings and community celebrations in Marseille and their country of origin. Part of the suitcase trade is intended to finance investments in the Comoros (construction of houses). Sometimes, they sell their wares on the Internet and social networks (especially Facebook). This merchandising on the Internet ties in with the plurality of digital practices found among the lower classes (Delacroix et al. 2018). These migrant women I interviewed are between 32 and 63 years old. The eldest arrived in Marseille (France) in the 1970s. All women are married, divorced, or widowed. Marriage is an important asset when it comes to plying the suitcase trade. It is deemed improper for unmarried Comorian women to go on trade trips since they are unable to provide the guarantees of an upright reputation and respectability. Families and the community are more wary of misbehavior by single women on trade trips than by married women. In addition to the matrimonial criteria, women who want to engage in the suitcase trade need experience in trade in the country of origin or need to know businesswomen who can introduce them in their circle of family and friends.

New mobility strategies have appeared in the new, post-Fordian economic environment of growing capital and manpower movements (Portes 1996). Transnational economic movements and the so-called ethnic male economic activities have long been thoroughly documented. Yet, it is only in recent years that researchers have started to study migrant women's economic initiatives, albeit often no more than partially.[4] Female work-driven mobility in general has long been overlooked, especially with respect to African migrant women. Abundant research is available on migration by Filipino, Latin American, and Eastern European women in search of upward social mobility through Western European labor market integration (Oso Casas 2002). Yet, in the case of North and Sub-Saharan Africa, there is a tendency to find stereotypical depictions of these women as seldom working "followers," although researchers are now being made to fill this theoretical and empirical void (Manry and Schmoll 2010). With the exception of R. Delafontaine (1998), and recently L. Monne (2016), migrant Comorian women have rarely been studied. Comorian women face a catalog of domination/constraints when endeavoring to organize their suitcase trade: organizational constraints (work schedules and family obligations), financial constraints, and family constraints (spouse or family insistence on group travel, a negative image of the trade, husband's permission, etc.). They constantly have to negotiate these dominant structures and rarely break the rules.

This study takes a different angle to the "victim" approach to research on migrant women—migrants as "victims" of human trafficking, especially for sex work (Guillemaut 2004), and capitalist, racist, and sexist exploitation of domestic and *care* workers (Hochschild 2000). As M. Morokvasic points out, this "victim" approach unwittingly reifies the stereotypical Cigrant woman as "passive, dependent, secluded, and in need of assistance" (Morokvasic 2011: 36). Our approach instead sets out to demonstrate that migrant women are not just victims, but can be channels for social change, ingenuity, gendered know-how, and resources, and that they can develop pathways to empowerment. Our purpose is to show that dominant relationships and normative structures can be both restrictive and empowering. As Sabah Mahmood puts it, "The capacity to act (agency) can be found not only in acts of resistance to norms, but also in the many ways norms are inhabited" (Mahmood 2011: 32). Norms are more than just imposed on individuals by society. They enable individuals to define themselves. This agency-based angle considers the "creative potential of acting individuals and groups in the face of social restrictions" (Strauss 1992: 270). Therefore, every system of domination—however inert and oppressive—is not only restrictive, but is also empowering through its interstices. We consider norms as empowering rather than merely subjugating or "opposed to counter-practices" (Cheikh et al. 2014: 8).

The purpose of this chapter is to analyze the action and organizational capacities (agency) of migrant women engaged in transnational economic activities as they contend with multiform, intersecting normative structures based on gender, class, race, and age (as in the traditional age-based social system in their native country) (Crenshaw 1991). In other words, we aim at showing how pluridominated individuals, migrant women in this case, use and "play" their subordinate position as leverage to develop strategies for action that can sometimes challenge, circumvent, or even strengthen dominant normative structures. This investigation into the dual work temporality of Comorian migrants seeks to identify how the marketization of their "off-work" or side-work (Weber 2009) is instrumental in their strategies to reduce or break out of their insecure situation in the host country. This transnational side-work takes the form of relatively regular trips back and forth, raising the following questions: how do these women convince their husbands, children, brothers, and sisters to support them in an unprofitable, unstable business, especially since some children have a hard time understanding the social implications of investment in the native country? What benefits do the Comorian women derive from this trade side-activity? Are there any symbolic or economic benefits? With migratory routes and marketplaces dominated and controlled by men, what gendered "knowledge" and resources do these women put to use to develop their transnational trade activities when their social skills are seldom recognized in their host country's labor market? What negotiating tactics do these women use to continue with their trade trips when faced with family responsibilities and bids for control by their husbands, family members, or the Comorian community?

Method

This chapter draws on an empirical corpus from a sociology PhD on Comorian women who live in Marseille and ply the transnational suitcase trade. The absence of men from this study is probably due to the fact that the suitcase trade is looked down on socially as economically wasteful and essentially women's work. The research on which it is based takes the form of a qualitative, inductive study of a working-class neighborhood in the north of Marseille, where most of the interviewed traders live. I used a snowball strategy to gain access to research subjects.[5] In-depth biographical interviews (n = 30) were combined with direct observations (n = 22) of trade-related spaces (community celebrations and *tontines*[6]). The biographical interviews focused on interviewees' reasons for migration, their migratory journeys, the network galvanized on leaving, arriving, and settling in the host country, and also the relationships built and sustained with the "community" (both in France and back in their native country). I then endeavored to understand the relationships between migrants and their families, in both their native and host countries. Lastly, I sought to reconstruct their professional pathways and reasons for their transnational trade activities. Given that their practices are actually illegal, there was concern among the interviewees that we would report them to the authorities. As a migrant man myself and a PhD student, I was able to conduct this study of older women with the same national origins. Their suitcase trade forms a partially illegal economic activity seen as an offense in a country such as France. The roots I share with these women opened doors, and respondent trust was facilitated by the fact that my investigative language was Comorian and that I knew a number of the businesswomen prior to starting my research. I was younger than all the traders, so some of them would call me "my son" and others "little brother." This generation difference also influenced data collection. In hindsight, I knew I was talking to the traders as if they were older family members. Sometimes, I adopted the behavior expected of a brother or son, steering away from certain issues such as trade profits, household income, and even their views on accusations of prostitution from the community. I am aware that we did not do enough to probe these areas for fear of losing that trust.

I studied tradeswomen with a range of situations—private and public sector service and care employees (personal assistant, home help, carer, chambermaid, or cleaner) (n = 21), jobseekers (n = 5), and women out of the labor force (n = 4)—over two and a half years of fieldwork (2013 to mid-2016). Aware as I was of the inherent limitations of biographical interviews in terms of their ex-post reconstruction of feelings and practices (Bourdieu 1986), we also used direct observation as a complementary line of inquiry to capture financing and retail strategies in situ. I observed ten *tontines* at work as funding spaces, and attended 12 cultural celebrations where

> women sold their wares and attracted new customers, mainly from the Comorian community. Traders are reluctant to sell on credit, even though some of them end up doing so. The most popular way to make a sale is what the traders call in Shikomori (Comorian): *towa wou rengue*, which means "pay and take away."

2 Traders with Atypical Profiles

2.1 Typical Profile of International African Tradeswomen

In precolonial Africa, female trading (in all its local, national, and/or transborder permutations) was a way of getting agricultural products from the fields to the weekly markets (Ki-Zerbo 1978). This form of trading first attracted attention in the late 1970s, with characters such as the *Nanas Benz*[7] of Lomé (Togo) and the *Driankés* of Dakar (Senegal), who were instrumental in the internationalization of Sub-Saharan African female trading (Diallo 2014). International trading by women from Africa is often associated with the *Nanas-Benz*, known as the greatest businesswomen of Lomé (Togo): "Like their role models, those millionaire Togolese tradeswomen trading in loincloths and riding in their Mercedes Benz through the streets of Lomé right up to the end of the 1980s […], these African women doing business in the heart of the city (Marseille) embody the new female African migrant success story" (Bredeloup 2012: 34). A. Lambert's studies (1987) show that the first international businesswomen in Western Africa were educated women with jobs, often in the civil service, which they combined with their international trading activities. They organized their trips during their vacations and stocked up in Europe or the United States, the main host countries for migrants from their native country. S. Bredeloup (2012) points out that differentiation is needed—albeit based on porous, complex categories—between female African migrants who trade internationally from their host space, as is the case with the Comorian women studied here, and international African traders who travel frequently from their native country to buy supplies, retail or wholesale, outside their national borders. These Comorian women have indeed settled in a host country from which they make their trade trips.

C. Lesourd discusses the ambiguous situation of women in the Mauritanian context: they are tied to the home, but enjoy a relative freedom of movement that allows them go on trade trips. In this research, she notes "the implications of being both a successful businessperson and 'being a woman', by comparing, in particular, the construction of success with negotiations in gender relations" (Lesourd 2009: 84). The Mauritanian businesswomen travel from Morocco to Thailand, from Algeria to Dubai, from the Canaries to China, and even to France, depending on their financial resources. The first international trading routes formed along the pilgrimage routes to Mecca (Saudi Arabia). Radiating out from Mecca, other marketplaces appeared in such places as Bangkok, Mumbai (Bombay), and Dubai. Unlike the pioneering Mauritanian tradeswomen who used the Hajj routes for their trading activities, the new international tradeswomen tend to prefer Dubai, which represents real opportunities. This internationalization of female African trade, initially the prerogative of a female elite, opened up at the beginning of the 1990s.

Our data suggest that trade is a common practice among Comorian women in Comoros. Half of the tradeswomen we met during our research had already engaged in trading activities at both the local and national levels before they migrated. They traded in groceries, local agricultural and fishing produce (seafood, fish, cassava, yams, etc.), embroidered caps (*Kofia*), manufactured products, and cosmetics in marketplaces in the villages and the capital, Moroni. In France, they consider they are resuming activities they have already conducted in their native country. Anthropologist S. Blanchy draws on an analysis of the gender-based division of domestic tasks on the island of Grande Comore[8] to show that many women take up trading activities: "Women set up profit-making gardening activities when they need money for a project such as the joint purchase of dishes for a party. In rural areas, they make money producing coconut oil and wickerwork.[9] In the towns and cities, they embroider male caps (*kofia*), which are very popular luxury objects in Grande Comore. Mostly women and young people are found working on cash crop programs (groundnuts, potatoes and tomatoes) whose profitability depends on trade channels" (Blanchy 2010: 47). This tradition of trade for urban and rural players in situations of social and economic insecurity is widespread in the native country and in many countries of the globalized South. Consequently, trade is common practice in the native country, but its increased transnationalization is largely due to the many opportunities offered by long-range migration.

These studies on African women's involvement in trade movements reveal the importance of traditional female trading in Africa and the active participation of women in "discrete globalization" (Pliez and Choplin 2016).

2.2 Profiles of Comorian Businesswomen

Suitcase trading is structured around networks of international players based largely on the models, norms, and resources of the constantly challenged traditional sociabilities. Using wages to finance trade movements is fairly common practice among tradeswomen with jobs. All those who have a job say they use their wages to finance their trade movements, even if their wages are low due to their job insecurity (part-time work, fixed-term contract, or low-waged job). In fact, 23% of working migrant women in our sample are employed in insecure jobs (fixed-term contracts, temporary employment, and government-subsidized employment) as opposed to 17% of the total female population (Arnault 2005). Migrant women "form a sort of low-skilled and unskilled employment 'sub-segment' of the female labor market, which is narrower than that for men" (F. Gaspard 1998: 188).

Works speak of dual casualization and dual ethnic discrimination inducing losses of skills when women are constantly having to change jobs at the end of their fixed-term contracts (Roulleau-Berger 2010). Maoulida[10] (mother of seven with no qualifications) is employed in the service sector as a cleaning lady on an atypical contract (part-time and irregular hours). In the company she works for, cleaning ladies start work early in the morning (at 6 a.m. or 7 a.m.) or else late (from 5 p.m. or 6 p.m. through to midnight). As C. Nizzoli puts it, "The conditions of part-time cleaning work splinter the work timetable: in most cases, these workers have to work early in the morning and late in the evening to keep from getting in the way of the company's employees and public on the premises" (Nizzoli 2014: 2). This irregularity in work timetable contributes to employer strategies to make invisible and lower the cost of a workforce that is both ethnicized and at the bottom of the female ladder (Chaib 2004):

> *Look, the last three days, I've been at Aérocoptère in Marignane, I get there very early. Basically, I start at 6 a.m. and finish at 8 a.m. And as work happens to start there at 8.30 or 9.00, I don't remember exactly but it's definitely after I leave, I don't meet anybody, except possibly in the evening, because I'm back in the evening for four more hours. From 5 to 9, and sometimes 10 at night. I've been doing this for ten years. I rarely meet an employee… only twice.* (Maoulida, cleaning lady, 47 years old)

Despite this objective job insecurity shared by half of the tradeswomen on the employment market (only five women have a "typical" job, working full-time on a permanent contract), the wage, low or high, remains their most stable income on which they rely to finance their trips. They can use their wages to buy tickets or book hotel rooms, to pay for the shipment of goods, or to pay into community-funding practices such as *tontines*.

Fahamoé, a 51-year-old home help working full-time on a fixed-term contract, told us that goods shipment is her main concern and that she therefore systematically sets aside part of what is left over from her wage after she has paid her domestic expenses:

> *I once had an arrangement with a cousin in Dubai to send my stuff to Mbeni [a village in her native country]. It was him who offered to help me for €300, for everything, shipment costs, taxes, and even clearance. I gave him the money and the goods without trying to check if he was telling me the truth, since he worked for an import-export company. The problem is that he lied, for his company didn't deal in clearance. So you see, he stole my money. When I went to customs in Comoros to get my merchandise with the ticket he had given me, they said, "No". Not only did I have to bribe every custom employee, but the money I had spent had vanished. So since that day I've been doing things straight, whether I send goods back home or here. I spend my wage so that I get*

my merchandise back. I never spend more than €100 from my wage. When I invest in a tontine, *it grows, but basically that's what I do. Now, I only negotiate with import-export companies when they are run by an Indian. Someone honest. With him, I know that what I spend depends on the amount of merchandise. When I go to Dubai, I don't even try to see my cousin.* (Fahamoé, home help, 51 years old)

The tradeswomen are members of joint, private *tontines*, wherein all members are supposed to know each other. The *tontines* are structured as much by family and friendship ties as by the aim to build up the maximum amount of capital possible for all the members. Since this economy relies essentially on networks of trust and word of honor (Portes 1995), scams are common and therefore condition a lot of the strategies used by the tradeswomen. One of Fahamoé's main concerns is that her merchandise arrives safely. It is the vital prerequisite for her activities to continue. So wages are invested in the shipment of merchandise. The income from *tontines* and other financing methods is invested in other parts of the business. Note that this case of someone using her wage exclusively to ship her merchandise is unique. Money from *tontines* and family donations is used to finance other trade stages such as travel, hotel accommodation, and purchasing goods. All the other tradeswomen use their wages for more than one step in the process (*tontine* funding and buying tickets, booking hotel rooms, and tipping "helpers" in marketplaces). Only unoccupied and unemployed women cannot claim to fund their business from their wages. These migrants draw on their family members' wages or welfare benefits.

In addition to their own wages, tradeswomen draw on welfare (child benefit, housing benefit, and unemployment benefit) and support and solidarity from family members (husband or children). It is only rarely that they invest all the welfare benefits in their business. They tend more to make strategic use of both welfare benefits and financial support from their family. These tradeswomen consequently have to convince their family members to help them out, which can cause problems in a household. How do they convince their husband, children, brother, or sister to support them in an unprofitable, unstable business, especially as some children have a hard time understanding the social implications of investment in the native country? So tradeswomen have many strategies in hand to drum up family support. Fara, for example, told us that the purpose of her trips was to pay for a house being built for the family in her native country. So everyone in the family had to make a contribution. Generally, this strategy should work on all family members when the goal is to finish a second home. Similarly, Karima makes her trips so that she can organize and plan weddings in the family. In these cases, then, financial support from the family is generally taken for granted since women's trips serve to help them carry out tasks that are their responsibility. As C. Schmoll points out that tradeswomen "embrace tradition whereby everything to do with planning and organizing weddings is their responsibility" (Schmoll 2005: 5). Here is what Karima, a 48-year-old, unemployed mother of six, has to say:

> The housing benefit is in my name. Our rent is €640. So when I need to organize a trip, I can go to my daughter and ask her to pay the rent so I can save the housing benefit, you see? I only do that from time to time, but it's a way for me to buy my ticket, generally it's for the ticket. It's not much, you see. But most of the time she turns me down. She works, she gets paid and she never does the shopping, so she should contribute a little. I have to insist. She makes a living thanks to us, her parents, so she can help out a little, especially since it's not often. But she always spins us the same line to get out of paying. Like she doesn't understand why I use the housing benefit for this unprofitable business. (Karima, unemployed, 48 years old)

Welfare benefits are used directly to buy tickets, book hotels, and/or pay into *tontines*. Welfare benefits such as the RSA (French working solidarity benefit) give recipients a way to be relatively "independent" with respect to household expenditure and contingencies, but tradeswomen who put these benefits into their business can find themselves dependent on family support:

> If you take your welfare benefits and put them into the business, how do you make a living? How do you feed your children? And what are you supposed to do if there's an emergency? I don't get it, these women who put their RSA and everything they have into their business, especially when customers never pay on time. (Boina, chambermaid, 35 years old)

Lastly, the *tontine* (*Mtsango*[11]) is another way to fund a business. The women find various ways of paying into these *tontines*: working women pay part of their wages, jobseekers use their unemployment benefits if they still have them, and housewives appear to juggle welfare with their husbands' wages. The tradeswomen use *tontines* to quickly make sizeable sums of money to fund their businesses and their trips to Euro-Mediterranean and Asian marketplaces. Semin (2007: 183) reports that female *tontines* are highly developed in Africa, "where they mark a clear divide between female and male activity spheres, and are part and parcel of the exchanges required for family ceremonies." Many women say they join a female *tontine* to start up or resume their business activities. Karima, mother of six and unemployed for a year, is one example:

> *We women can do the* Mtsango [tontine] *to start our small* Uchuzi [trade]. *Each woman puts into it. For example, you have an* Mtsango *of a hundred euros a month and there are twenty of you. So you take it in turns to take 2,000 euros, and then you go with that to buy* Nkandous [agbadas], *rings, a few plates and you come to sell it here. Your sister who can't move, who can't do what you do, she'll take it from here and give you 50 euros. With that, we get by. We can't get by without trade. With that, we meet in a group, we do* Mtsango *and take it in turns every month to get our share. Sometimes, after the* tontine, *we go into the city because some of us are a bit old and you can't go into the city all the time. It's not easy when you live north of Marseille. So us traders, we go into the city to buy some things and we come to sell them for five euros to those who didn't get out. With that, I do my food shopping.* (Karima, unemployed, 48 years old)

All the traders interviewed practice this group way of funding individual or joint projects. They say that *tontines* have the advantage over bank loans as there is no steep interest rate to pay. The *tontine* practices observed among the Marseille tradeswomen correspond to this mode of social relations whereby "space is decreasingly a territory and increasingly a place of mobility" (Semin 2007: 186). It is possible to join a number of *tontines* at a time and to live in Marseille and be a member of a *tontine* in Marignane (a city near Marseille), and vice versa.

> **Ethnographic observation:** *Tontine* **meeting in Marseille (January 2015)**
>
> The meeting was held at Halima's home, the respondent who gave me permission to observe the *tontine*. There had been eight members at the previous meeting, but one participant had asked to bring a friend on board and so now there were nine. The group meets every six months, which gives members the time to raise their contribution of €250. Halima lives in Castellane (a working-class neighborhood in the north of Marseille). From what I understand, only two members of the *tontine* live nearby. The others come from districts further afield. One of the members (with a car) is from Belsunce (Marseille city center), and offered to pick up the other members on her way. The meeting was set for 7 p.m. on a Saturday, a day when most of the women do not work, except for the one missing member who is a home help and gave her contribution to the "secretary" (*tontine* treasurer). I arrived at Halima's at 6 p.m., with some drinks in hand as my contribution to the expenses. Halima had been cooking all afternoon, and was still cooking when the contributions were due to start. She finally left the kitchen at 7.15 p.m. She kept saying, "*We're Comorians, we're always late,*" as if to say that not only was she late with the preparations for the *tontine*, but that the members were late as well. By 7.30 p.m., eight members had arrived, with the home help held up at work. As the meeting starting, Halima offered traditional "*tchayi,*" tea and coffee, accompanied by appetizers such as samosas and traditional Comorian bread (*mkatre siniya*). Meanwhile, the television was switched onto ORTC, the Comoros national television channel.
>
> Halima: "*It's easy to figure out who'll get their money first. The eldest decides. At least, that's the way it's always done in our group.*"
>
> Respondent 2: "*It's true we ask the eldest to decide. The young people now draw lots, that's why we don't invite them. When they need money, they put pressure on everyone to get their money when it suits them.*"
>
> Respondent 3: "*That's so true. They're always bickering in their* Mtsango. *There are no rules.*"
>
> For the older generations, *tontine* rotations are decided mainly by the eldest members. So they refrain from deferring to individual needs at a given time or drawing lots as the "young people" always do. For these merchants, the *tontine* normative order is the elders' right to decide on the order of rotation and thus avoid conflict. The question is not who gets their money first or last. It is about asking the elders their opinion as to the order of rotation.

These *tontines* are female spaces from which men are excluded.[12] As J. Semin has shown, *tontines* serve many and varied purposes. *Mtsango* are used to rapidly raise capital to pay for family ceremonies such as "big weddings," substantial funds to invest in personal projects such as building or finishing a house, and money to pay for a child's schooling or studies abroad. Above all, they serve as a social meeting place for members. So *tontines* are effectively spaces that facilitate the migrant integration in the land of immigration and prevent new newcomers from being isolated.

In addition to the *tontine* networks, community network solidarity takes the shape of shopping missions in marketplaces such as Istanbul. Shopping missions are a form of solidarity offered by traders to women who do not get out much and need certain products that can only be found in larger stores and markets. A customer gives a sum to a trader with precise instructions as to the prices to pay for the products. Most shopping missions mentioned in the interviews are for products for big wedding celebrations in the home or host country. Sometimes, traders are asked to buy more everyday products such as Indian fabric held in high esteem in Comorian society. And then there are the shopping missions by traders in the host country and those dispatched by freight and cargo to the country of origin when goods and products are needed for projects such as house building. For this type of project, the shopping mission may consist of asking the businesswoman to buy building materials that the customer is responsible for clearing through customs in the country of origin. The customer has to provide the trader with enough capital to provide the service. Yet, as with any exchange, a system of give and take is the norm, and it can be both social and economic in this case. For example, customers may provide capital over the sum of the prices of the products to be bought, with the remainder to be used for the traders' traveling expenses. This is actually an explicit part of the negotiating strategies used by female "customers" to persuade traders to provide them with the service. The capital provided for a shopping mission can sometimes be used to part-finance *tontines*. In the case of social returns, tradeswomen who accept these missions expand their customer network and build up symbolic capital (prestige) that can advance their sales activities. One trader (Halima, 60 years old) told us that she gets the impression that she is known by everyone in Marseille as a "great trader" because she accepts certain shopping missions.

3   Contentious Travel: Negotiation and Compromise in the Household?

Married migrants (70% of the businesswomen we met) and those with young children have to conduct a number of negotiations in the household for every business trip they take abroad. This marital status widely shared by migrant women clearly has an impact on the different strategies to seal approval to travel. Married women prefer to travel as a group to persuade their husbands to give their approval, considering that the group is supposed to be able to control and call to order any unseemly behavior or waywardness. Husbands tend to find it safer and more reassuring, even if some of them feel that a stop should be put to their wives traveling altogether. Although the reason for travel is considered legitimate, the women know that a trip on their own, outside of a group, is stigmatized by the community in the host country and by their families because there is a strong chance they would be suspected of abandon or even prostitution. Group travel, albeit making it easier to control the women's movements, enables migrant women less endowed with cultural, social, and symbolic resources to take part in trade movements accompanied by women with broader knowledge networks and especially makes for economies of scale by sharing the different costs (hotel room, filling a container, shipping goods, etc.). For married women, group travel makes it easier for them to obtain their husband's consent, provided they have a legitimate reason for the trip.

In the case of Baraka—a 41-year-old cleaning lady and mother of four, two of whom have stayed back in the home country—her husband insists on very short trips and finds it hard to totally accept his wife's trade-related movements:

> *It's complicated with my husband. That's why I can't do trade as I would like to. It's a pity that we have to yell at each other every time I want to leave. For him, two days with four children is too much. Sometimes to set his mind at rest, I send them to my cousin in Soli (neighborhood of Solidarity, North of Marseille). But that's not enough. He has even asked me to stop trading. He knows it's how he has been able to have a great marriage full of things he's proud of like his father's Hajj [Muslim pilgrimage to Mecca]. It's because I'm in this business.*

He's right to say we're not paid sometimes, but it still helps a lot. So it's the same scene every trip. We have to fight over it. I get tired of it, especially since we are doing nothing wrong. All my friends go on trips without a problem. Their husbands either look after the children or find someone to look after them. Sometimes it's their husbands who make them trade. My best friend, for example, often travels alone and her husband approves. I can't even get away with travelling with other women. And yet I know the roads and places where I can travel alone well. (Baraka, cleaning lady, 41 years old)

V. Zelizer (1994) talks about gender differences in the perception and use of money. There is not much value placed in the household on fluctuating incomes from the women's trading activities. Consequently, not much value is placed on the trade itself, which might well be stopped by recalcitrant husbands. Funding their trade activities from their spouse's or children's wages or money has a direct impact on the family budget, especially when goods are sold on credit and reimbursed late. It is this group travel and the networking it creates that enable Baraka and other married traders whose husbands disagree with their transnational trade activities to continue with their activities and their travels, albeit with difficulty. The information, assistance, and, most importantly, supervision of the network of travelers constitute a form of guarantee that the trader can provide her skeptical husband. In this way, the network of traders resembles a social resource brought into play to lend credibility to travel plans and to convince husbands as well as the entire extended family.

Sitty, a 35-year-old cleaning lady and mother of two, considers her husband to be "*understanding and accommodating.*" Her unemployed husband agrees to her business trips without any trouble and, more importantly, takes care of their children while she is traveling:

My husband regularly babysits for me without any problem whenever I go on a trip. But for a few months, my own family was trying to change that. Two months ago, I went to Istanbul. When I got back home, my husband told me that my own cousin who I had helped come to France with my own money had dared tell my husband that I was the husband and he was the wife. So I get the feeling that it does bother him even if he says he doesn't care. I told him a while ago that there are many mashouhoulis *[weddings] coming up. It's the best period to sell. He pretends he doesn't understand. He even told me he has to look for work. I knew my family wasn't keen on me travelling, but they are warping my husband's mind.*

Commercial travel brings a form of independence that conflicts with traditional gender roles. Unemployed husbands are more likely to agree to babysit (and even tolerate their wives' travels even though they may consider them inappropriate). On the other hand, non-trader women can be quick to criticize the female traders.

In their country of origin, women are used to conducting business activities without any trouble from their family. In France, however, the possibility for women to work and earn a stable income for the household has completely reshaped how families see women in trade. Families in Comoros find it hard to accept the idea of women going on business trips, as this is a mainly male activity on the archipelago. Obviously, the activity is usually seen as nothing new, but its transnationalization is breaking with the stereotypes that underpin the gendered distribution of tasks and social spaces. This transnational trade activity means that women are entering a public space usually frequented by men.

In the face of such resistance and moves to control their movements, migrant women learn to use ploys and tactics to facilitate their travels. The main tactic used to prevent family-based systems of control from prohibiting their trips is to line up people to stand in and attend to the domestic duties during their absence from the family home. Mkaya, a 43-year-old cleaning lady and mother of three, arranges everything that needs to be done in the home a week before her departure. She rallies her network of friends to take care of her children during her absence. Despite the fact that she is divorced, her family in the Comoros do not understand her travels and talk of frequently abandoned children. So to reassure them, she has to call on her friends to take care of her children. And, as with any exchange of favors, she brings gifts to the friends who look after her children when she comes back.

For married women like Boina, a 55-year-old cleaning lady and mother of three, rallying her network of friends to look after her children is not enough for her husband to allow her to go on a trip. She has to take care of all the household tasks ahead of time, such as preparing enough food for the family during her absence. In addition to these household management strategies, some women readily bring back gifts for the entire family unit—husbands and children—to win their support for future trips. There are also women like Karima, a 48-year-old jobseeker and mother of six, who point out the utility of trade for the family, particularly in terms of investments in the country of origin such as the construction of family houses. It is clear in all cases that trade trips are not exempt from any of the forms of social control exercised over women. So the trips can be made legitimate in the eyes of the migrant family circle by investing (or the promise of investment) in real estate in the home country and/or by the promise of valuables to family members, especially husbands. It is reasonable to say that the suitcase trade empowers women and drives a change (albeit slight) in the gendered, traditional relations in the family and the community.

4   Shipping and Selling Merchandise on a Transnational Scale

These "non-professional" economic players define their trade routes and organize their purchases and main delivery strategies on the basis of merchant and circulatory know-how acquired in part before emigration. Research has shown that the form of entry into trade has an impact on "access to information on profitable trade routes and how to purchase, ship and sell goods" (Dicko 2013: 137). The interviewed traders' previous commercial experience has given them knowledge of the merchandise supply channels, and enabled them to activate or reactivate certain transnational networks and organize goods delivery strategies. They were not actually transnational traders in their country of origin. They were supplied by international merchants working in *biachara* (international trade) and were therefore able to become acquainted with at least some trade routes. The migrant women have drawn on this knowledge acquired from past experience to deploy new transnational supply channels.

4.1 At the School of Dubai: First Steps in a Cosmopolitan Trading Center

The "supermarket city" of Dubai is a central hub for all international traders from North and Sub-Saharan Africa. It is in Dubai, a cosmopolitan trading center, that the majority of the traders interviewed took their first steps in transnational trade (25 of the 30 women first started trading transnationally from Dubai). And it is from this cosmopolitan trading center that Chinese goods (mainly second-hand clothes) are distributed in the country of origin, as they are in a number of African countries: "At the time, the other logic identified led the African traders who travelled up to that point from the Black continent to Dubai, the global platform for re-exports of Chinese products, to trace the chain back to the source" (Bertoncello and Bredeloup 2009: 56). In this regard, one trader speaks nostalgically about how she used to shop in Moroni (capital of Comoros), buying Chinese goods and products that had transited through Dubai. She illustrates this ascent of the commercial chain to the source with the example of a friend:

> *Chinese clothes are very successful over there in Volo Volo [main market of Comoros]. Since my family had a grocery store, I often went to buy them. They were always snapped up very quickly. People fought over them. So, yes we knew that it all came from Dubai, but I wasn't aware back then that they came from China and went through Dubai before the big traders took them to send up-country [Comoros]. I was told by a friend, who travels with me and who went to China to buy things. She told me: 'Everything there is half the price it is in Dubai', when Dubai is already cheaper to start with. So now everyone goes to China for that. Some send back here and others send over there.* (Rikinaza, child care, 34 years old)

Therefore, this trade route to Dubai frequented by all the traders interviewed is part of a supply chain that starts in China. It is a chain made up mainly of entrepreneurs and importers from the country of origin who travel between the trading platforms of Dubai and China, activating, as they go, transnational social networks and networks in places joined by these traders.

In 1995, with the arrival of Emirates airline, the Comorian government broke the monopoly of Air France airline, which stopped serving Comoros from France for strategic and profitability-related reasons (El-Amine Souef 2009). Up to that point, Air France had been the main airline providing the France-Comoros connection. M. A. H. Meran, T. Gullian, and B. Bertoncello estimate that Dubai-based Emirates used to fly "between 5,000 and 6,000 Comorians" to their country of origin via Dubai every year (Meran et al. 2000: 67). During this period, a significant number of Comorian migrants would stop over in Dubai to make purchases, a large proportion of which was sent in container to Comoros. Zaoudja, who arrived in France in 1982 and frequently makes round trips between the host country and the Comoros, is one of those Comorians who used to fly with Emirates to shop in Dubai:

I know Dubai from the beginning when we used to stop over there with Emirates airline. At the beginning, I was always with my husband. We always took flights with a stopover of five hours, because it was cheaper when the stopover was long. With my husband, we used to go to Dubai looking for clothes, bracelets and handbags that we took as presents to the family back home, especially when we had had the time to find them things there. Before going to Istanbul, I went to Dubai for at least ten years. (Zaoudja, jobseeker, 54 years old)

Emirates airline stopped flying to Comoros on January 15, 2000. Although Emirates stopped serving Comoros, for five years, Comorian migrants had the opportunity to get acquainted with Dubai marketplaces on trips back home, among others, and subsequently take flights with stopovers in Dubai aboard other airlines as a leg of their trade trips. Even today, Dubai is the favorite marketplace for storekeepers and traders, in particular due to the ease of shipment of goods to the country of origin. Since the 1990s, then, Dubai has been the most buoyant trading center for traders from Comoros, and has served as a hub of commercial socialization for many Comorian women.

The businesswomen stock up in the United Arab Emirates (Dubai) mainly with fabrics (varieties of colored fabrics, Indian sari fabrics, cotton fabrics, and silk pashmina for the women to make shawls and scarves), clothes (shawls appreciated by the migrant women, scarves, Indian-style dress, *agbada* for men, and keffiyeh), prayer mats, religious books bought by traders keen to attract a religious clientele, silver-plated costume jewelry (earrings, bracelets, and necklaces), cosmetics, jeans for men and women, other female beauty accessories (bags, vanity cases, perfumes sold in Europe at knockdown prices), shoes for men and women, suits (for men), and spices. Such a wide range of products in one place like this can only be found in Dubai's marketplaces, making them a must for all the traders we spoke to.

As O. Pliez puts it, "Dubai is particularly symbolic as that moment where the roads of Mediterranean, Middle Eastern, East African and Eastern European trade converge and cross" (Choplin and Pliez 2016: 3). The Emirate's marketplaces form a trading floor for businessmen from the country of origin and the tradeswomen living in France to come and stock up on goods to be forwarded to both Comoros and France. However, the Istanbul trade route was discovered and established by the tradeswomen themselves traveling from the host country and did not need fellow Comorians living in Turkey for them to take it. The traders base their trade movements on female solidarity rationales. The women are not well-endowed with cultural capital, but they use social resources (transnational social networks in particular) to conduct their trade. Here is where traveling in a group comes into its own, because the women least endowed with social capital can take advantage of others' networks. The traders with the largest transnational relational networks are asked to email or telephone the "helpers" (Sakoyan 2011), who will welcome them at the airport, take them to the best hotels, and pick them up from their hotels to "better marketplaces."

Helpers or business intermediaries are individuals from the same village, family relations, or mutual acquaintances who operate as guide, adviser, translator, and negotiator for the traders. They are students or Comorian expatriates working in the marketplaces. Helpers on trade trips are paid, in either cash or kind, and rates vary by trader. Some tradeswomen can only pay for a meal, or products requested from their shopping trips, such as brand shoes. Note here that women can sometimes act as a helper for their fellow travelers, in particular on group journeys. However, although solidarity rationales may appear to preclude competition and jealousy between tradeswomen, the group journeys do have their drawbacks. Customs and airport services responsible for controlling border flows are more likely to check groups of women than women traveling alone.

In the marketplaces, the tradeswomen show no lack of social creativity. We have identified three categories of negotiating and purchasing strategies: independent bargaining (20%), partial use of a helper (57%), and/or total use of a helper (23%). Independent bargaining is where the women ask for no outside help to negotiate their purchases in the marketplaces. The leading independent bargaining strategy entails the use of a calculator. Among the other strategies are consideration of the financial market situation and collective transmission of information on gold prices to facilitate negotiations; exhibiting shared religious and cultural affiliation with the seller(s) (some women speak in Swahili in Kenya, Malagasy for the natives of Madagascar, Arabic in Dubai, and Turkish in Turkey); showing previous receipts to the sellers to prove customer loyalty when asking for a discount; and writing down the prices of sellers visited in a notebook to be able to make comparisons. The partial use of a helper concerns migrants who start negotiating alone, but need to bring a helper on board when they cannot manage to lower the price any further. Total use refers to women who want assistance right through the bargaining process. These negotiating strategies are porous and depend on the marketplace. An independent bargaining strategy might be adopted in Nairobi (Kenya), in a space of cultural and linguistic proximity, whereas a helper may be needed in China.

4.2 Transporting the Merchandise to France and Comoros

Two main goods transport networks and two main trade routes are used. Goods are transported to the host country often in suitcases and sometimes by contracting goods suppliers or helpers to make the purchases and arrange for the goods to be transported on the trader's behalf. Goods are transported to the country of origin in suitcases or are shipped by air or sea.

The women have to contend with strict customs systems when transporting goods to the host country and have learned to deal with these obstacles by developing "ingenious" transport strategies such as "physical" transport, in the shape of wearing certain products such as clothes and jewelry or carrying products in a suitcase:

> *Sometimes, you run into customs officers. When they stop you, that hurts. When you are found with gold on you, you get a €2,000 fine. I once got a €1,000 fine one day when I had some gold on me. But that didn't put me off. Not at all. I keep going whenever I can. It's a bit like playing the lottery. Sometimes you win and sometimes you lose. That day there I lost. But I can't forget all the times I've got through with no problem at all. From that day on, whenever I've had gold on me, I pretend it's mine. I wear it.* (Karima, unemployed, 48 years old)

Products sent to the country of origin are subject to a less restrictive legal system. Large quantities of goods are consequently sent to Comoros, sometimes in containers rented or purchased by a group of traders. These container rentals and purchases bring the migrants into contact with importers in the country of origin, who are sometimes met in the marketplaces. These contacts with importers give rise to complex arrangements.[13] Importers can ship large quantities of goods at knockdown prices, remotely receive purchase orders from the country of origin, share the costs of purchasing containers between traders, and sort out customs clearance in the country of origin with the tradeswomen. This can considerably reduce the cost of customs clearance for the tradeswomen in the Comoros and avert systematic taxation of their goods.

4.3 Selling the Merchandise in France and Comoros

Traders—working on their own or in a group—report encountering huge problems when it comes to selling the products and goods they have bought. The merchandise is sold in both the host country and the country of origin. The women attend community celebrations and weddings in the host country. Sometimes they work door to door and sometimes they market their products on the Internet and social networks (especially Facebook). They also market their products in places and on platforms online dedicated to the "Comorian community" in France, such as Facebook groups.

My observations of social networks such as Facebook have led me to conclude that online socialization by these migrants not well-endowed with cultural capital channels passes through two forms of solidarity: intergenerational mutual aid within the family in the host country and solidarity between women. It is often the tradeswomen's children or other family members who post the products on the Internet platforms. These IT-savvy children or family members are generally "second generation migrants" and have been socialized and schooled in France, unlike their mothers or grandmothers who have rarely attended school in the country of origin. We observe that selling can also be conducted by family members, without any division of tasks between mother and daughter. Sales assistance is a girls-only practice.

The most common selling strategy is product sales on credit. However, as Maoulida, a 47-year-old cleaning lady and mother of seven, explains, delays with payment mean that this sales strategy is inefficient and puts the business in jeopardy:

> *I cannot spend €3,000 to €4,000 to go to Dubai, buy my wares and come back. And there's another worry, which is the recession. And in addition to the recession, there are poor payers. People do not want to pay their debts. Because of that, I cannot risk telling Zaza [her daughter], because she works, to loan me €4,000 or €5,000 so I can concentrate entirely on this business. And the products that sell well are the products for women [...]. For example, I go to Dubai and when I get back, someone takes the products on credit. There's a problem there, because we find ourselves with far too many goods in the house. I went to Dubai in 2011, and I can tell you that there is an untold amount of money outstanding. Someone owes me €370 alone, another owes me €220, and another person recently gave me checks. I was pleased about that at least, because at least I have a guarantee. I'll collect on them every month. That's what I advised the other traders to do. I have a Maore Comorian customer and it's as if I was the one who owed her money, she avoids me all the time. But maybe she's not as bad as all that. Because her problem is that when she sets an appointment with me, and when I don't get there on the precise date she's fixed, then the money has already been spent on something else or used to pay other creditors.* (Maoulida, cleaning lady, 47 years old)

Two women (Halima and Aturia) have set up strategic *tontines* to rope in customers in debt. When it comes round to the debtor's turn to collect their money, the amount is automatically used to pay off their debts first. Some traders like Chando, a 42-year-old cleaning lady, prefer to sell at weddings held at the local community hall to celebrate a union in the host country. Chando believes that it is at these "hall marriages" that customers are most likely to buy, since wedding attendees always make provision for sums of money to help newlyweds set up home. So Chando's aim is to cash in on part of the sums in question. In addition, she often refuses to sell on credit, since she has frequently been left unpaid. Her selling method is called *towa ourenge* (literally, "give and take"), used by only a minority of traders, since clientele generally insist on credit. She sells gold in the main to the bride and groom. Traders are seen in a positive light and can earn their reputation at weddings, as they bring the gold and wares needed for the wedding.

5 Conclusion

The Comorian women engaged in trade on a transnational scale can be considered as transmigrants in terms of their skills and their capacity for action. They are consequently able to straddle two worlds between "here," where they have settled and live, and "there," where they come from and in which they invest (real estate investment and small shops) (Tarrius et al. 2013). M. Granovetter's words are resonant here in that "Individuals do not have purely economic goals, but they also seek sociability, gratitude, recognition from others, status and power" in their economic actions (Granovetter 2000: 112). International trade by migrant Comorian women is an economic activity structured around the mobility of women in situations of insecurity and professional discrimination.

Groups of women from Sub-Saharan African countries who have settled in a Euro-Mediterranean country find in this activity a way to supplement their earnings from host-country jobs with strong social insecurity, giving them little room for maneuver in their different projects. This sideline brings them social recognition. Ultimately, this transnational business activity appears to affect some empowerment configurations constantly renegotiated within the households and in the migration spaces, which have less to do with economic independence than with social gender roles.

Appendix

Table 5.1 The interviewees mentioned in the chapter

Pseudonym	Marital status	Age	Occupation	Number of children	Level of schooling	Markets and public squares
Aturia	Married	59	Cleaning lady	8	Unschooled	Dubai (UAE), Istanbul (Turkey), Nairobi (Kenya)
Baraka	Married	41	Cleaning lady	4	Unschooled	Dubai (UAE), Istanbul (Turkey)
Boina	Married	35	Chambermaid	3	High school	Dubai (UAE), Istanbul (Turkey)
Chando	Married	42	Cleaning lady	1	Unschooled	Dubai (UAE), Istanbul (Turkey), Ventimiglia (Italy)
Fahamoé	Divorced	51	Home help	4	Primary level	Dubai (U AE), Istanbul (Turkey)
Fara	Divorced	58	Dressmaker	4	Unschooled	Dubai (UAE), Istanbul (Turkey), Nairobi (Kenya)
Halima	Married	60	Cleaning lady	3	Unschooled	Dubai (UAE), Istanbul (Turkey), Antananarivo (Madagascar), Nairobi (Kenya), Ventimiglia (Italy), Barcelona (Spain)
Karima	Married	48	Unemployed, jobseeker	6	High school	Dubai (UAE), Istanbul (Turkey), Nairobi (Kenya)
Maoulida	Married	47	Cleaning lady	7	Unschooled	Dubai (UAE), Istanbul (Turkey), Antananarivo (Madagascar), Ventimiglia (Italy)
Mkaya	Divorced	43	Cleaning lady	3	High school	Dubai (UAE)
Rikinaza	Married	34	Child care	0	High school	Dubai (UAE)
Sitty	Married	35	Cleaning lady	2	Primary level	Dubai (UAE), Istanbul (Turkey), Tunis (Tunisia)
Zaoudja	Married	54	Unemployed, jobseeker	3	Unschooled	Dubai (UAE), Istanbul (Turkey)

Notes

1. This work is supported by Aix Marseille University, CNRS, LEST (France).
2. This term refers to the heavy suitcases and bundles in which informal traders carry items bought abroad and sold as contraband.
3. Including several coups d'état where French mercenaries regularly intervened, notably led by Bob Denard, and so on.
4. See, for example, Bouly de Lesdain (1999) on Paris-based Cameroonian food traders, Peraldi (2001) on female Maghrebi suitcase traders, and Sandoval (2012) on *chiveras*, that is, Mexican tradeswomen dealing in clothes and other cheap products from Texas in the US-Mexico transborder space.
5. That is to say our respondents suggested other people we could speak to after our interviews with them.
6. A *tontine* is a rotating credit and savings association whereby members make regular payments (weekly, monthly, quarterly, or annual) into a fund run by a trustworthy person and collect a share of the proceeds in return.
7. The *Nanas-Benz* are tradeswomen from the Lomé market in Togo, who got rich by selling woven loin clothes. This name was coined as they were the first women in Africa to drive cars from the Mercedes-Benz brand.
8. According to the last Comorian census, approximately 95% of Comorian migrants living in mainland France are from the island of Grande Comore. As J. Sakoyan (2011: 6) points out, "Anjouan 'migration know-how' extends across the archipelago, whereas Grand Comorians have developed global networks."
9. Cf. Chap. 6 which analyzes the process of food production and home-based marketing in rural Russia (G. Mainguy).
10. All names have been changed to keep respondents anonymous.
11. Fee, in Comorian.
12. In this regard, as a male researcher, I found it very hard to observe the tradeswomen's *tontines*. I was de facto excluded and my presence was not really "welcome."
13. Importers are import-export companies or retailers in the country.

References

Arnault, S. (2005). Le sous-emploi concerne 1,2 million de personnes. *Insee Première*, 1046. Retrieved July 2014, from http://www.epsilon.insee.fr/jspui/handle/1/222.

Barbey, A. (2008). *La Socialisation des Comoriens à Marseille, Conservation et métamorphose des rôles et des usages sociaux en migration*. PhD in Ethnology, Université d'Aix-Marseille I.

Barreau, L. (2016). *Les Mules de la mode: mobilités de commerçantes angolaises au Brésil et en Chine*. PhD in Political Science, Université de Bordeaux-Sciencespo.

Bertoncello, B., & Bredeloup, S. (2009). Chine-Afrique ou la valse des entrepreneurs-migrants. *Revue européenne des migrations internationales, 25*(1), 45–70.

Blanchy, S. (2010). *Maisons des femmes, cités des hommes, filiation, âges et pouvoir à Ngazidja (Comores)*. Paris: Société d'ethnologie.

Bouly de Lesdain, S. (1999). *Femmes camerounaises en région parisienne. Trajectoires migratoires et réseaux d'approvisionnement*. Paris: L'Harmattan.

Bourdieu, P. (1986). L'illusion biographique. *Actes de la recherche en sciences sociales, 62–63*, 69–72.

Bredeloup, S. (2012). Mobilités spatiales des commerçantes africaines: une voie vers l'émancipation? *Autrepart, 61*(2), 23–39.

Chaib, S. (2004). Femmes, migration et marché du travail en France. *Les cahiers du CEDREF, 12*, 211–237.

Cheikh, M., Anglade, M. P., Bouasria, L., Debarre, F., Manry, V., & Schmoll, C. (Eds.). (2014). *Expérience du genre. Intimités, marginalités, travail et migration*. Paris: Karthala.

Choplin, A., & Pliez, O. (2016, octobre 4). Des mondialisations plus discrètes. Vers une nouvelle géographie des échanges mondiaux. *La Vie des idées*. Retrieved from http://www.laviedesidees.fr/Des-mondialisationsplusdiscretes.html

Crenshaw, K. (1991). Mapping the Margins: Intersectionality, Identity Politics, and Violence against Women of Color. *Stanford Law Review, 43*(6), 1241–1299.

Delacroix, E., Parguel, E., & Benoit-Moreau, F. (2018). Digital Subsistence Entrepreneurs on Facebook. *Technological Forecasting and Social Change*, 1–13. Retrieved October 2018. https://doi.org/10.1016/j.techfore.2018.06.018.

Delafontaine, R. (1998). Les femmes et la famille, au cœur de la communauté comorienne de Marseille. *Hommes et Migrations, 1215*, 21–31.

Diallo, A. (2014). Yakaar, Dakar-Dubaï-Guangzhou: trajectoire des commerçantes de Dakar. *Revue Tiers Monde, 217*(1), 97–112.

Dicko, B. E. (2013), *Les Ressources de la migration: les activités commerciales des maliens en France et au Mali*. PhD in Sociology and Anthropology, Université Paris Diderot.

Gaspard, F. (1998). Invisibles, diabolisées, instrumentalisées: figures de migrantes et de leurs filles. In M. Maruani (Ed.), *Les Nouvelles frontières de l'inégalité. Hommes et femmes sur le marché du travail* (pp. 183–192). Paris: La Découverte-Mage.

Granovetter, M. (2000). *Le Marché autrement, essais de Mark Granovetter*. Paris: Desclée de Brouwer.

Guillemaut, F. (2004). Trafics et migrations de femmes, une hypocrisie au service des pays riches. *Hommes et migrations, 1248*, 75–87.

Hochschild, A. R. (2000). Global Care Chains and Emotional Surplus Value. In W. Hutton & A. Giddens (Eds.), *On The Edge: Living with Global Capitalism*. London: Jonathan Cape.

Ki-Zerbo, J. (1978). *Histoire de l'Afrique noire: d'hier à demain*. Paris: Hatier.

Lambert, A. (1987). Femmes commerçantes dans la région du Cap-Vert (Sénégal). *ORSTOM Fonds Documentaires, 79*, 6–15.

Lesourd, C. (2009). Routes des commerçantes. Itinéraires de femmes. De quelques businesswomen Mauritaniennes d'hier et d'aujourd'hui. In M. Cheikh & M. Peraldi (Eds.), *Des Femmes sur les routes, Voyages au féminin entre Afrique et Méditerranée* (pp. 73–93). Paris and Casablanca: Le Fennec Éditions and Karthala.

Lesourd, C. (2014). *Femmes d'affaires en Mauritanie*. Paris: Karthala.

Mahmood, S. (2011). *Politics of Piety. The Islamic Revival and the Feminist Subject*. Princeton: Princeton University Press.

Manry, V., & Schmoll, C. (2010). «Le bizness des femmes » : Nouvelles figures des mobilités maghrébines dans l'espace euro-méditerranéen. *NAQD, 28*(1), 111–138.

Meran, M. A. H., Gullian, T., & Bertoncello, B. (2000). Les Comoriens de Marseille, entre coutume et commerce. *Hommes et Migrations, 1224*, 62–70.

Monne, L. (2016). *"Voix" de femmes comoriennes à Marseille: étude anthropologique de subjectivités dans l'espace migratoire*. PhD in Anthropology PhD, Paris, EHESS.

Morokvasic, M. (2011). L'(in)visibilité continue. *Cahiers du Genre, 51*(2), 25–47.

Nizzoli, C. (2014). Étudier le syndicalisme par les pratiques. Approche comparée du secteur du nettoyage. *XVIII ISA World Congress of Sociology*, July 2014, Yokohama, Japan. Retrieved June 2016, from https://hal.archives-ouvertes.fr/hal-01059042.

Oso Casas, L. (2002). Stratégies de mobilité sociale des domestiques immigrées en Espagne. *Tiers-Monde, 43*(170), 287–305.

Peraldi, M. (Ed.). (2001). *Cabas et containers. Activités marchandes informelles et réseaux migrants transfrontaliers*. Paris: Maisonneuve and Larose.

Pliez, O., & Choplin, A. (2016). Des mondialisations plus discrètes. Vers une nouvelle géographie des échanges mondiaux. *La Vie des idées*. Retrieved April 2017, from https://halshs.archives-ouvertes.fr/halshs-01400055.

Portes, A. (Ed.). (1995). *Economic Sociology of Immigration: Essays on Networks, Ethnicity, and Entrepreneurship*. New York: Russell Sage Foundation.

Portes, A. (1996). The Globalization from Below: The Rise of Transnational Communities. In W. P. Smith & R. P. Korczenwicz (Eds.), *Latin America in the World Economy* (pp. 151–168). Westport: Greenwood Press.

Roulleau-Berger, L. (2010). *Migrer au féminin*. Paris: Presses Universitaires de France.

Sakoyan, J. (2011). Les frontières des relations familiales dans l'archipel des Comores. *Autrepart, 57–58*(1), 181–198.

Sandoval, E. (2012). *Infraestructuras transfronterizas. Etnografía de itinerarios en el espacio Social Monterrey—San Antonio*. Mexico: Publicaciones de la casa chata.

Schmoll, C. (2005). Pratiques spatiales transnationales et stratégies de mobilité des commerçantes tunisiennes. *Revue européenne des migrations internationales, 21*(1), 131–154.

Semin, J. (2007). L'argent, la famille, les amies. Ethnographie contemporaine des *tontines* africaines en contexte migratoire. *Civilisations, 56-1*(1), 183–199.

Souef, M. E. (2009). *Le Transport aérien aux Comores. entre sécurité et souveraineté*. Paris: De la lune.

Strauss, A. (1992). *La Trame de la négociation*. Paris: L'Harmattan.

Tarrius, A. (1992). *Les Fourmis d'Europe. Migrants riches, migrants pauvres et nouvelles villes internationales*. Paris: L'Harmattan.

Tarrius, A., Missaoui, L., & Qacha, F. (2013). *Transmigrants et nouveaux étrangers. Hospitalités croisées entre jeunes des quartiers enclavés et nouveaux migrants internationaux*. Toulouse: Presses universitaires du Mirail.

Weber, F. (2009). *Le Travail à-coté: une ethnographie des perceptions*. Paris: EHESS.

Zelizer, V. (1994). *The Social Meaning of Money: Pin Money, Paychecks, Poor Relief, and Other Currencies*. Princeton: Princeton University Press.

6

Domesticity as Value: The Commodification of Foodstuffs in Precarious Rural Russia

Glenn Mainguy

1 Introduction

> Ioura: *In Russia, we have a stand-up comic Винакур. Do you know Винакур?*
> Me: *No*,
> Ioura: *Vot! He said, "What kind of strawberries do you buy? The very red ones with no spots or mold, or the wormy ones the babushkas sell?" And he answered, "I buy the wormy ones, of course, from the babushkas." "And why are they better?" "Because if the worms can eat the strawberry, so can I. But the ones the worms don't want to eat, they're already...."* (Ioura, 60 years old)

This chapter analyzes the process of domestic activity commodification by people living on the edge.[1] More specifically, it focuses on the case of individuals whose professional situation has been profoundly changed and entire spheres of their lives destabilized by an economic crisis or major upheaval. As the professional world loses its centrality in structuring their daily lives, these people develop another steady non-professional

---

G. Mainguy (✉)
Centre Emile Durkheim (UMR CRNS 5116), Sciences Po Bordeaux, Bordeaux, France
e-mail: mainguyglenn@gmail.com

© The Author(s) 2020
S. Naulin, A. Jourdain (eds.), *The Social Meaning of Extra Money*, Dynamics of Virtual Work, https://doi.org/10.1007/978-3-030-18297-7_6

activity that is marketable, but not black market, and profitable, but not adequately so: they start to commodify their domestic activities.

How do these people in precarious situations become market players? Why do they choose to take up these types of activities: for economic reasons or for others? How do they commodify their domestic activities? What is the role of such practices for people living in precarious situations? What is the social significance of these activities? To address these questions, this chapter analyzes the phenomenon of the commodification of domestic activities based on a study of household-farm practices. More specifically, we examine home-based market activities—selling meat, vegetables, dairy products, and honey—of rural people in precarious situations living in Russia.

The question of the commodification of domestic activities through the lens of rural Russian society is worth investigating for two main reasons. Firstly, the socioeconomic transformations that have taken place in Russian society since the fall of the Soviet Union could be called a process of marketization. This process was due to the collapse of the planned economy and the introduction of a market system as the dominant regime for the governance of the circulation of goods and allocation of resources. Thus, the market should be understood as an agent of social change and Russian society can be seen as a laboratory in which this process and, more generally, the transformation of contemporary capitalism may be studied (Alacovska 2018).

Furthermore, rural Russian society, built on the model of agricultural labor and Soviet paternalism, went through a deep crisis in the 1990s. Privatization of *sovkhozes* and *kolkhozes* and state withdrawal from the financing, management, and administration of the agricultural sector resulted in a drastic drop in production and farm bankruptcies (Nefedova 2003; Hervé 2007). Alongside the Russian agricultural system's structural changes, the labor market metamorphosed, and changes to employment-related social protection led to the formation of a rural "precariat" (Mainguy 2018). As illustrated by the trajectory of Kolia and Natasha described below, socially integrated workers in skilled employment either withdrew from the labor market or became poor workers, often in intermittent, low-paid and low-skilled jobs. To cope with this situation, many households engaged intensively in household-farm production. The

6 Domesticity as Value: The Commodification of Foodstuffs… 153

expression household-farm production refers to all agricultural production activities, but also, more generally, to food and nutrition activities conducted within the family unit (market gardening and animal husbandry). This defines the scope of activities included in the food production and acquisition process, as well as activities associated with the use of the produce—storage, consumption, circulation, and marketing.

This type of production is officially referred to as *khoziaistva nacelenia*. The Russian National Statistics Office defines it as agricultural production on plots of land (*outchastok zemli*) within the family, intended mainly for own consumption.[2] The 2003 law passed "on personal subsidiary farming" defines this agricultural production as a non-entrepreneurial activity. Although individuals are required to declare ownership of the agricultural land used, the agricultural activities carried out on it (number of head of cattle, quantity of vegetables produced, etc.) do not have to be declared. This definition as a non-entrepreneurial activity is important insofar as income from the production of *khoziaistva nacelenia* is no longer liable for taxes.[3]

Whereas household production represented 25% of Russia's agricultural production in 1990, individual plots accounted for more than 50% of total agricultural production by 2000 (Nefedova 2003). This rise in household agricultural production was due mainly to the development of a survival strategy—produce to eat—among populations hit by the economic crisis and loss of their jobs (Bridger and Pine 1998; Burawoy and Verdery 1999). By 2014, while the share of household agricultural production remained high at over 40%, its structure had been profoundly transformed.[4] The last decade has seen a gradual decline in household production as a survival economy—essentially for own consumption— and a shift toward the commercialization of this production (Pallot and Nefedova 2007). In effect, contrasting realities lay behind the still relatively large share of very poor households dependent on their household production to survive (about 33% of households in household agricultural production). The figure includes some 12% of households whose production is mainly market-oriented and for whom selling is a major source of income, and around 55% of households whose production is both consumed and marketed, providing them with monetary and non-monetary income (Wegren 2008: 7).

The choice of the home-based commercialization mode was made further to observations realized during my fieldwork—the importance of this distribution method to the surveyed families—and a shortfall in the literature on the subject. In the post-Soviet context, the circulation of household agricultural goods was perceived mainly as being external to the market, centered on the village and conducted in the form of non-market trade or gifts (Gambold Miller and Heady 2003; Paxon 2005). When market commercialization is addressed, it is to explore the meaning of the market act and its morality in the post-Soviet context (Humphrey and Mandel 2002). Little work has been done on either home-based commercialization activities or, more specifically, the reasons that drive individuals to engage in these practices and how those in precarious situations become market actors.

This chapter draws on an ethnography of economic practices used in household agricultural production and the construction of market trade to show how we can rethink the place of the market and trade logic in the everyday lives of individuals in precarious situations. Following a description of how people get involved in household-farm production, the chapter considers the ways in which the activity is organized and analyzes the impacts of market entry on production choice. It then explores vulnerable individuals' marketization activities and, more specifically, the mechanisms they put in place to singularize their foodstuffs for sale. Lastly, beyond the activity's economic determinants, the chapter shows that taking up commodification practices give men a way to recover their position in the domestic sphere and gain access to certain forms of social re-legitimation.

Method

The fieldwork was conducted on two missions to Russia (September 2012–June 2013 and February–July 2014), with visits to around 40 villages in the Kolomna and Zaraisk *raions* some 150 kilometers southeast of Moscow. The field research did not set out to produce a monograph of a village or a family, but an ethnography of rural people's daily lives in different places with different families. The main principles governing the investigation were to listen and observe in order to describe and explain. In keeping with these principles, a large number of people were met to enrich the study's empirical corpus. In addition to many informal interviews and one-off meetings, I forged sound ongoing relationships with five families during my fieldwork: Sacha and Marina's family in the village of Astapovo, Babushka Valentina's family in Sovkhoz Industria, Kolia and Natalia's family in Letunovo, Ioura and Irma's family in Shkin', and Father Jean and his wife also in Shkin'. These families were central to my fieldwork and are prominent throughout this chapter. The large number of visits to these five families during the survey provided the material for a discontinuous, but iterative, ethnography. Time spent with the families varied from one afternoon to immersion lasting several days. During these stays, I tried to take part in all the daily activities. For example, I dug the garden, picked berries, planted vegetables, led the cattle out to pasture, took part in slaughtering animals, watered gardens, worked the hay, repaired tractors, went to the shop, looked after children, and helped with the sheep shearing. In addition to these activities, I also spent a lot of time with my hosts, eating, drinking, walking around their village, and so on, or waiting on a bench in front of their house. My participation in domestic agricultural practices and all those everyday moments spent with the families and people I met formed a rich source of heterogeneous empirical material made up of recorded interviews, collections of discussions and stories heard, informal conversations, in situ observations, and photographs.

2 Taking Up Household-Farm Production: Kolia and Natalia's Pathways

2.1 Retreat into the Household

When I first met Kolia in May 2013, he was 55 years old. He and his 60-year-old wife Natalia lived in a house on the edge of the village of Letunovo (844 inhabitants). Kolia worked, mainly in winter and mostly in intermittent, low-skilled, and low-wage jobs. Kolia and Natalia coped with the situation by working almost every day on their household-farm production. In 2014, they had 12 goats, 5 ewes that birthed 6 lambs, and a large number of chickens. Behind their house, the plot of land on which they grew their vegetables was divided into two. In the first part, they grew potatoes, cabbages, beets, and onions. In the second, they had set up a greenhouse where they grew tomatoes, cucumbers, peppers, and herbs. All the goods produced were for consumption, even marginally in the case of the mutton. Kolia and Natalia sold mutton, goat's milk, tomatoes, cucumbers, potatoes, cabbages, and onions.

Although they are Russian, they were both born in Uzbekistan. Their parents had emigrated to Uzbekistan after the Second World War. They wanted to "*postroit' kommunizm*" (build communism), to use Natalia's words. Kolia started working at the age of 15, first as a cotton picker while he was training to be a welder. Following his military service, he worked as a mechanic specialized in welding (*cvarchtchik*) on the collective farms in his home village. He held that job for nearly 20 years. Natalia went to university. On graduation, she started working in the Soviet administration. She was in charge of Komsomol organization[5] through to the early 1990s. As with many, the story of Kolia and Natalia's social slide began with the collapse of the USSR in 1991. Natalia was first in line. She soon lost her job and was out of work. Kolia kept his job as a welder until 1996, when the *sovkhoz* closed. A year later, in late 1997, they had to move away. They sold their house along with Kolia's father's apartment and they—Kolia, his father, Natalia, and their two children—moved to Letunovo in Russia. After losing her job in the Soviet Administration, Natalia never found employment again. She was the first of the couple to withdraw from the labor market and "work at home" as she put it, that is, take charge of household-farm production.

Kolia and Natalia's story is typical of many pathways whereby engagement in household-farm production is driven mainly by a crisis caused by the collapse of the Soviet economy and the breakup of the USSR. Since 1991, "shock therapy" reforms in an environment of market transition have profoundly disrupted the agricultural sector (see Fig. 6.1). The crisis has brought agricultural production crashing down, collective farm bankruptcies (*sovkhoz* and *kolkhoz*), and a sharp increase in the number of unemployed. The effects of the agricultural sector breakdown have been aggravated by soaring inflation, which has drastically cut back living standards, and by a deep crisis in social services.

The crisis in the Soviet agricultural sector and Soviet society as a whole has prompted a sudden, sharp, and massive retreat into the household by *kolkhoz* and *sovkhoz* workers. Engagement in household-farm production on individual plots appears to be a response to everyday upheavals and problems. As F. Pine notes, "In one sense what appears to have happened

Fig. 6.1 *Коровник—korovnik*—dairy cow barns, 24 April 2014, *Совкоз Родина* (*Sovkhoz Rodina*), Letunovo, Russia (photo: Glenn Mainguy)

in rural areas, very crudely, has been a retreat into subsistence production" (Pine 2002: 98). In the initial years following the breakup of the USSR, people perceived this retreat into the household as an economic, social, and identity tragedy. Job losses exposed individuals to uncertainty and extreme poverty. Along with their work, individuals lost a network of social interaction, a space of autonomy within which they could thrive, and a raft of social protection. Retreat into the household was also seen as an identity tragedy, since individuals perceived it as a return to a past identity as an ordinary peasant, a *moujik*.

2.2 Withdrawal from the Labor Market

Kolia's professional trajectory in the post-Soviet economy is much more complex. Unlike Natalia, Kolia carried on working even after losing the job he had held for 20 years. He did not take up household production following the collapse of the USSR or the first hiatus in his professional career. When he told his story, he described three singular experiences.

Following their arrival in Letunovo, Kolia found a position as a welder in a construction company in Moscow. Despite a good pay package, he was forced to resign from his job after three years with the company because of the working hours (15 days of work in Moscow and 15 days of rest at home) and his family's precarious living conditions. Kolia's professional career then continued on a local farm in Letunovo. He was hired as a farm worker. The low wages and the intermittent nature of their payment forced him to quit once again. He was unable to support his family. After that, he was hired as a manual worker by a plastic products manufacturing company in Zaraysk. This time, he left to escape the terrible working conditions at the factory. He described the furious work pace and inhuman environment, which prevented him from accomplishing his set tasks.

Kolia did not stop working altogether after that. When I met him in May 2013, he still worked intermittent low-skilled jobs, usually in winter, as a manual worker, warehouseman, or the like. Nevertheless, the experience was a turning point for him. Working up until that point had been not only his main activity, but also a goal and a desire. Yet now, his professional activity had dropped in status and taken a back seat as a sort of supplement. Having a job no longer seemed central to structuring Kolia's daily life: "*After that, I decided to stay at home and work here.*"

Engagement in household-farm production is not only the consequence of a sudden retreat into the household, but it is also, as we have seen with the case of Kolia, the result of gradual withdrawal from the labor market. Rural people have experienced severe downward social mobility from their status as socially integrated workers in skilled employment. They have become poor workers, often in intermittent, low-paid and low-skilled jobs. These vulnerable individuals' perceptions of the world of work have been altered. The world of work has changed from a valued social sphere underpinning a strong, central, professional identity and structuring individuals' daily lives into a neglected, depreciated social universe in which personal investment has become severely limited. To cope with the crisis in the world of work, people take up household-farm production. The following section describes how this household economy works.

3 Household-Farm Production

3.1 A Collective, Daily Activity

I first met Sacha and Marina's family on a cold February day. I took the bus from the town of Kolomna to the village of Astapovo with its 155 inhabitants. After over an hour-long trip, the No. 31 bus stopped along the road to Zaraysk. I, and one other man, got off the bus. The sun was high in the sky at the start of the afternoon. I had to walk more than 30 minutes to get to the village. It was only about a kilometer from the bus stop, but the snowy road made it quite hard to make headway. Sacha and Marina's house was at the end of the village, at a dead end. I passed no one on my way to the house. The doors were closed. Smoke rose from the chimney, and the windows were fogged up and icy. Some people had put newspaper or aluminum foil between the window frames and the glass to protect their house from cold draughts. The temperature that day was −20°C. When I finally reached Sacha's house, he was about to go out. He was dressed in warm clothing, ready to go and feed his sheep hay. His wife was on her way to the house with a large milk pail.

Sacha was 47 years old, and Marina was 32. They spent most of their time working on the household's farm production to keep their family. Sacha and Marina's household was run collectively by themselves and their five eldest children: Ivan, 13, Sania, 12, Ludmilla, 10, Vera, 9, and Stas, 7. On my last visit in July 2014, their household-farm production was divided between animal husbandry and market gardening. They owned 100 ewes that had birthed some 60 lambs (see Fig. 6.2), 2 cows, and a multitude of chickens that provided them with meat, eggs, and milk. They had a meadow to feed the animals. Every year in June and July, they made hay.

They also had a large garden (see Fig. 6.3), half of which was reserved for growing potatoes. The other half was divided more or less equally between carrots, onions, cucumbers, cabbages, and a few tomato plants. Although all the different types of produce were for the family's consumption, Sacha and Marina also sold some. There was no sign or advertisement informing people of the existence of a sales outlet. Sacha and

Fig. 6.2 Part of Sacha and Marina's sheep, 26 April 2014, Astapovo, Russia (photo: Glenn Mainguy)

Fig. 6.3 Sacha and Marina's vegetable plot behind their house, 19 July 2014, Astapovo, Russia (photo: Glenn Mainguy)

Marina sold mainly mutton along with some potatoes, onions, eggs, and milk.

As can be seen from the case of Sacha and Marina, household-farm production is handled collectively by the family members. In Sacha and Marina's family, household-farm production has seven people working as a cooperative. In Kolia and Natalia's case, two people work as a cooperative. However, although all the household members take part in the agricultural activities, not all participate in the same way. My field observations revealed a gendered division of labor. On one side, men are in charge of all activities that require mechanical tools (lawn mowers, chainsaws, tillers, etc.) and in command of agricultural machinery (tractors, in particular): "Men work with tractors and machines" (Pine 1993: 238). These activities include animal shearing, hay harvesting and transportation, and plowing the plot to prepare the soil for growing vegetables. Men are also responsible for the construction and maintenance of the facilities required for household agricultural production. On the other side, there is a set of tasks carried out mainly by women. Women rear cattle, put them out to pasture, and milk them. They also grow vegetables. They plant, harvest, weed, and water the vegetable plot every day. And the women process the harvested fruits and vegetables, usually canning the produce. This gendered division of labor can also be seen when it comes to marketing the produce. Retail sales—especially of vegetables, milk, and dairy produce—appear to be handled entirely by women. Men seem more involved in the meat trade side of the farm. They are responsible for negotiating animal prices in particular, but they are also in charge of slaughtering and butchering (Boxes 2 and 3). In all cases observed, market transactions were always concluded by women, and it was the women who received the cash payments.

3.2 Taking Up Commodity Production: Targeting Profitable Produce

When I met Sacha and Marina, neither of them was in stable employment. Marina was a *domokhoziaynka* (housewife) and had never been employed. Like Kolia, Sacha's professional career was marked by downward social mobility. Part of Sacha's right foot had been amputated following a domestic accident when he was 14 years old. Since then, he had worn an orthopedic prosthesis and walked with a limp. Despite his handicap, he studied at Zaraysk Agricultural High School and was hired as a driver at Astapovo's *sovkhoz* in the late 1980s. He worked there for about ten years. In 1997, he was dismissed when the state farm was restructured into a *zakrytoe aktsionernoe obchtchectvo* (closed joint-stock company). He acquired a tractor and some farmland, and set up as a farmer. Three years later, he had to wind up the farm as it was no longer viable and was a victim of the economic crisis that had hit the Russian economy in 1998. With his farm bankrupt, Sacha took up household-farm production: "*I stopped being a farmer. I kept just a few horses, a dozen sheep and a few chickens for us to keep the family going and sell a little. I gave the rest away.*" After that, Sacha's employment path took a turn into casual labor. He never got a stable job again and he worked intermittently, mostly in low-skilled and low-wage jobs. For example, he worked as a night security guard on a building site in Kolomna for one month from March to April 2014.

Sacha and Marina started selling their domestic produce when Sacha gave up the farm, but sales were initially slow. Sacha and Marina's family have only been "*earning money from it*" since 2008. The increase in sales of their domestic production has led them to specialize in and scale up their sheep farming. Their flock has grown tenfold, from a dozen in 2000 to just over a 100 at the time of the survey in 2014. They now sell some 40 sheep every year. Based on the data collected by the fieldwork, their sales of mutton generate an estimated 15,000 rubles (375 euros) per month—minus costs—for Sacha and Marina's family.

3.3 The Economic and Domestic Profitability of Sheep Farming

What prompted Sacha and Marina's and Kolia and Natalia's family to specialize in sheep farming? Why did they choose to raise sheep? The answers to these questions can be found from the examination of the logics governing these choices.

6 Domesticity as Value: The Commodification of Foodstuffs…

Sacha initially explained in our interviews that they raised ewes mainly as a means of subsistence, to feed the family:

> *I get a state pension of 7,000 rubles [175 euros]. What can I do? How can I do anything? I've got seven people, six children. They [welfare] give me 6,000 rubles [150 euros] in child benefit every month. Fortunately, we have our own meat. I raise ewes already! There are eight of us, and if I didn't have the ewes, we'd starve! You'd die! They'd be nothing you could do about it, nothing at all!* (Sacha, 47 years old)

Sacha's reasoning here corresponds at first glance to the development of a subsistence logic. As outlined by A. Chayanov (1966 [1925]), this logic holds that production choices are induced by household food needs and that the level of production is defined by the group's physiological needs. Nevertheless, the choice of ewes is not just indicative of the application of a subsistence logic. Sacha also explains his engagement in ewe farming in terms of its economic profitability. He explains his preference for sheep farming by comparing it to cattle farming. In his own cost-benefit analysis, he shows that it is more advantageous to raise ewes than cows:

> *Cattle rearing is not profitable. It involves more work every day. For example, you have to milk the animals every day. Production costs are also higher. And you need more resources and equipment to store and sell dairy produce.* (Field note, Sacha and Marina's house, Astapovo, May 18, 2014)

Sacha's cattle comparison highlights the fact that products are never strictly substitutable. As F. Vatin points out by taking the example of milk, the economic logic applied to each product always has to consider the materiality of that product (Vatin 1996). Furthermore, whereas the question of the market profitability of farm production is present in the choice of the type of livestock, the question of economic profitability can also be observed in the way farm production is managed. Coming back to the story of his livestock expansion, Sacha explained that he started to specialize in rearing ewes six years before not only to feed his family but also to "*earn money*":

I've been doing this for six years. I've been raising ewes for six years. I didn't earn any money from it for one and half years. For one and half years, I waited. I waited for my business to develop. And, I've been earning some money from my ewes for nearly five years now. I started to make money from rearing ewes five years ago. (Sacha, 47 years old)

Sacha's narrative with respect to his specialization in sheep farming shows that his reasoning is associated not only with subsistence, to feed the family, but also with economic profitability, to earn money. Specialization in sheep farming appears to offer the most effective combination of economic profitability in the market sphere (lower production costs) and "food" profitability in the domestic sphere, that is, meeting the food needs of a family in a precarious situation.

In Kolia and Natalia's case, their engagement in the commodification of household agricultural produce led them to gradually diversify and scale up their production. They invested in a greenhouse and a cultivator, increasing the surface area of their garden and upgrading from manual to mechanical digging. This enabled them to move into tomatoes and peppers. They also started farming sheep and goats. In 2014, the last time I saw them, they had 12 goats and 5 ewes that had birthed 6 lambs. A probe into why the couple chose to raise sheep reveals slightly different reasoning to that of Sacha and Marina.

Kolia and Natalia explain their choice to raise sheep based on three considerations. The first is their very low consumption of mutton; the second is the high price of this type of meat on the conventional market; and the third is their low income:

Me: "Can *I buy some mutton from you?*"
   Kolia: "*No, we don't have any yet. We will slaughter the animals in the fall and then sell the meat. For the time being, we're not selling meat. We only have lambs. We'll slaughter them later in the fall. We won't keep the meat for ourselves. We'll* sell *it.*"
   Me: "*You'll sell it?*"
   Kolia: "*Yes, because mutton is very expensive for us.*"
   Me: "*What do you mean?*"
   Kolia: "*We don't have enough money to buy this kind of meat. So we sell it. We kill chickens for ourselves, but not sheep. They're too expensive for us.*"

Natalia: "*It's not profitable! It's not profitable. If we have to, we slaughter sheep for ourselves. But we don't eat a lot of mutton. We're too old already. This kind of meat is not very good for our heath. We rarely eat it.*" (Kolia, 55 years old; Natalia, 60 years old)

Kolia and Natalia's reasoning shows that their choice of sheep breeding is based not so much on feeding the family, as they eat very little mutton, but on economic and commercial considerations, that is, the high profitability of mutton in the market sector.

3.4 Home-Based Foodstuff Commodification and Demographic Change in the Village

The development of farm produce commodification by people in precarious situations is also the result of an internal metamorphosis in rural society, which has significantly reduced access to food shops in villages. The collapse of the Soviet Union and the great transformation of the agricultural sector saw not only the closure of the collective farms—*sovkhoz* and *kolkhoz*—but also the demise of a food distribution system—*produokty*, *kolkhoz* markets, and state shops (Ioffe et al. 2006). In the villages, many shops directly dependent on the collective farms have closed. This phenomenon is exacerbated by the rural exodus with its impact on suburban and rural areas. "*No one lives here anymore, so why have a store?*" Between 2002 and 2010, the population of Astapovo—where Sacha and Marina's family live—fell by 14%. In Shkin'—another village central to my fieldwork—the population shrank by 27%. In 2010, there were 75 inhabitants in Shkin' and 155 in Astapovo. When I first arrived in the villages, I used to ask people I met whether there was a shop. The answer was often the same: "*No, not anymore, my son! You have to go over there. Take a bus and go to the next village*" (Informal discussion with a babushka, February 2013, Tumenskoe).

During my fieldwork, I went to more than 30 villages. In more than 60% of them, shops had closed over the last 20 years. Even where *produokty* have not closed, only basic foodstuffs are sold, usually cereals, pasta, rice, drinks, cakes, bread, cigarettes, alcohol, ice-cream, and household cleaning products.

With most shops in rural areas closed, access to stores outside the villages—in larger urban areas—is constrained by restricted mobility. It is often hard for rural people to get to a market. The majority of individuals I met during my fieldwork had no means of transport. Some families—like that of Sacha and Marina—owned a tractor. Others—like that of Kolia and Natalia—had built their own means of transport from a cultivator with a trailer attached. But people rarely own a car. In some villages, buses run only in summer. They cannot run in winter because the roads are not cleared of snow. In other cases, buses simply stop on the main road, and people have to walk miles to reach the village. Figure 6.4 illustrates this situation. It shows a babushka I met on the road to the village of Tumenskoe in February 2013. She was on her way to a bus stop two kilometers from her village. From there, she was going to the nearby village of Biorki to do her shopping.

As shown above, the internal metaphors of rural Russian society and village demographics have led to the creation of a new type of customer: a default clientele. These are people who are forced by the closure of

Fig. 6.4 Babushka walking to a bus stop from the village of Tumenskoe to go shopping, because the village shop has closed down, February 2013, Tumenskoe, Russia (photo: Glenn Mainguy)

produkty and the difficulties of moving to obtain supplies and foodstuffs in the villages.

4 Marketization: Household Origin as a Source of Value

4.1 Singularization Efforts

While access to shops, supermarkets, and markets, that is, conventional outlets, is hard or restricted, buying foodstuffs in a village is no easy task either. Customers need to know of the existence and location of outlets. Yet, they are not easily identifiable. Signs and boards advertising sales outlets are scarce. Sacha and Marina have no board to inform people that they sell foodstuffs. Kolia and Natalia have just a wooden sign bearing the words Молоко Козье (*Moloko Koz'e*: goat's milk) (see Fig. 6.5). In both cases, customers often have to call and make an appointment to buy goods. There are no given opening hours and no shopkeeper. Neither

Fig. 6.5 Kolia and Natalia's house and wooden sign *"Молоко Козье,"* 24 April 2014, Letunovo, Russia (photo: Glenn Mainguy)

does the producer's presence guarantee that they will serve a customer if they are too busy or tied up with other business.

This lack of information is not restricted to the location of the sales outlets. It also concerns the quality of the foodstuffs. Unlike goods sold in the conventional sector, there is no authority on hand to check, certify, and guarantee the quality of produce sold from the home. Consequently, uncertainty surrounds the quality of household-farm-produced foodstuffs that are sold from homes by people in precarious situations. This configuration creates a situation of asymmetric information, as in the case of the "market for lemons" analyzed by G. Akerlof (1970). How do households manage to sell their foodstuffs in these circumstances? How do they guarantee the quality of their produce? How do they price their produce?

These questions call for a study of the food marketization process. I. Kopytoff states that "The production of commodities is a cultural and cognitive process: commodities must be not only produced materially as a thing, but also culturally marked as being a certain kind of thing" (Kopytoff 1986: 64). So the commodification process is, firstly, a branding operation. And the observable social processes used to brand these products as goods need to be described in order to explore how rural people in precarious situations marketize foodstuffs.

Rural people in precarious situations develop the singularization (Karpik 2010; Jourdain 2010) of their produce in order to sell their foodstuffs. They accordingly seek to differentiate their production from foodstuffs that can be bought at conventional outlets (shops and markets). This singularization effort is based on pushing the "quality" of their foodstuffs by making a distinction between two categories of agricultural produce: *domachnie prodoukty*—which means "homemade products"—and *pokoupnie prodoukty*—which literally means "bought products."

The distinction between *domachnie prodoukty* and *pokoupnie prodoukty* is based primarily on differentiation between foodstuffs defined as good, authentic, and pure—*domachnie prodoukty*—and foodstuffs portrayed as bad, impure, and unhealthy—*pokoupnie prodoukty*. Yet beyond these positive and negative tags, how do precarious households engaged in the commodification of their produce justify the authenticity and purity of their foodstuffs? As we will see, singularization efforts center on the promotion of two main characteristics to give the goods value: domestic origin and domestic modes of production.

4.2   Singularization Based on the Origin of the Foodstuffs

The branding of foodstuffs as *domachnie prodoukty* is grounded in a definition in terms of origin. It labels foodstuffs whose provenance is known … unequivocally. When interviewees spoke about the foodstuffs they sold, they would say, "*They are our products*" or "*They come from our home.*" Conversely, the term *pokoupnie prodoukty* labels goods whose origin is uncertain. They are described as products from abroad, particularly China:

> We do everything ourselves. Products [in the shops] are too expensive and they aren't good. They're all Chinese and they're no good. So we buy the minimum and do the rest ourselves. (Dima, 53 years old)

Whereas interviewees often mentioned that foreign products were bad, they made a strong connection between local production and good production. The two words—local and good—were treated as synonyms. An illustration of this parallel between "local" and "good" can be found in the respondents' answers to my question about the good quality of their produce. They would say, "*Of course, it's from here,*" as they pointed in the direction of their garden. What frames this link between good and local? In what way is domestic origin a guarantee of the value and quality of foodstuffs?

Firstly, there is the link between local and good, the nature of the produce, and, more specifically, its subsistence function (Caldwell 2011). As seen earlier, although engagement in a commercialization process may change the structure of production, it does not necessarily lead to the development of a specific output. While not all types of farm produce consumed are sold, all types of goods sold are consumed, even marginally as in the case of Kolia and Natalia. Indeed, interviewees seek to prove the quality of their goods by explaining that they themselves consume these products: "*We eat them!*" (Sacha). It could be said that the original connection between farm production and subsistence acts as a justification, an assurance given by the households of the better quality of the foodstuffs they sell.

Secondly, the *domachnie prodoukty* label not only helps identify the origin of the produce, but it more importantly identifies the individual who produced them:

> Me: "Where *do you buy food?*"
> Father Jean: "*Here, in the village… Honey, for example. Ioura's honey. Honey that Ioura produces.*"
> Katia: "*It's real* honey. *We only buy from him. He's the only person we believe in and the only person we trust.*"
> Father Jean: "*It's pure honey, nothing more, no additives. It's natural.*"
> Katia: "*And we buy honey from him alone! […] It's the same for milk. In the village, we have 'clean' milk,* 'tchistoe moloko' *[pure milk]. We buy from a man we know. We buy milk from a man who has his own cows… But if you buy it in the shop… Now then! Of course! It's powdered milk and they put products in it to make milk… No! We know what we're buying and the taste is completely different. We have* 'nastoiachtchoe moloko' *[real milk].*" (Father Jean, 39 years old; Katia, 29 years old)

As the above excerpt from the interview with Father Jean and his wife shows, *domachnie prodoukty* are "*better,*" purer, and more authentic, as they are produced in the village by someone who is known and trusted.

In addition, specifying the domestic origin of these goods also protects customers against fake products and possible changes to product quality by dubious production processes used by some unscrupulous traders. It has become a guarantee. Following our conversation, Father Jean told me a story about a honey trader and his honey production method:

> *The trader bought honey in cans. Then he got a mixer. Not a little one, but the kind you use on a building site to mix quickly. Then he made a sort of sugar syrup in a can. After that, he filled three other cans with sugar syrup and added a little bit of honey. Then he used his mixer to mix it again! And there you have honey!* (Father Jean, 39 years old)

Here, the term *domachnie* transcends pure location to extend to the social group and the network of friends and acquaintances in particular.

This notion of friends and acquaintances can be also found in Sacha's statement about the way he sells: "*Those who know me, they come here and buy meat or dairy produce.*" So in a situation of uncertainty over the quality of goods and in the absence of quality controls or a certification body, the social network plays an important role in regulating trade.

4.3   … And on the Mode of Production Used

Description of the origin of the produce is a defining element in the distinction between *domachnie prodoukty* and *pokoupnie prodoukty*. Consumers who know where a product was produced can identify how that product was produced. In their narratives, my interviewees associated each type of goods —*domachnie* or *pokoupnie*—with a particular production process and assessment of it:

> Ioura: "*We grow our own potatoes and vegetables ourselves. We know there's nothing added to our produce, no chemical products, none of* that."
> Me: "*You can't buy that sort of produce in the shops?*"
> Ioura: "*Shop-bought products contain a lot of nitrates.*"
> Irma: "*You need to really clean shop-bought produce a lot.*"
> Ioura: "*A lot, a lot.*" (Ioura, 60 years old; Irma, 53 years old)

Father Jean made similar remarks about potato production:

> *Potatoes! Why potatoes? Because we grow them simply, we don't add any products, fertilizers or pesticides. We pick them by hand. Whereas at the* sovkhoze, *they add products to the potatoes. That's why we don't buy potatoes from them. They always add a lot of chemical products to the potatoes. So we don't buy them* (Father Jean, 39 years old)

What Ioura, Irma, and Father Jean say shows that the justification for the quality of household-farm production is based on a comparison with and rejection of the food industry mode of production. In this case, the term *pokoupnie* refers to food industry goods. They are suspected of being poorly produced, that is, of having been heavily sprayed with chemicals. By contrast, the term *domachnie* refers to homegrown products, to foodstuffs that people produce themselves. People know everything about the production process. These goods are produced "*simply*," meaning by a production method that makes minimal use of mechanical means—"*we collect them by hand*"; "*everything is done by hand*"—and minimal use of chemicals.

Over and above the narratives, the importance of production methods to the definition of food quality can also be seen from the households' selling practices: visits to the vegetable plot, barns, or paddocks, participation in slaughtering (Box 2), description of the production process, origin of the hay, and so forth. Visits to the production sites are also marked by a permanent reminder that the traders alone are the producers. Their farming descriptions stress the fact that these activities are performed by them alone—"*We plant ourselves*" or "*We work on our own*"— and that no tasks are delegated—"*Everything comes from us. We do everything ourselves*" (Ioura). These practices exhibit the modes and sites of production to the customers. They are displayed and become visible. They could be interpreted as advertising materials in the construction of the singularity of homegrown goods.

Observation of a mutton sale at Sacha and Marina's home (28 February 2013)

The slaughter
   When I first met Sacha, I asked him if I could buy some meat from his farm. When people need meat, they have to place an order. Usually, the orders are taken directly in the barn or by phone. Sacha suggested I come back at the end of the month when he had scheduled to slaughter some sheep. So, on 28 February, I again took bus 31. I arrived at Astapovo bus stop at 5 p.m. That time, I was the only one to get off the bus. It was very cold outside. The temperature was −28°C, and the icy, biting wind meant I felt even colder. Sacha was in the backyard with his son Ivan. His blue Belarus tractor, which dated back to the USSR era, had broken down. After Sacha had explained that he had problems with the tractor, Sacha, his, son and I went to the barn to slaughter the sheep. There is no lighting in the barn. We had to hurry: everything had to be done before nightfall. When we got to the barn, Sacha asked his son to go and catch the sheep he had marked the previous day, "*The one with the bleeding ear, the one that had cut its ear.*" As his second son wasn't there, he asked me to go and help Ivan. Catching the sheep wasn't very easy, but we finally managed and brought the animal to Sacha. Meanwhile, he was sharpening a long knife with a thick metal disc. Before

cutting the sheep's throat, Sacha crossed himself asking for God's blessing. Twenty minutes later, after skinning the front legs, we hung the animal from a piece of wood by its hooves. Sacha started to cut up the sheep. When the animal had been cut up, it had to be emptied. Sacha cut the stomach out of the sheep, removed the intestines, and took the offal and threw it on the roof. I asked Sacha why he did this, and he answered that it was an old tradition. His grandmother had taught him to do it, because it is supposed to bring peace and happiness. Finally, Sacha crossed himself once more and thanked God for having given him the sheep.

The sale

After crossing himself, Sacha asked us to bring the sheep's carcass into the vestibule and place it on a wooden table covered with a plastic film. Everything was there in Sacha and Marina's vestibule: everything that could withstand the cold and did not have its place in the house, like winter coats, winter shoes, and tools. While Ivan and I were placing the carcass on the table, Sacha called Marina. He asked me how much meat I needed. I didn't know how much or which cuts I could have. I asked his advice. He advised me to take the shoulder and some ribs. He cut the carcass again and weighed the pieces of meat on a steelyard. All the pieces were weighed at the same time. He didn't differentiate between the different cuts of meat; each piece was the same price. There were four kilos. The price of the meat was 250 rubles a kilo, so I gave Marina a thousand rubles. Then Marina wrapped the meat in plastic film, put it in a bag, and gave it to me. Whereas Sacha had started the transaction, Marina concluded it by giving me a bag containing four kilos of mutton in exchange for the sum of 1000 rubles in notes. The transaction was now complete.

The entire food marketization process uses the precarious means of production (Box 2)—modest technical means and manual work—as a guarantee of the quality of the produce. Here, we observe an inversion of values. In the productive sphere, precarious production means are negatively perceived by households as they limit production and make agricultural work harder:

But when everything has to be done by hand, of course it's impossible! But we do everything by hand. No, no, there's a tractor, but it's too old. It's terrible! (Sacha, 47 years old)

In the market sphere, however, precarious means of production become an advantage because they add to the value of the produce by guaranteeing respect for "natural" production methods.

5 The Non-Economic Determinants of Marketization

5.1 Restoring the Legitimacy of Unemployed Men

Engagement in a commodification process is not just about selling products. For individuals seeking social recognition, it is about becoming integrated into a world of rewarding practices. This last section focuses on the situation of vulnerable men and the non-economic determinants of their engagement. The decision to concentrate on men is the result of the constraints of the ethnographic work, in that it was easier to talk to the men and observe their practices.[6] Yet restricted access to the female world is not the only reason for centering this part of the study on the condition of men in precarious situations. Post-Soviet economic trajectories, marked by social downgrading and a retreat into the domestic sphere, have had particularly tragic repercussions for men (Kiblitskaya 2000; Ashwin 2000). The particular intensity of this phenomenon for men is due to the historical definition of male and female social roles and the place assigned to each person in the domestic sphere. "The dual-earner family in which the man is the chief breadwinner and the woman takes primary responsibility for household management remains the norm in Russia" (Ashwin and Lytkina 2004: 193). Therefore, since a man's status and legitimacy are based mainly on his professional position, withdrawal into the household sphere makes it impossible for men to maintain their position in the social world and perform their role. We will now see how engagement in commodification practices enables men to recover a place in the domestic sphere and gain access to certain forms of social re-legitimation.

5.2 Commodification: A Space to Reward Individual Skills and Enable Men to Resume a Legitimate Place in the Domestic Sphere

For men engaged in the commercialization of foodstuffs, the domestic division of market labor is not restricted to mechanizing activities directly associated with the production process. Firstly, selling from home gives them a set of market relations tasks to accomplish (Box 3). For example, in livestock marketing, it is the men who are in charge of market relations. Contact with buyers is made through them, and they take charge of the negotiations. Negotiations concern both the choice of animal and its selling price.

---

12 July 2014—Division of market labor and negotiation of sheep prices. A sales scene in Sacha and Marina household

While Ivan, Vassia, and I were removing a hay bale from the trailer, a car driving along the dirt road leading to Sacha's house stopped, not far from us. Two Caucasian men—in the ethnic, not the morphological sense—got out and came up to us. One of them asked, "*Who is the* khoziain *here?*" As I was the oldest person in the group, he naturally turned to me and said, "*Is that you?*" I didn't have time to answer, as Ivan responded in my place, "*No, it's not him, it's my father. He's in the field. What do you want? He's busy right now, can you come back later?*" The two men wanted to buy a sheep and had heard from one of their relatives that there was someone here who was selling sheep. After a brief discussion between these two men and Ivan, they decided to come back later to see the *khoziain*, that is, Sacha.

When they returned, Sacha was there to receive them. The two Caucasian men wanted to buy a live animal. Sacha was in charge of the first stages of commercialization. He negotiated the chosen animal and its selling price. In the sale of a live animal, the selling price is set by the price per kilo. At the time of my investigation, this was 175 rubles (4.40 euros). Note, however, that the price per kilo corresponds to the price of the meat. When people buy a live animal, its weight includes both meat and the inedible parts: bones, offal, skin, and so forth. So the final price will be the sum of the weight of the animal minus the weight of the non-edible parts. Therefore, the negotiation between Sacha and the two buyers focused on the weight of these non-edible parts. On that day, once the animal had been chosen, its weight was determined using a scale. It weighed 40 kilos. A first price was established at 7000 rubles (175 euros). Following negotiations on the weight of the inedible parts, the price fell to 5000 rubles (125 euros).

Once the choice of animal and the price had been fixed, the work changed hands. The other tasks were carried out by Marina. She finalized the sale by taking charge of catching the animal, delivering it, and receiving payment. Later, in her account of the marketing scene, Marina told me: "*They [the two Caucasian buyers] thought that as the* khoziain *[Sacha] had left and as I was a woman, they could renegotiate the price. But I said 'No', because the price had already been decided and they'd already got significant reduction.*"

Secondly, a commercial activity in rural Russia entails far more than just the tasks associated with the sale of goods. It also involves dealings with administrative and law enforcement officials. Here again, Sacha's example is very enlightening. The land on which he grazed his animals was the former property of the *kolkhoz*. The land now belonged to what he called "*administratsia*" (the administration). He had to go "*to the* sovkhoz" regularly to renegotiate the right to keep using the land with members of the administration. During my last field visit, between February and July 2014, important negotiations were held regarding the future of this farmland. The administration wanted to use the land to build a rural tourism center. Sacha opposed this project for a number of reasons, and the issue of land tenure was at the crux of the debate.

In addition to negotiations on land use rights, other less formal discussions are called for with law enforcement officials to be able to pursue the agricultural goods marketing activities. The case of Pacha, a home-based watermelon trader in the Volgograd region, illustrates this situation well. Pacha regularly had to renegotiate the right to sell his agricultural production. Negotiations concerned small, regular, daily arrangements between Pacha and the authorities: the right—or possibility—to sell at a discount or give "*gifts*" of produce. In Sacha's case, negotiations to conduct sales activities also related to the payment of *vziatki* (bribes). These were paid mainly from the household's farm production. Yet, sometimes, the negotiations involved the "obligation" to spend the afternoon drinking with a police officer who had a *vykhodnoï* (day off) and came to have a look at the farm.

Male investment in marketing activities enables men in precarious situations to combat their marginalization within the domestic space. Their management of a range of responsible tasks gives them a significant place in the domestic division of market labor. They are no longer mere farm workers, but also traders, negotiators, and go-betweens with officials.

5.3 The Title of *Khoziain*: The Social Recognition of Male Traders in Precarious Situations

The validation and social legitimacy of the position occupied by men who market their produce from home is confirmed by the term used to define them: the *khoziain*. This term was used by the two Caucasians who came to buy a sheep: "*Kto khoziain zdes'?*" ("Who is the *khoziain* here?"). The word is also present in Marina's account ("*They [the two Caucasian buyers] thought that as the* khoziain *[Sacha] had left and as I was a woman, they could renegotiate the price*") (Box 3). Analysis of recurrences of the term *khoziain*—heard during interviews and observations—shows that it is used mainly to refer to certain men in a social situation relating to farm activities, either in discussions or conversations about the management of agricultural production: "*On [Sacha] khoziain doma, on znaet, On sam reshaet!*" ("He's the *khoziain* here"). He knows and he decides alone: "*Ia [Sacha] zdes' khoziain, Ia reshaiu*" ("I'm the *khoziain* here, I decide"). A similar use of this term can be noted in the words pronounced by Pasha, the godfather of one of Sacha's children, who had come to help bring in the hay bales. Faced with the orders given by Sacha, which he did not always consider fair, Pasha confessed his powerlessness by telling me: "*He [Sacha] is the* khoziain *here, so we can't say anything or do anything.*" Moreover, the term *khoziain* is never used to refer to other people in the household (women or children). And there can be only one *khoziain*. The term is never or very rarely used in other social settings. Indeed, when the family was no longer at work, when the children had become children again and behaved badly or did not listen to their mother, Marina said: "*Otets boudet rougat'sia*я" ("Your father will get angry"). Here, Sacha is referred to in his role as a father (*Otets*). When the relatives ate together to celebrate the return of Sacha's sister to the village for the holidays, Sacha was once again, for a photo with Marina, the husband (*mouj*).

Thus, the word *khoziain* is mainly related to the lexical field of the household economy. It refers to a place occupied by men in this social sphere and, more particularly, to a hierarchical position, that is, a leader or a manager. As shown by an analysis of the previously transcribed language elements, the *khoziain* is the person who knows (*znat'*), the person who decides (*reshit'*), and the person who directs, in the sense of managing or leading (*dirjit'*). From these three functions is derived a fourth as the person who exercises "absolute" power over the other members of the family. "*He [Sacha] is the* khoziain *here, so when he makes a decision we shouldn't protest*," Marina told me. As M. Paxon (2005) writes: "The *khoziain* of a household has special decision-making powers. […]. Ideally, he is in charge […] of running the household. Any failings are on his shoulders as well. The *khoziain* of a house is the symbol of leadership" (Paxon 2005: 74).

Thus, the development of home commodification has opened up a social space in which men can develop a set of individual skills and be socially recognized as someone: a *khoziain*. Everything points to a process of commodification leading to the "normalization" of relations within the domestic sphere and enabling men to resume their "legitimate" place in the domestic sphere, that is, the role of breadwinner.

6 Conclusion

The analysis of home-based foodstuff commercialization by people in precarious situations living in rural Russia describes (i) the pathway that led them to take up marketing farm produce, (ii) the work done by households to market their own production, and (iii) the social and symbolic reasons for this engagement.

In addition to exploring the home-based commercialization of agricultural produce by households in precarious situations in rural Russia, this analysis looks into how the norms and values of "the domestic city" overlap with those of the "merchant city" (Boltanski and Thévenot 2006) in the process of the commodification of domestic activities. In keeping with Viviana Zelizer (1994) and contrary to the argument of a "great divide" between the two types of economy based on incompatible rules, this analysis demonstrates, first, that the process of the commodification of domestic activities contributes to the creation of a new market space within which the value of the goods derives from their inclusion in the domestic sphere. Second, this chapter takes the example of men to show how people in precarious situations, by means of their engagement in a marketized activity, can embark upon a pathway leading out of precarity and to emancipation. Thus, in analyses of precarity, the market can be reexamined (Fontaine 2014) by shifting the focus from its negative effects to thinking of it as a possible space within which precarity-exit strategies can be deployed.

Appendix

Table 6.1 The interviewees mentioned in the chapter

Household/Place of residence	Name	Age	Professional occupation	Main product sold	Fixed monthly income
	Pacha	38	Unemployed	Watermelon	n/a
Kolia and Natalia's household Letunovo (844 inhabitants)	Kolia	55	Intermittent low-skilled jobs (manual worker, warehouseman, etc.)	Mutton, goat's milk, vegetable	6000 rubles (old-age pension)
	Natalia	60	Retired		
Sacha and Marina's household Astopovo (155 inhabitants)	Sacha	47	Intermittent low-skilled jobs (security guard, etc.)	Mutton, vegetable	13,000 rubles (325 euros)—welfare.
	Marina	32	Unemployed		
Father Jean and Katia's household Shkin' (75 inhabitants)	Father Jean	39	Pastor	Vegetable	n/a
	Katia	29	Unemployed		
Dima and Macha's household Tcherebaïevo (486 inhabitants)	Dima	53	Tractor driver	Vegetable, pork	19,000 rubles (475 euros)—wage.
	Macha	48	Trader		
Ioura and Irma's household Shkin' (75 inhabitants)	Ioura	60	Retired ex-army/security guard (part-time)	Honey/Vegetable	15,000 rubles (375 euros)—old-age pension + wage.
	Irma	53	Unemployed		

Notes

1. This work is supported by the Conseil Régional d'Aquitaine, the Centre d'études franco-russe de Moscou (UMR MEAE CNRS USR 3060), and the Moscow Region State Institute of Humanities and Social Studies in Kolomna.

2. Note that this form of agricultural production did not appear in Russia until after the collapse of the USSR. The *khoziaistva nacelenia* are the successors to the individual plots of land—also referred to as personal subsidiary plots—access to which was granted to *kolkhoz* and *sovkhoz* workers by Joseph Stalin in 1935. This right was then extended to the entire Soviet population, as with the development of the *dacha*.
3. The definition of these farms as non-entrepreneurial activities differentiates them from another type of farm in the official nomenclature, peasant (farm) enterprises (individual entrepreneurs)—(*fermerskie khoziaistva*). This status was created by the 1991 agrarian reforms, whose purpose was to create a new category of farmer. In 2014, some 10% of Russia's national agricultural production was produced by these farms (*Federal'naia sloujba gosoudapstvehhoy statistiki, prodouktsia sel'skogo khoziaistva po kategoriiam khoziaistv po Rossiïskoy Federatsii 1990–2014*).
4. *Federal'naia sloujba gosoudapstvehhoy statistiki, prodouktsia sel'skogo khoziaistva po kategoriiam khoziaistv po Rossiïskoy Federatsii 1990–2014*.
5. During my investigation, it was often hard to gather information on women's social origins and pathways. In many situations, the information was given by the husband. In Natalia's case, she was also reluctant to talk about her personal life and her professional occupation in Soviet times.
6. During the fieldwork, access to the female domestic universe was restricted. So, very little material was gathered on this dimension, making it hard to construct a sociology of women's involvement in the commodification of agricultural goods.

References

Akerlof, G. (1970). The Market for 'Lemons': Qualitative Uncertainty and the Market Mechanism. *Quarterly Journal of Economic, 84*(3), 488–500.

Alacovska, A. (2018). Hope Labour Revisited: Post-socialist Creative Workers and Their Methods of Hope. In S. Taylor & S. Luckman (Eds.), *The New Normal of Working Lives. Critical Studies in Contemporary Work and Employment* (pp. 41–63). Cham: Springer International Publishing.

Ashwin, S. (2000). *Gender, State and Society in Soviet and Post-Soviet Russia*. London: Routledge.

Ashwin, S., & Lytkina, T. (2004). Men in Crisis in Russia: The Role of Domestic Marginalization. *Gender and Society, 18*(2), 189–206.

Boltanski, L., & Thévenot, L. (2006). *On Justification: Economies of Worth*. Princeton: Princeton University Press.

Bridger, S., & Pine, F. (1998). *Surviving Post-Socialism. Local Strategies and Regional Responses in Eastern Europe and the Former Soviet Union*. London: Routledge.

Burawoy, M., & Verdery, K. (1999). *Uncertain Transition. Ethnographies of Change in the Postsocialist World*. Lanham: Rowman & Littlefield.

Caldwell, M. L. (2011). *Dacha Idylls. Living Organically in Russia's Countryside*. Berkeley and Los Angeles: University of California Press.

Chayanov, A. (1966 [1925]). *The Theory of Peasant Economy*. Homewood, IL: Richard D. Irwin.

Fontaine, L. (2014). *Le Marché. Histoire et usages d'une conquête sociale*. Paris: Gallimard.

Gambold Miller, L., & Heady, P. (2003). Cooperation, Power, and Community. Economy and Ideology in the Russian Countryside. In C. Hann and the 'Property Relations' Group (Ed.), *The Postsocialist Agrarian Question. Property Relations and the Rural Condition* (pp. 257–292). Münster: LIT.

Hervé, J. J. (2007). *L'Agriculture Russe. Du kolkhoze à l'hypermarché*. Paris: L'Harmattan.

Humphrey, C., & Mandel, R. (2002). *Markets & Moralities. Ethnographies of Postsocialism*. New York: Berg.

Ioffe, G., Nefedova, T., & Zaslavsky, I. (2006). *The End of Peasantry? The Disintegration of Rural Russia*. Pittsburgh: University of Pittsburgh Press.

Jourdain, A. (2010). La construction sociale de la singularité. Une stratégie entrepreneuriale des artisans d'art. *Revue Française de Socio-Economie, 2*(6), 13–30.

Karpik, L. (2010). *Valuing the Unique: The Economics of Singularities*. Princeton: Princeton University Press.

Kiblitskaya, M. (2000). 'Once we were Kings': Male Experiences of Loss of Status at Work in Post-Communist Russia. In S. Ashwin (Ed.), *Gender, State and Society in Soviet and Post-Soviet Russia* (pp. 56–67). London: Routledge.

Kopytoff, I. (1986). The Cultural Biography of Things: Commoditization as Process. In A. Arjun (Ed.), *The Social Life of Things: Commodities in Cultural Perspective* (pp. 64–94). Cambridge: Cambridge University Press.

Mainguy, G. (2018). Figures du précariat rural. Supports et capacités d'agir des individus précaires dans la société rurale russe. *Nouvelles pratiques sociale*, 30(1). Retrieved February 17, 2019. https://doi.org/10.7202/1051405ar.

Nefedova, T. (2003). L'agriculture russe après 10 ans de réformes: transformations et diversité. *L'espace géographique, 4*(32), 289–300.

Pallot, J., & Nefedova, T. (2007). *Russia's Unknown Agriculture: Household Production in Post-Socialist Rural Russia*. Oxford: Oxford University Press.

Paxon, M. (2005). *Solovyovo. The story of memory in a Russian Village*. Washington, DC: Indiana University Press.

Pine, F. (1993). The Cows and Pigs are His, the Eggs are Mine': Women's Domestic Economy and Entrepreneurial Activity in Rural Poland. In C. Hann (Ed.), *Socialism. Ideals, Ideologies, and Local Practice* (pp. 231–248). London: Routledge.

Pine, F. (2002). Retreat to the Household? Gendered Domains in Postsocialist Poland. In C. Hann (Ed.), *Postsocialism. Ideals, Ideologies and Practices in Eurasia* (pp. 95–113). London: Routledge.

Vatin, F. (1996). *Le Lait et la raison marchande. Essais de sociologie économique*. Rennes: Presses Universitaires de Rennes.

Wegren, S. (2008). Typologies of Household Risk-Taking: Contemporary Rural Russia as a Case Study. *Paper Prepared for Agrarian Studies Colloquium*, Yale University.

Zelizer, V. (1994). *The Social Meaning of Money: Pin Money, Paychecks, Poor Relief, and Other Currencies*. Princeton: Princeton University Press.

7

Nonstandard Working Hours and Economic Use of Free Time in the Upper Class: The Gender Gap

Anne Lambert

1 Introduction

Nonstandard working hours and shifts have dramatically increased since past two decades.[1] Reasons for these include changes in labor legislation, administrative exemptions in the retail and tourism sectors, greater demand for healthcare due to population aging, and changes in patterns of consumption and way of life of many households in developed countries. Atypical work schedules have greatly increased in OECD (Organisation for Economic Co-operation and Development) countries generally, but especially in the United States, which some have called a "24-hours-a-day-and-7-days-a-week global economy" (Presser 2003; Presser et al. 2008). In France, 44% of salaried workers (10,4 million) work nonstandard hours, voluntarily or not, as do many self-employed people, mainly in the trade and catering sectors, in the social services sector (health care, police, etc.), and in the transport industry (Letroublon and Daniel 2018).

A. Lambert (✉)
National Institute for Demographic Studies, Paris, France
e-mail: Anne.lambert@ined.fr

A growing body of studies measures the impact of nonstandard work schedules on employees' health and family life (Schulz and Grunow 2012; Matthews et al. 1996; Schulz et al. 2004). Most studies conclude that flexible work schedules affect both child and adult outcomes, even though the impact is different for men and women (Lozano et al. 2016). Nonstandard work schedules appear to have harmful effects on couples: people working nonstandard hours have higher divorce rates (Täht and Mills 2015), spend less time with their partners, and report lower satisfaction with the marital relationships (Perry-Jenkins et al. 2007; White and Keith 1990). Nonstandard schedules are also reported to put pressure on marital relations by causing unequal sharing of household tasks (Hertz and Charlton 1989; Perry-Jenkins et al. 2007), reduce the amount of time spent with the family (Zuzanek 2000), and increase the stress levels reported by parents (Davis et al. 2008; Bulanda and Lippmann 2009). However, some recent studies tend to suggest that nonstandard work schedules could, under certain circumstances, facilitate the work–family balance (Lozano et al. 2016).

While very important for public policies and work organizations, the questions of health conditions and work-life balance have occulted another major aspect of the nonstandard working hours issue: its impact on the social status of such workers and the gender gap. How is "free" time spent, used and valued by men and women working offset? Are flexible work schedules always associated with temporal constraints and negative effects on the individuals? And how such a temporal organization of work (from a marginal one in the 1980s to a dominant one today) participates more generally in the global process of economization of the post-Fordist societies (Adkins and Dever 2016)?

Anthropologists offer us a more complex view of the interaction between shift work and social status. In the 1980s, F. Weber first showed that in heavy industry, shift work (with 12-hour rather than 8-hour shifts) was not only a source of stress and domination for workers but also a key condition that enabled them to "work on the side" and make economic profit of their free time (Weber 1989). Coming from socioeconomic backgrounds where money was scarce, blue-collar workers were taking advantage of the time slots and tools available in the factory to make extra money and to improve their living conditions. Doing so, they

7 Nonstandard Working Hours and Economic Use of Free Time...

were also fighting against a form of downgrading due to standardized work and repetitive gesture; side activities such as gardening and DIY helped them (mainly men) restore a sense of dignity. In this chapter, I apply the same kinds of questions to upper-middle-class occupations, in line with E. Hughes' recommendation that labor sociologists use the same tools to address humble and prestigious occupations alike. I examine the process of marketization of off-work time among integrated categories of salaried employees, using a survey conducted among a major European airline between 2014 and 2017 (see Box). I thus show that side job is not only frequent among upper class, but it is also constitutive of its class identity: side job, or "multi-positioning," is part of the dominant (and male) ethos.

To do so, I conduct a case study based on cabin crew (flight attendant, purser) and airline cockpit crew (pilot, co-pilot), who belong to the top 1% labor earners in France. All of them work at night, weekends and bank holidays, have stable working contracts, and gain high levels of financial compensation for the night shift. I show that far from using their "free" time for relaxing, sleeping, leisure, and family time, they develop a range of economic activities that enhance their social status.

As flight crew comprise both men and women (66% of cabin staff and 7% of pilots are women), I can compare the cross effects of gender and social status on the use of free time and the propensities to do other paid work alongside their main job. While being specific to the airline studied, the working conditions are quite similar to those of major airlines. Pilots are mostly men, and flight attendants are mostly women. Pilots earn much more money than flight attendants: varying according to the amount of flight hours, the annual gross salary ranges from 200,000 euros (in Great-Britain) to 250,000 euros (in France) for a captain; and from 30,000 euros (in Great-Britain and Germany) to 46,000 euros (in France)[2] for cabin crew. Moreover, in Western countries, the maximum legal working time is fixed by the EU and cannot exceed 900 hours per year.

In the airline studied, full-time flight crew work 12 days per month, in blocks of one to six consecutive days depending on whether they work on short-, medium-, or long haul flights. Long-haul rosters involve overnight layovers. Maximum working time is set at 92 hours a month (784 hours a year) for cabin crew, and 75 hours a month for pilots. Rosters are defined from month to month for cabin crew and every two months for cockpit staff, depending on the airline's needs. The rest of the month, flight staff is "free," that is, they have no professional obligation under their contract with the airline.

The chapter shows that multiple job holding is not incidental: on the contrary, it is part and parcel of the flight attendant life. It is for the male pilots that sidelines are the most profitable, and routinely practiced, even though these activities are scarcely visible. They succeed in monetizing their professional skills in leisure-time activities, they invest in the housing market, and they spend time making assets work—without considering changing jobs. In comparison, their female counterparts—women pilots—spend much more time parenting and engaging in leisure activities, making almost no extra money, since they consider that their position provides them high standards of living and great financial autonomy compared to other women on the labor market. The purpose for which flight attendants undertake sidelines activities is quite different: while being overqualified (a lot of them holds a bachelor or a master degree), both air hostesses and stewards consider their job (serving meals, taking care of passengers) as being quite "superficial" and "meaningless," and they expect to change positions as they get older—but only a few pay for professional training and actually hold multiple jobs.

Finally, what this chapter shows is that under specific conditions (predictable working hours, stable work contracts, high level of income), nonstandard working hours facilitate sidelines and reinforce social status instead of being a sign of precariousness and economic domination. This is the case of wealthy people—mainly men—who take advantage of such a work organization to multiply profitable activities. More generally, pilots' behavior reminds us that the members of the upper class structurally hold multiple positions that facilitate the accumulation of different types of capital and increase its economic returns (Boltanski 1973; Bourdieu 1989; Wagner 2007).

Method

This study is based on a survey carried out between 2014 and 2017 in a major airline in Europe. Three types of material were collected:

(1) The HR files of cockpit crew (pilots and co-pilots) and cabin crew (flight attendants, pursers, and chief pursers), covering all the 24,000 flight crew who worked for the airline between 1997 and 2015. They supplied sociodemographic information (sex, age, marital status, children's dates of birth, number of dependent children) and data on position in the firm (rank, long- or medium-haul, full- or part-time contract, percentage of working time, and date of and reason for end of contract). These data, which are kept for HR management purposes, provide no information on the employee's situation prior to joining the firm (social background or level of education).

(2) Biographical interviews enabled us to fit professional careers into broader social and family histories and find out about the flight crew's private worlds and domestic practices. We conducted 53 in-depth biographical interviews with flight crew on long-term contracts with the airline—23 cockpit crew and 30 cabin crew. Half were men and half women. Their ages and family situations varied. The interviews, lasting between 1 hour 30 minutes and 4 hours 15 minutes, took place in their homes. Half the interview concerned how they had joined the profession and how their career had unfolded; the other half addressed their off-the-job activities, domestic arrangements, and leisure. We also took six flights in two rotations to observe practices on board and during layovers (purchasing small items for gifts or resale, remote-managing everyday business or tenants) which might be too informal or illicit to be mentioned in a sociology interview (Schwartz 2011). The nondirective nature of the interviews and their taking place outside the work setting (not during duty hours, on layovers, or at the airport) proved decisive for finding out about the flight crew's off-the-job activities. In a situation where competition is fierce and the airline is chronically overstaffed, flight crew might otherwise feel threatened and disinclined to talk about activities that might seem to compete with their main salaried job.

(3) We collected and analyzed institutional documents: employer union agreements for cabin crew since 1997, company annual reports, comparative situation reports, and three-yearly agreements on employment equality between men and women. These gave us a better knowledge of the flight crew's working conditions and of the institutional, financial, and symbolic incentives around part-time working which, since 2009, have encouraged staff to reduce their working hours. With these data, we were able to see individual trajectories against the broader institutional background and understand the macro-sociological drivers of behavior that at first sight looked like purely personal choices.

2 Institutional Incentives and Material Conditions for Working on the Side

2.1 Growth of Part-Time Working

Historically, an air hostess' job was considered temporary, and careers were short. Until 1963, hostesses had to resign if they got married (Barnier 1997). A report by the French transport ministry noticed that "according to the airlines' promotional literature, the job of air hostess has never been considered a 'true profession' but rather a job, i.e. gainful employment for a limited period and without career prospects" (Florence-Alexandre and Ribeill 1982). Today, though careers are longer, many more cabin crew are working part-time and so too, to a lesser extent, are cockpit crew. The HR files show that 39% of cabin crew are working part-time, which is far more than the national average. The figure for pilots is 16% (see Table 7.1).

Working part-time has increased rapidly since the mid-2000s for economic and managerial reasons. The proportion of full-time employees fell by 15 percentage points between 1998 and 2014, and the trend is more marked for women (–20 points) than for men (–7 points). At the same time, the air transport business—because of its cyclical nature, the long shifts, and the desynchronization from ordinary social rhythms due to time-zone changes, night flights, and irregular schedules—allows flight crew's working hours to be concentrated into short periods and facilitates sidelines.

Table 7.1 Full- and part-time work by PNT (left) and PNC (right) in 2014 (%)

	Pilots			Flight attendants		
	Total	Women	Men	Total	Women	Men
50%	0.2	0.7	0.1	4.9	6.8	1.3
66%	0.1	0.7	0.1	5.1	7.1	1.2
75%	2.2	7.0	1.8	9.8	13.4	2.9
83%	4.7	11.8	4.2	10.1	12.6	5.2
92%	8.4	10.7	4.2	9.5	10.1	8.3
100%	84.4	69.1	85.6	60.7	50.1	81.1

Source: Company personnel files
Population: Cabin crew employees on permanent contracts in 2014

The reasons for this are both structural and contextual: (a) because of the physical difficulties of the work, flight crew careers are organized for a fairly short term; although the legal retirement age has been pushed back several times since the airline industry's initial expansion after World War II, flight staff are encouraged to prepare for their retirement in a situation where their salaries, being indexed to flight bonuses, are reduced by half when their shift ends; (b) the airline business is seasonal (summer/winter), with slack months when there is only half as much flying time. This explains chronic overstaffing in the company; (c) the situation since 2008, with an international economic crisis and the competition of low-cost airlines and Gulf's airlines, has persuaded many staff to switch to working part-time or to take occupational retraining under voluntary redundancy schemes. Indeed, the company's restructuring plan and the four successive voluntary redundancy schemes since 2009 have encouraged staff to shift to working part-time, resign, or take retraining/redeployment, and seem to favor multiple job holding. Various agreements also seem to encourage multiple job holding, the foremost being the "assisted split-month arrangement," a temporary measure to encourage the move to part-time work under which staff received a 7.5% to 10% addition to their fixed salary. Another, more generous arrangement was the *Temps alterné hors quota exceptionnel*, organized by whole calendar months. Employees received a monthly incentive bonus of 32% of the fixed pay. The bonus for month M was shown on the pay slip for month M−1 (e.g. a December payment on November's pay slip), helping to smooth the income fluctuation (Fig. 7.1).

These temporal changes in work organization are presented as a response to the employees' deepest aspirations, allowing them to adjust their working time in line with their age, family situation, and life cycle position: "Alternating work schedules have been introduced to meet the aspirations of flight crew and allow voluntary work sharing and consequently the creation of permanent jobs" (2014 voluntary redundancy scheme). According to a major union representative, flight crew are keen on the new assisted split-month system:

> Less working time is a demand among flight crews. Because it's tiring, desocializing work. And the assisted split month has been a success. Before, there was

1.a. Split-month alternating work schedule, with a release period of 7 or 10 days in a calendar month that also includes a period of airline work with social insurance contributions

A month
0 1 2 3 4 5 6 7 8 9 0 1 2 3 4 5 6 7 8 9 0
Airline work   No airline work

1.b. Whole-month alternating work schedule: periods of airline work with social insurance contributions and periods with no airline work last one or more full calendar months

A year												
Jan	Feb	March	Apr	May	June	Jul	Aug	Sept	Oct	Nov	Dec
Airline work	off	Airline work	off	Airline work	off	Airline work	off	Airline work	off	Airline work	off

Source: SNPNC, 2015

Fig. 7.1 The new part-time work schedules

only month-by-month alternation. The split month is a way to cope with the load month by month; you can better organize your private life, and your cash flow is smoother. (Paul, ex steward, human resource manager, 55 years old)

As the same time, the human resources department finds it easier to manage chronic overstaffing and the seasonal nature of the business if staff have income-generating sidelines. It also helps to improve the training and skill levels of cabin staff, who are theoretically recruited at upper-secondary (*baccalauréat*) level.

Finally, the recent debates over the economic uses of "free time" reveal that sidelines and multiple job holding are not scarce among the cabin crew. Indeed, the company-union agreement for the 2013–2016 voluntary redundancy scheme stated that "flight staff working under the alternating work schedule shall not, during their unpaid release period, perform any gainful work in the air transport sector or in the organization or sale of travel or holidays as defined by the law of 13 July 1992." At the same time, an internal union memo explicitly states the conditions for multiple job holding: "Flight staff working under the whole-month alternating work schedule may perform *another professional activity during their OFF months* (periods not working for the airline) on condition, notably, that they obtain permission from their main employer" (emphasis in the original).

2.2 Short Careers and Abundant Free Time

In talking about their jobs, flight staff very often point out their ample free time and the flexibility of their working hours, often comparing themselves with managers in the private sector who work regular, long hours (Stenger 2017). However, while opposition to office working hours is often expressed, there are differences between men and women. Women more often associate free time with parenting and family occupations, as if the two were contiguous. They often stress the importance of free time for a balanced family life and, increasingly, so do young male co-pilots socialized in a context more favorable to paternal involvement in the family sphere. To Eliane, a co-pilot aged 57 and mother of one child, working conditions that reconcile work and family life are an asset of the job:

> *I'd completely recommend this job to women, even with a family life, because one can ask, one has a selection of rest days every month that one can ask for, plus one flight. That means we have half our month that we can manage. And most of the time rotations are fairly short, we leave for four days, we don't leave … on average it's four days. In the old days, people were away for ten, 15 days!* (Eliane, co-pilot, 57 years old)

Such family involvement also emerges in the younger pilots' narratives. Pierre-Henri, a 35-year-old co-pilot with two small children, embodies the figure of the new father who has taken on board the idea of joint parenting. Son of a primary school teacher, he has cut his working hours and his earnings for the sake of a balanced sharing of work in the home:

> *As I'm a fairly new father, I asked for short rotations. I only do day flights. That means I generally get home every night. If I take off at 6 a.m., I'm home by 2 p.m. If I take off at 2 p.m., I'm home by 10 p.m. That means I miss either the morning or the evening. I rarely miss both. So in general I do one. She does the other. (…) Anyway, I think unbalanced situations are not tenable for a couple.* (Pierre-Henri, co-pilot, 35 years old)

This is also the case for co-pilot Pierre-Louis, aged 36, whose wife is a freelance photographer. He presents a flight crew job as more compatible with family life than other occupations:

Flight crew, when they're at home, unlike senior managers or other kinds of work, the difference is that for flight crew, when you're at home, you're at home. I don't have my work, my computer under my arm. In fact, you're often at home, and especially you can be there in the week. So you can take care of the children. That's how I see it. (Pierre-Louis, co-pilot, 36 years old)

Nonetheless, the use of free time seems to be conditioned by family roles much less for the men than for the women. Some single pilots, and some who had been through the intensive preparatory courses (*classes préparatoires*) and the French Civil Aviation University (*École nationale de l'aviation civile*), where classes and training had taken up all their time, seem disconcerted by the on-and-off nature of the job and the great amount of free time. On pilots' web forum, discussions about leisure time and the economic use of free time are frequent. One pilot posted[3]: "*Hi. I have 13–15 days off per month and, frankly, sometimes I want to do something with that free time. Anyone else in that situation?*" Some replies spoke of the other aviation work they did such as working as instructors at flying clubs and piloting light aircraft for tourism. Others replied that they were "*setting up their own business*," "*creating companies*," "*starting their own company*," and so forth. All of the comments were written by men, with no more details. None of them mentioned family and domestic activities.

3   Gendered Use of Free Time and Unequal Profitability

While the increase in sideline work has been encouraged by organizational incentives in a political and social context that promotes self-employment and values entrepreneurship (Abdelnour 2017; Taylor and Luckman 2018), flight staff choose their sidelines according to their personal aspirations, as shaped by their social and family background. Their free-time activities vary widely in terms of content, status, amount, and form of payment. Sidelines can be of many kinds (from making craft jewelry to working as a banking broker franchise, and from catering and hospitality to farming). In this respect, prior social resources are decisive for understanding the sidelines people choose and the conditions for their success. In practice, in the eyes of many men, the organization of work in the air transport industry has some specific features that seem favorable to income-generating sidelines: the basic schedule (concentrated work schedules on a few days); job security (permanent contracts), which reduces the economic risks involved in a freelance sideline; and fairly high salaries, allowing spending on other things than basics and essentials (flight crew get a guaranteed basic salary plus a flight-time bonus). Women less often have income-generating sidelines or, at least, tend to have sidelines that take up less time and pay less well.

3.1 Women's Sidelines: Creative Leisure Activities and Professional Training without Subsequent Paid Work

Observation and statistical analysis show that men and women do not use their free time in the same way. Women are more often on split-month or parental part-time work, with high working-time percentages (66%; 75%); they less often have a paid sideline and, if they do, it is less economically profitable. Men are more often on a whole-month alternating schedule with low working-time percentages (92%), and more often have leisure or business activities. The women, whether pilots or flight attendants, mainly use their free time for parental and educational activities in the family. When they do have a sideline, it is likely to be less income-generating than men's sidelines.

Their nondomestic, nonsalaried activities are of two kinds. One kind is creative leisure activities such as making jewelry or children's clothes from fabrics brought back from work trips. The products are not necessarily put up for sale (boutique, own website, or sale via a platform); they are mainly marketed by word of mouth in the family and in the broader social circle. They are seen as unique craft products (usually made of materials, shell, stones, cloth, etc. bought from abroad, during layovers) and are not intended to be replicated or sold on a large scale. The other kind is continuing education courses that, in practice, do not lead to paid work. For example, many women flight attendants continue their education via university-run training courses for paramedical occupations (osteopathy, psychology, sophrology, etc.). These occupations are fully in line with the gendered division of labor—requiring empathy, emotional labor, and interactional skills. But, at the end, it is rare for these women to practice their new profession and to set up as a liberal profession. The link between the training they take and the prospect of having two jobs or switching to a new profession seems sometimes very loose, as we see from the interview with Estelle, a 38-year-old purser on long-haul flights who is married to a steward and has two children. Her case is emblematic of those who take a training course but do not use it professionally. Estelle, from a working-class family, was recruited by Air France as a flight attendant at the age of 21, armed with a two-year university degree (DEUG) in languages. She had been a shop steward for eight years, was finding it increasingly difficult to cope with long-haul schedules, and felt strongly that her job has been devalued:

> *I don't want to be a flight attendant any more. People speak to us with absolutely no respect. And discussions with colleagues … My husband too, it's hard, he's fed up with it. But he hasn't had the opportunities I've had thanks to the union.* (Estelle, purser, 38 years old)

Estelle had started learning about labor law through her union responsibilities, developed a taste for the discipline, and was able to benefit from the in-service training fund (FONGECIF) to take a university law course in the town of Sceaux, in the suburbs of Paris:

> *These days I do more company-union negotiation; before, I was handling disputes a lot. That made me want to learn law. So I took a law degree through the FONGECIF fund, a 12-month intensive course in Sceaux, and got a licence degree. Then I did a Masters 1 and Masters 2 Professional in labour law at the same time as being a flight attendant and shop steward, so as to have more leverage with management. [And what do you want to do now?] I don't know what I want to do. In fact, at one point, I was thinking I might go over to the other side, work in HR in fact. But that scares me, I don't know.* (Estelle, purser, 38 years old)

Nearly five years had passed since Estelle took her training course, and she had not changed jobs. While many other air hostesses seem to have a long-term aim of switching to a ground job in a profession they deem compatible with their job as a mother, there are few who have a specific occupation in mind. No doubt they have less time available when at home to think about personal projects and career development. Not to mention the fact that for some, their fairly high salary, in some cases higher than their spouse's, can block any career change projects.

3.2 Stew's Sidelines: Long-Term Dual-Job Holding and Dreams of Independence

Among male flight attendants, the time freed up by alternating work schedules is more often used for leisure activities, often practiced at a high level (e.g. cycle racing, martial arts), but also for income-generating activities that can hold the prospect of a career change (leaving a job that is unrewarding although well paid and with company benefits and perks). Their aim is to escape from their situation as a "basic" employee (a service worker, producing "nothing" concrete in their eyes) whose status is drummed into them by onboard service conditions, passengers' attitudes, the hierarchy on the ground, and the pilots. Their position is reinforced by the sociopolitical context where independent workers are credited with many merits and enjoy greater symbolic prestige than salaried workers (Abdelnour 2017). The stewards' sidelines seem to reflect such dreams of independence: the desire for self-determination in one's movements, work, management, and time; self-realization in a productive activity rather than a service job that is seen primarily as women's work and described as low-skilled.[4] But these sidelines are also a response to the very weak career prospects at the airline; there are no openings in the company's internal labor market. The freezing of promotions to purser and chief purser has discouraged many cabin crew from committing to their career.

The diversity of income-generating sidelines reported by male cabin crew is striking. They include investing in rental housing, financial brokerage, managing a filling station for boats, running a car hire website, conjuring, and running a campsite. What these activities have in common is the effort involved in gaining professional status, with a training course that is obligatory in many cases (e.g. agricultural diploma, broker's license). Economic profitability is also often an explicit aim. In this context, the (partial) switch from salaried work to self-employment can be interpreted as a step up in status rather than an income supplement needed to improve living standards.

With the two cases described below, I analyze the men's pathways to starting a sideline and the personal resources they mobilize to achieve it. The new activity is taken on as a reaction against their main, salaried job, which they consider unrewarding ("just" serving, not producing anything with one's hands, etc.); it comes late in the person's career; and it uses resources acquired in initial education or training. But by no means are all these men aiming for total independence; no action is taken to relinquish the salaried status they still see as protective.

Patrick, aged 46, defines himself as a "farmer-steward." He is a purser, married and with three children, living in the South of France near an airport hub the airline opened in 2011. He earns about €3000 net per month, plus perks through the airline's works council (language trips and summer camps for the children, reduced-rate air tickets, supplementary health insurance, etc.). Patrick has a post-secondary catering and hospitality qualification (BTS) and was working in catering before he joined Air France as a flight attendant in 1997 at the age of 25. He was attracted by the good pay and stable employment status; the appeal of exotic travel was secondary. In 2007, he was promoted to purser before being assigned to a regional hub, at his own request, in 2011. He wants to do shorter rotations, which will give him time for sideline activities: "*I think at my age you realize you want to leave something. Ours are jobs that leave no trace. We don't build anything. We don't make anything. We don't leave anything.*" In 2012, Patrick and his wife bought a farm in the South of France, which he means to convert to organic farming; in the long run, the farmhouse will be turned into a guest house.

More broadly, the change in his career plans was prompted by the changes in cabin crew employment conditions under collective bargaining agreements since the mid-2000s: passenger greeting and in-flight service procedures have been standardized, the pace of rotations and duty shifts accelerated, and cabin crew numbers reduced. All these changes give Patrick and many of his colleagues a sense that their job has been devalued and even downgraded. In this situation, gradual disengagement from their work and the greater symbolic distance they express have been reinforced by the voluntary redundancy plans introduced since 2011:

> We all have one idea in mind, and that is to quit Air France. I set June 2017 as the date. June 2017. … They want us to work more and earn less. Which is shitty, obviously. In a training session one day, they said if we're hostile to change, it would be better to leave. I've told my superiors, I'm not putting all my energy into this firm, it's over. I took promotion to purser because I wanted to. Now, I have no desire to go for promotion to chief purser. (Patrick, steward, 48 years old)

Patrick's career path is determined by both personal and institutional factors, and was made possible by his use of various kinds of capital amassed in the family and professional spheres in the course of his career:

> I want to go back to cooking, that's what the farm idea is all about. Organic food and the guest house. My son would say I have a shitty catering baccalauréat, he made me quite a speech over his science baccalauréat. But the two-year BTS hospitality degree I did gives you a lot on labour law, book-keeping, taxation, really a lot of stuff. It prepares you for quite a few lines of work. … There are Parisians who say 'We'll drop everything and set up in farming and sell saffron'. So they no longer have a job, which is a pity because they've been told saffron is a money-spinner. They haven't done their research, the market research. I look at my overheads and at the money coming in, and I come out all right … The saffron gives a surplus. (Patrick, steward, 48 years old)

Also, with a stable job in a major firm, Patrick has enjoyed an income high enough to set aside "a little starting capital" to buy the farm buildings and adjoining land. As he confidently says, "I know I'm very well paid at Air France. That enabled us to launch our project. … I'm going to apply for a training grant from the FONGECIF fund this year; I'll take a farming diploma." The social conditions for Patrick's dual-job holding also include the presence of his wife, who is not economically active under the official definition but does the day-to-day book-keeping and management of the farm. "She's the one who is the farmer, I just give a helping hand from time to time." The work of women, which is frequent but particularly invisible on family farms, enables farm work to keep going when the spouse is away. But the farming Patrick and his wife have been doing for five years does not appear to pay well; the debt incurred for machinery purchases is colossal, and the restoration of the building costly. So far, Patrick has not earned any income from the farm. "*I don't need it to live on … You have to realize that you don't generate income with organic farming.*" All in all, with the cost of quitting his salaried job so high and getting started in farming so difficult, his shift to independence is more than uncertain. The pattern that seems to be becoming established is one of long-term dual-job holding.

Other cabin crew also start, like Patrick, by acknowledging the repetitive and unrewarding nature of their work and the lack of career prospects. Fabrice, a 36-year-old steward on medium-haul flights, is also a housing loan broker:

> *In my job you have so little need to think, it's just automatic and completely mind-destroying. The work itself teaches you nothing. And I needed to … not to fulfil myself, but to feel useful in a different way. And I couldn't take the pace any more. Not the hierarchy, the pace. I was whacked out. Anyway people say after 45 you're done for.* (Fabrice, steward, 36 years old)

But unlike Patrick, these stewards see dual-job holding as a lasting and desirable solution in terms of living conditions and status. The appeal of dual-job holding may be a generational phenomenon connected with the situation in which they came to the job (in 2009, France introduced a new "*auto-entrepreneur*" status facilitating self-employment, at the same time as the airline had entered a period of economic crisis and had put a freeze on hiring and promotion). It also reflects the changing conditions for entry to the job. After a period around 2000 when many flight crew were being hired, recruitment dried up and cabin staff seemed to be both older and more highly educated (Lambert and Remillon 2018).

Fabrice joined the airline as a flight attendant in 2004 at the age of 24, with a two-year technical diploma (from an Institut universitaire de technologie, or IUT) and a three-year degree (*license*) in law:

7 Nonstandard Working Hours and Economic Use of Free Time... 199

I did an IUT and a law licence. At the same time, I was doing internships; I did three months of long-haul flights when I was 20, 21, and 22. My sister was an air hostess, too. So I decided to join, and I joined XX when I was 24. That was in 2004. (Fabrice, steward, 36 years old)

Single, with no children and living in Paris, in the late 2000s he trained in his free time to be an "intermediary in banking operations and payment services" and was officially registered as an "intermediary" by ORIAS (Organisme pour le registre unique des intermédiaires en assurance, banque et finance), the body responsible[5]: "*I did it with the guy I work with now, who gives officially certified training. You are not responsible, or rather, you are in a brokers' order that gives you a card enabling you to do that job.*" In 2013, after nine years working full-time at the airline, Fabrice decided to switch to an alternating work schedule and devote more time to his banking brokerage work. He chose medium-haul flights to be able to reach his clients on the phone during stops. As this case shows, the marketization of free time seems to be strongly supported by the development of technological devices that play a crucial role by enabling "ordinary salaried workers" to reach their own "clients" at any time (in spite of the jet lag) and from anywhere in the world. Nonetheless, Fabrice does not want to give up his salaried job, even under the financially advantageous conditions of the airline's voluntary redundancy scheme:

Have you always worked full-time?
No, I've been at 80 for two years, on a split-month basis, so I have eight unpaid days in the month.
Why did you change?
To do other things on the side. I work 11 days in fact. And alongside that, for two years, I have been working... I work with a housing loans broker. So I do a thing completely on my "off" days. That's why I am on medium-haul flights, it matches well. It would be more difficult with long-haul.... Afterwards, to do only that, I have wondered about leaving. And that would be to give up everything I have set in place. I mean, to have choice over my whole life... over everything I do ... to get into a system where I would have goals. With the brokerage, I'm not paid a salary. I'm an agent; I bill for my services. In fact, I'm hyper-independent.

You're not interested in the voluntary redundancy scheme?

No. No. No, because … I'm too scared to not have my salary to fall back on. I don't have the balls to switch completely and, for the moment, what I have set up suits me well: alternating between the two, and having a salary, I find that comfortable too. (Fabrice, steward, 36 years old)

4 The Male Pilots: From Marketization to Multi-positioning

At the other end of the social scale, nonstandard working hours are not considered a professional constraint; on the contrary, they are seen as one of the conditions for accumulating wealth. Pilots commonly have several paid activities, holding different positions in different social spheres which generally increase the overall yield on their capital. Their day-to-day practices fit with Boltanski's theory that multiple position holding seems to be part and parcel of membership of the upper middle class (Boltanski 1973). They do not seek to switch careers completely, and their sidelines are not seen as ways to compensate for the subordinate nature of the main job. Their sideline may be a long-term business; it is partly subcontracted (the financial side) and partly put on display (the cultural and political side). Three types of male pilot sidelines can be distinguished, which are not mutually exclusive.

4.1 Tax Optimization

Part of the work pilots do on the side is designed to maintain the economic wealth accumulated through their main, salaried job and make it yield a profit—what C. Herlin calls "*le travail du capital*" (the work of capital) (Herlin-Giret 2017). These activities are, by definition, hard to pin down because, though not illegal, they occupy a place on the edge of legality (Barrault-Stella and Spire 2017). The most common is investment, for example, in real estate (buying to rent under tax-friendly arrangements like the Scellier and Robien laws and *Société*

Civile Immobilière status). Other activities are designed more directly for tax optimization (opting to be taxed under the "real expenses" system rather than a lump sum reduction for expenses; moving their tax residence abroad if the number of nights spent outside France is more than half the year, etc.). These practices require time investment and specific skills (calculation skills and financial literacy, knowledge of the law, IT competencies, etc.); they involve intermediaries such as the pilots' unions and tax consultants. Fiscal optimization appears as a collectively rooted practice, as the annual tax guide (*Précis Fiscal*) published by the main pilots' union shows. The guide explains the main changes in the law and gives advice to the pilots: "If you enter into the complicated calculations for 'tax niches', check with a specialist to see which niche you fit into (see page 4, real estate)." For example, the expenses that count under the "real expenses" deduction system are very varied: the cost of running two homes, travel expenses, clothing costs, and meals away from home if not covered by an allowance, and so forth. This means acquiring knowledge of tax law and taking care to file all the bills, invoices, and vouchers needed in the event of a tax inspection.

Finally, tax optimization can be considered as a proper job, in the sense that it requires technical knowledge and is both time-consuming and income-generating. However, the time put into this work is not very visible; it is often done in the pilot's home and/or subcontracted to a private intermediary (for knowledge of French and foreign tax laws, relevant networks, different investments and their respective yields, etc.). Moreover, tax optimization work is seen as a normal part of life. Members of the upper class have been socialized to financial and fiscal analysis by their family or their relatives. Those who have property justify their financial work as fulfilling a duty of foresight and preparing for a drop in income when they retire (half of a pilot's pay is in the form of flying time bonuses on which pension and health insurance contributions are not paid). It is a matter of looking ahead to ensure future consumption for the household, whose living standards depend very largely on the pilot.

4.2 Leisure Activities That Pay

Male pilots in particular may earn money from leisure activities, mainly in aviation, which is directly linked to their main occupation. Some work as flying school or flying club instructors, or as pilots subcontracted by charter companies in the summer, even though this type of activity is forbidden by their main employer. Some have leadership roles in local aeronautics-related social circles. Others practice high-level sports, often aviation-related sports like free-fall parachuting, which reinforce their image as a committed pilot by vocation and increase their symbolic capital because such activities fit the model of dominant masculinity (Connell 2014).

Pierre, a 40-year-old co-pilot on medium-haul flights, has worked on several paid jobs in the aviation industry. A pilot's son and a flight attendant's partner, Pierre became an airline pilot after finishing his studies. For the last few years, he has taken advantage of the chronic overstaffing of pilots in the European sector. He works 92% of the time and uses his off-month to work for another airline company that offers charter flights to the Antilles in the summer. So, during the month of July, Pierre works weekly connections between metropolitan France and Martinique for a net compensation of over 10,000 euros. He finds this supplement especially valuable, since the downturn in airline activity in the European sector has cost him a loss of income linked to the part that is indexed on flight hours. Although this is a relatively marginal case in the company under study, needs for technical personnel in airlines from emerging countries might favor this type of skills transfer and multiple job holding.

Ultimately, pilots use their aeronautical skills that they sell and monetize in the leisure market. In return, such activities constitute a body of experience that can be used advantageously in a pilot's workplace and career; they are what M. Bozon and Y. Lemel have called "the small profits of salaried work" (Bozon and Lemel 1989). Indeed, sidelines in the aeronautical sector contribute to maintaining skills and keeping them up-to-date (turnaround, take-off, approach and landing procedures, flight manual emergency procedure, etc.) in a context where more and more pilots are working part-time and where flight controls are increasingly automated.

4.3 Symbolic Activities and Social Prestige

A quite different type of activity, carried out in complementary manner to the financial work, is non-traded productive work whose remuneration is essentially symbolic. A number of pilots were mayors, deputy mayors, or other elected officials in small rural communes or urban districts. Some take up functions on consultative bodies or the scientific councils of non-profit organizations. Or they invest time and energy into worthy and prestigious local causes, for example, conservation of natural or built heritage (regional nature park, getting a building onto the national heritage list, organizing private concerts in a château or second home, parish work). These unpaid activities contribute to the financial valorization of the pilots' own assets.

Clément's trajectory is exemplary. A 54-year-old long-haul flight captain, he has held multiple jobs in the aviation industry and in local politics. He lived for 20 years between Paris and the Alps to practice mountain sports, which was his passion. There, while working full-time at his main job, he carried out different electoral functions, directed a regional park, and was a member of the local flying club. He still regularly practices paragliding in different areas of the Savoy region, weather permitting, although he now aspires for a calmer life. This sustained multiple job holding has given him access to a certain high standing on the local scene. Known by the citizens as "the left-wing pilot," he has long been elected to head the local council.

All in all, these activities help to build up and maintain a social status, whether inherited (for the "airline pilot dynasties," though these are a minority) or under construction (for pilots coming from elsewhere within the salaried middle class). The use of collaborative platforms and digital tools to find customers and sell services or commodities does not seem to be central to these kinds of activity. Internet is mainly used for gathering information or acquiring new skills during self-training (finance, law, accounting, etc.); for many of these activities, it is the invisibility of the activity that counts more.

5 Conclusion

Since the end of the Glorious thirty years and the entry into mass unemployment and economic crisis, working on the side and holding several (part time) jobs at the same time have been seen as a working-class practice.

The French term, *le travail à-côté*, was initially taken up by the anthropologist F. Weber to refer to the practice among heavy industry workers in rural areas in the 1980s, who were fighting to improve their living conditions, to make extra money and at the same time to regain their autonomy and dignity. The literature review also shows that working on the side was also considered essentially a male activity; women were mostly absent from the factories, or simply not mentioned in research studies on the working class. My survey of people in stable, well paid, salaried jobs in the air transport industry shows a different part of the reality. Working on the side is by no means the prerogative of the working class. The upper middle class also make economic use of their free time; some of their sidelines are income-generating and are performed with a view to practicing a new profession; some women also do productive work that is not solely domestic, though proportionally fewer women than men are involved.

Although the sidelines of stewards and pilots are notably different from those of manual workers, the practice as such fulfills social functions common to both groups, thus justifying the comparison. Working on the side is fostered by the time schedule; it can be encouraged by work organization and trade unions; it can be attractive in a situation of economic crisis and a restricted internal labor market, when full-time jobs are scarce and promotions are blocked. In the transport industry, side jobs are thus becoming more common, partly as a result of the economic downturn and partly because the democratization of air transport has led to a relative devaluation of flight crew occupations: long-haul flights are not seen as a luxury anymore nor seen as a technical advance. However, considering a longer period of history, sideline activities seem to have deep roots and to be integral to a certain position in society. This is what the pilots' situation reveals. The sideline is not secondary to the main job; it is a fully fledged job that helps to establish the person's social status when backed up by stable, salaried employment. The wide range of sideline activities and their diversity explain why the survey respondents did not apply a single, indigenous classification principle to their sidelines; among cabin crew, the way they referred to their sidelines varied according to its status, extent, and remuneration.

Appendix

Table 7.2 The interviewees mentioned in the chapter

Pseudonym	Function	Age	Number of children
Eliane	Co-pilot	57	1
Pierre-Henri	Co-pilot	35	2
Pierre-Louis	Co-pilot	36	0
Estelle	Purser	38	2
Patrick	Purser	46	3
Fabrice	Steward	38	0
Pierre	Co-pilot	40	2
Clément	Captain	54	2

Notes

1. My thanks to Delphine Remillon (INED-CEE) and Maxime Lescurieux (INED-CMH) for their help in processing the data from the databases.
2. http://www.europe1.fr/economie/air-france-trois-questions-autour-du-salaire-des-personnels-navigants-3628883. Accessed 17 May 2018.
3. http://forum.aeronet-fr.org/viewtopic.php?t=29259. Accessed 10 February 2018.
4. Theoretically, the baccalauréat is all that is required for a cabin crew job.
5. Under Article L. 519-1 I, paragraph 2 of the Financial and Monetary Code, a person may work as an intermediary in banking operations and payment services as a second or complementary business to a main professional activity.

References

Abdelnour, S. (2017). *Moi, petite entreprise. Les auto-entrepreneurs, de l'utopie à la réalité.* Paris: Presses universitaires de France.

Adkins, L., & Dever, M. (2016). *The Post Fordist Sexual Contract: Working and Living in Contingency.* Basingstoke: Palgrave Macmillan.

Barnier, L.-M. (1997). *Personnels navigants commerciaux: valorisation et dévalorisation du travail.* mémoire de DEA de sociologie, Université Paris X—Nanterre.

Barrault-Stella, L., & Spire, A. (2017). Introduction: Quand les classes supérieures s'arrangent avec le droit. *Sociétés contemporaines, 108*(4), 5–14.

Boltanski, L. (1973). L'espace positionnel: multiplicité des positions institutionnelles et habitus de classe. *Revue française de sociologie, 14*(1), 3–26.

Bourdieu, P. (1989). *La Noblesse d'État*. Paris: Éditions de minuit.

Bozon, M., & Lemel, Y. (1989). Les petits profits du travail salarié. Moments, produits et plaisirs dérobés. *Revue française de sociologie, 31*(1), 101–127.

Bulanda, R. E., & Lippmann, S. (2009). Wrinkles in Parental Time with Children: Work, Family Structure, and Gender. *Michigan Family Review, 13*(1), 5–20.

Connell, R. (2014). *Masculinités: Enjeux sociaux de l'hégémonie*. Paris: Éditions Amsterdam.

Davis, K. D., Goodman, W. B., Pirretti, A. E., & Almeida, D. M. (2008). Nonstandard Work Schedules, Perceived Family Well-Being, and Daily Stressors. *Journal of Marriage and Family, 70*(4), 991–1003.

Florence-Alexandre, H., & Ribeill, G. (1982). *Le Personnel des compagnies aériennes: les évolutions majeures de l'après-guerre à nos jours*. Mission de la recherche, Ministère des Transports.

Herlin-Giret, C. (2017). Quand les héritiers deviennent des « entrepreneurs »: les nouveaux appuis rhétoriques et pratiques de l'accumulation. *Revue de la regulation*, 22. Retrieved February 16, 2019, from https://journals.openedition.org/regulation/12388.

Hertz, R., & Charlton, J. (1989). Making Family under a Shiftwork Schedule: Air Force Security Guards and Their Wives. *Social Problems, 36*, 491–507.

Lambert, A., & Remillon, D. (2018). Une marche vers l'égalité professionnelle en trompe-l'œil. *Travail et Emploi, 154*, 5–41.

Letroublon, C., & Daniel, C. (2018). Le travail en horaires atypiques: quels salariés pour quelle organisation du temps de travail? *DARES Analyse, 30*, 1–12.

Lozano, M., Hamplova, D., & Le Bourdais, C. (2016). Non-Standard Work Schedules, Gender, and Parental Stress. *Demographic Research, 34*(9), 259–284.

Matthews, L. S., Conger, R. D., & Wickrama, K. A. S. (1996). Work-Family Conflict and Marital Quality: Mediating Processes. *Social Psychology Quarterly, 59*(1), 62–79.

Perry-Jenkins, M., Goldberg, A. E., Pierce, C. P., & Sayer, A. G. (2007). Shift Work, Role Overload and the Transition to Parenthood. *Journal of Marriage and the Family, 69*, 123–138.

Presser, H. B. (2003). *Working in a 24/7 Economy: Challenges for American Families*. New York: Russell Sage Foundation.

Presser, H. B., Gornick, J. C., & Parashar, S. (2008). Gender and Nonstandard Work Hours in 12 European Countries. *Monthly Labor Review, 131*(2), 83–103.

Schulz, F., & Grunow, D. (2012). Comparing Diary and Survey Estimates on Time Use. *European Sociological Review, 28*(5), 622–632.

Schulz, M. S., Cowan, P. A., Pape Cowan, C., & Brennan, R. T. (2004). Coming Home Upset: Gender, Marital Satisfaction, and the Daily Spillover of Workday Experience Into Couple Interactions. *Journal of Family Psychology, 18*(1), 250–263.

Schwartz, O. (2011). L'empirisme irréductible. La fin de l'empirisme ? In N. Anderson (Ed.), *Le Hobo: Sociologie du sans-abri* (pp. 333–384). Paris: Armand Colin.

Stenger, S. (2017). *Au cœur des cabinets de conseil et d'audit. De la distinction à la soumission*. Paris: PUF.

Täht, K., & Mills, M. (2015). *Out of Time: The Consequences of Non-standard Employment Schedules for Family Cohesion*. Dordrecht: Springer.

Taylor, S., & Luckman, S. (Eds.). (2018). *The New Normal of Working Lives: Critical Studies in Contemporary Work and Employment*. Basingstoke: Palgrave Macmillan.

Wagner, C. (2007). *Les Classes sociales dans la mondialisation*. Paris: La Découverte.

Weber, F. (1989). *Le Travail à-côté: étude d'ethnographie ouvrière*. Paris: Institut national de la recherche agronomique.

White, L., & Keith, B. (1990). The Effect of Shift Work on the Quality and Stability of Marital Relations. *Journal of Marriage and the Family, 52*, 453–462.

Zuzanek, J. (2000). *The Effects of Time Use and Time Pressure on Child-Parent Relationships*. Waterloo, ON: Otium Publications.

Part III

Low Labor Income

8

Performing Amateurism: A Study of Camgirls' Work

Pierre Brasseur and Jean Finez

1 Introduction

This chapter studies sexcamming, an economic activity whereby individuals sell their charms on the web to an audience of Internet users.[1] These individuals—or sex models to use the generic term—pose in front of a webcam chatting live with viewers or giving erotic or pornographic performances in return for payment in tokens. Contact is made between the sex models (called "camgirls" or "camboys") and their viewing customers on dedicated platforms, serving as intermediaries and charging a commission that generally ranges from 40% to 70% of payments. Sexcamming first emerged in the early 2000s and is today one of the facets of a sweeping game change on the sex markets. The development of the web and, more generally, the boom in the new information and communication technologies have transformed the traditional forms of pornography and sex work in terms of both work organization and sex workers' living conditions (Bernstein 2007; Jones 2015; Sanders et al. 2017).

P. Brasseur • J. Finez (✉)
Université Grenoble Alpes, CNRS, Sciences Po Grenoble, PACTE, Grenoble, France
e-mail: brasseurph@gmail.com; jean.finez@univ-grenoble-alpes.fr

Although sexcamming is a key line of business in the new sex economy, it remains relatively uncharted territory (Jones 2015; Henry and Farvid 2017). In the 2000s, some groundbreaking studies did look into the nascent industry (see, in particular, Knight 2000; White 2003; Dobson 2008; Senft 2008), but this research and other more recent studies often consider the business from the angle of the feminist "sex wars" controversy. These studies, whether for or against the controversy (Jones 2016), generally discuss the trade's coercive or empowering nature (Cruz and Sajo 2015; Jones 2016; Henry and Farvid 2017). Some authors show how sexcamming is an integral part of an international sex economy exploitative of women, namely Filipino, Colombian, and Romanian women (Mathews 2010; Davies 2013). Others focus on camgirls in rich countries, describing the mechanisms involved in the reproduction of inequalities and gender stereotypes (Dobson 2008) and race (Jones 2015). Some studies, however, point up the activity's subversive aspect (Knight 2000). By considering sexcamming from the angle of identity construction, this research shows how broadcasting erotic shows can give women a way to regain control over their bodies and their sexuality (White 2003; Senft 2008; Nayar 2017).

Although close attention should be paid to the risks and opportunities of sexcamming for women, it is important not to lose sight of the activity's socioeconomic dimension. Like all the new forms of online sex work, sexcamming should be viewed as one of the aspects of platform capitalism run on a workforce—generally flexible, underpaid, and feminized (van Doorn 2017)—competing for work.

This chapter analyzes women's professional engagement in the sexcamming economy. From this point of view, our work echoes the study by N. van Doorn and Olav Velthuis (2018) on how sex models devise strategies to give meaning to what they do and cope with uncertain market mechanisms. In our case, we study camgirls' professional engagement logics through the lens of *amateurism* (Nayar 2017). Like the logic described by Brooke Erin Duffy in the world of fashion blogging (Duffy 2015), the sexcamming economy is based on a "myth." To attract viewers, sexcamming platforms claim that the sex models are not professionals and that they broadcast shows for fun, from their own homes and in their free time. Our survey reveals, however, that camgirls take their work very seriously. The women interviewed are generally full-time camgirls, and sexcamming is their main (or only) source of income.

Unlike most of the other cases in this book, the camgirls' line of work therefore equates less with the marketization of everyday life than with the commodification of the *so-called everyday life*, as its clients imagine it to be. In what circumstances do certain women decide to start broadcasting sexual content on the Internet? Once in the business, how do they learn how to meet their clients' expectations? What do they do to make an economic return on their shows and differentiate themselves from the competition? Such are the questions addressed in this chapter.

The chapter is divided into four sections. The first section discusses the research methodology and justifies the framing of the field survey, a stage we feel is key to "defuse" a subject that is a source of so many misconceptions and often the target of sanctimonious analyses. The second section analyzes camgirls' entry into sexcamming: entry is the result of a convergence of capture devices (websites that promise easy money for a few hours' work) and a captive audience (women, often young women, with socioeconomic difficulties). As the symbolic cost of entry is high and profits are often low, the women who engage long term in sexcamming are generally those with particular marketable skills who are prepared to put their all into the business. The third section analyzes how camgirls collectively monetize sexcamming. Camgirls' success in business depends on their ability to stage amateurism: it is by negating the commercial aspect of the activity that the sex models authenticate the principle of an economic return on it. The fourth and last section discusses individual strategies for earning a living from sexcamming: success depends, first, on the capacity to produce shows that meet a solvent audience's demand, and, second, on building a lasting relationship, at a safe distance, with the viewers.

2 Why Study French-Speaking Camgirls?

Our survey focuses on a specific group of actors: French-speaking camgirls (generally French and occasionally Belgian or Swiss) who target a male audience. This narrow framing may come as a surprise to readers considering that sexcamming covers an array of models (generally classed in four categories on the platforms: "women," "men," "couples," and "transsexual," with no gender distinction) and situations (shows for a straight, gay, lesbian audience, etc.). In reality, the sex entrepreneurs' promise of diversity—with the use of platform-framing devices (key words, content filters, etc.)—is misleading. In France, the sexcamming economy is a heteronormative economy (Rubin 1984) in which women sell sexual services to men. For example, a count of the sex models broadcasting on French platform *Ufancyme*, set up in spring 2017, shows that sexcamming is worked predominantly by women. Of the website's 470 broadcasters, we counted 438 women (93% of the total), 24 men (5%), 6 couples (1.5%), and 2 "transsexuals" (0.5%).[2] In addition, an exploratory study based on personal accounts and data collected from the broadcast platforms and Twitter suggests that customers are predominantly men, which is in keeping with the literature on pornography audiences in France (Bozon 2008).

Turning now to the justification for the survey's spatial scope, despite the emergence of an international pornography market driven by the development of the digital economy, we felt it a sounder method to focus solely on French-speaking camgirls for a number of reasons. The first reason is *analytical*: a contained study of a population living in a given geographical, political, and cultural era restricts variations in social context. This is especially important in that the pathways of the people working in sexcamming are largely dependent on the institutions of the country in which they live: legal regulations on sex work, the extent of moral censure of pornography, the population's standard of living, and so on. The restriction of the survey frame is also justified for *empirical* reasons. Despite the possibilities opened up by the new technologies for ease of contact between supply and demand the world over, the sexcamming economy is not a uniform, globalized social universe: the camgirls interviewed generally have French customers, most of the sex models mentioned in the interviews are French-speakers, and so on. This is what *Le Tag Parfait*, an online porn culture magazine, calls a *PCF* for *Paysage de la Cam Française* (French Camming Landscape). Lastly, there are *practical* reasons for concentrating on French-speaking camgirls: easier access to interviewees, gaining respondent trust, perfect command of the interview language, and so forth.

Our survey material is based mainly on 21 semi-structured interviews with women between 20 and 47 years old. These one-to-three-and-a-half-hour interviews held between September 2017 and November 2018 were conducted by three interviewers of different sexes (two men and one woman), allowing for a control for gender effects on interviewer/interviewee interactions.[3] Drawing on the advances of other research on sexuality (Riandey and Firdion 1993), stating that "a conversation about sex—even in the form of a scientific interview—is, in itself, a form of sexual interaction" (Devereux 1967: 107), we sought to keep a distance from respondents by using a video conference system for the interviews (Skype). In a few rare cases where respondents preferred not to reveal their face or voice in order to protect their identity, the interviews were conducted by telephone or instant messaging. As distancing devices, video conferencing and the telephone facilitate the acceptance of interviews by women who might otherwise balk at the physical proximity of interviewers whose sociodemographic profile equates them with potential clients.

The respondents were contacted on the Twitter social network (124 contacts resulting in 21 actual interviews). The use of Twitter proved particularly effective as it is a key medium for the online promotion of this line of work. The first sex models contacted were dubious as to whether our inquiries were in earnest, despite our many precautions to avoid being taken for free riders in search of free shows. Gradually, wariness waned as the positive responses, recommendations by other camgirls, and new contacts came in, and the positive response rate rose substantially. It is difficult to establish the respondent sample's representativeness of the population of French-speaking camgirls. We simply do not know how many of them there are, although they must run at least into the thousands. However, although the camgirls had been sexcamming for highly variable lengths of time (two months to 13 years) at the time of the interviews, a number of elements suggest that camgirls with a high level of sexcamming activity are overrepresented: a number of sex models approached refused to be interviewed on the basis that they had little experience and considered themselves unqualified to express an opinion.

Alongside the interviews, this study draws on a series of exploratory observations in different digital spaces where the sexcamming economy operates. The first of these are devices employed by sexcamming entrepreneurs to entice the sex models and incentivize them to broadcast on their platforms: advertising, recruitment websites, blogs promoting the activity, and so forth. Second, the camgirls' Twitter pages were observed, in particular to understand the self-presentation strategies behind the choice of pseudonym,[4] profile description, and photos and messages posted. Lastly, public show broadcasting platforms (see Box) used by the French-speaking sex models were observed, namely, Ufancyme, Cam4, and Chaturbate.

> **Private shows and public shows**
>
> The sexcamming economy is based on two forms of paid show. The first are *private shows*: a client who wants an individual interaction with a sex model pays an hourly rate in *tokens*, whose value varies from one platform to the next. During the show, the sex model fulfills the client's wishes. The second form concerns *public shows*, which are viewed simultaneously by a variable number of Internet users: generally ranging from dozens to hundreds. These shows are performances conditioned by meeting *goals* for a rate of payment set in advance by the sex model: for example, 20 tokens to take off her bra, 50 to take off her knickers, 100 to start to masturbate. In the public show model, although Internet users can behave as free riders and enjoy the show free of charge, the show can only be viable if some accept paying for the others.

3 Starting Work in Sexcamming

How do women become camgirls? Far from being spontaneous, initial contact between sex models and platforms relies on soundly developed capture devices: sexcamming promoters seeking to grow their business create recruitment websites that present the activity in an appealing light. However, these devices can only work if they reach a captive audience. So, the first broadcast generally occurs following a life event that disadvantages the life course. For some women with capital they can sell on the sexcamming market, this entry into the business converts into a commitment. These women then take the risk of pursuing a difficult, restrictive, and often low-paid job despite the platforms' initial promises.

3.1 Capture Devices and Captive Audiences

As with other sharing economy activities (Schor and Attwood-Charles 2017), sexcamming relies on the existence of web platforms to help match supply and demand. Yet this match first requires enough people to be broadcasting shows to attract customers. Part of the sexcamming entrepreneur's job is therefore to capture sex models using ad-hoc devices: recruitment websites that present an idealized image of the business. These websites, despite their individual particularities, present some recurring sales pitches. Firstly, in spite of the reality of sexcamming, they understate the pornographic nature of the business: the websites present demure photos (bare-chested men wearing trousers and women always in underwear) and use vocabulary closer to the glamorous world of modeling than pornography ("become a hostess," "choose a life in modelling," etc.). Secondly, the recruitment websites plug the supposed absence of constraints in sexcamming: freedom of initiative ("decide for yourself what you do in your shows"), flexible hours ("work how you want, when you want"), and a job that is fun ("have fun and meet great people all over the world"). Thirdly, they use implausible testimonials to push the particularly lucrative nature of sexcamming ("I doubled my earnings (…) working just five hours a week"). Lastly, they assure women who are interested that it is easy to get into the business and that the commitment is minimum, so they have the option to stop broadcasting at any time.

Although recruitment devices are necessary to get camgirls into sexcamming, they are not enough on their own. The women first need to find these websites before they can become sex models. Yet, like other pornographic activities, sexcamming is a morally questionable activity, which limits the possibilities of promotion on conventional recruitment websites. Understanding the drivers of working in sexcamming therefore calls first for a grasp of how the women find out about the activity in the first place. Many camgirls interviewed said they first heard about sexcamming from a TV show. Some mentioned TV series, and press articles and reports on the Internet. Some also said that they found out about sexcamming by word of mouth or while chatting with friends. Yet, according to their personal accounts, aside from the women who were familiar with sex work or promiscuous, the initial contact with the activity generally prompted no more than amusement. It was only months or years later, when faced with a financial problem, that they really looked into it and considered working in the business, just like Eurydice:

> *The first time I heard about sexcamming was in Desperate Housewives. That was two years ago, but I've actually only been doing it for eight months. I did it thinking back to that TV series because I needed the money. That's really what it was… In the series, it's Susan. She films herself doing the housework in her underwear. That's how I came to think of it. When I really looked into camming, I signed up straight away. That was in March 2017. I didn't think twice really. At the time, I simply had to earn a living. I lost my job for personal reasons and wound up at the job center. I'd just bought an apartment a few months earlier and was in urgent need of cash. So I signed up straight away. I found out how to cam on the job, like all the other girls I should imagine. It started out as kind of a last resort. But it turned out to be fun, so I stayed.* (Eurydice, 27 years old)

Eurydice's tale, as a young woman previously in relatively well-paid skilled employment (master's degree), is significant. Entry into sexcamming generally coincides with a life event with socioeconomic consequences. These biographical ruptures are contributory factors to engaging in sexcamming, whether they are due to an affective event (breakup of a cohabiting couple or leaving home after a family row), a work-related event (an incapacitating occupational injury or dismissal), an education-related event (leaving the education system with inadequate qualifications), or an unfortunate accident in life (a car crash resulting in disability). These breaks and misfortunes can be considered as *turning points* (Hughes 1971) in disadvantaged life courses. However, it would be oversimplistic to equate them with situations of high socioeconomic insecurity. Whereas some camgirls may well have started broadcasting shows to meet their basic needs (rent an apartment, and clothe and feed themselves decently), others started out to maintain their standard of living or gain financial independence from their partner. In any case, they generally had much more leeway than in the case of the more conventional forms of sex work, particularly street prostitution (Weitzer 2009). For example, the camgirls interviewed generally said that they weighed up the job against other lines of work available to them: waitress, child minder, specialized educator, or check-out clerk. Aware that staging their sexuality on the web is clearly not an inconsequential act (fear of being discovered by friends and family, and repercussions on future career), they give careful consideration to the decision to broadcast.

3.2 Women with Marketable Assets

The symbolic cost of entry into sexcamming varies from one woman to the next. It depends in particular on the woman's attitude to sex before starting work in the business. The cost can be relatively low, as is the case, for instance, with women who have an extensive previous sexual repertoire compared to ordinary practices (Bozon 2008) and those who have specific professional skills due to past experience in a listening job or as a sex worker. Such is the case with Ophelia Shibari, a former peep-show employee who was the victim of a car crash in the early 2000s. Having lost the use of her legs and unable to resume her former job, she then had to face a steady slide in her disability allowance, down to just 800 euros at the time of the interview. For Ophelia Shibari, who has to receive daily treatment at home and spend long weeks away in treatment facilities, sexcamming is a godsend. It gives her more flexibility than other jobs and puts to use the skills acquired from her peep-show years in the Netherlands in the late 1990s:

> *I'd already done it back in 1998. That was in another life, you might say. It was on a set with professional direction for a production company in Amsterdam. I lived there and went to the set every day. A production team managed everything. I was paid by the hour and given hours every day. (…) So when I start camming, I was already familiar with it and, in a way, I'd already done it. Even if it was different. How can I put it… Now, I do it from home. But, if you like, when I started to broadcast, I knew what I was going to be asked to do.* (Ophelia Shibari, 45 years old)

Ophelia Shibari's case demonstrates one possible pathway into sexcamming, but it is not one that is representative. Only three of the women interviewed worked directly in sex work before they started broadcasting.

Although the other camgirls were often strangers to this world, a number of them suggested that they were open to the idea based on their previous sex life, and virtually all the camgirls interviewed said they were bisexual. Moreover, a number of camgirls had previously frequented pick-up joints or sex clubs. Others mentioned having a particular body image (weight problem, difficulty accepting their physical appearance, eating disorder, etc.). These women see working in sexcamming as a long learning process in the techniques of the body (Mauss 1973), generally offset by having other assets that can be put to good use in the business. While some are perfect *digital natives* with a command of particularly useful techniques (communication on social media, website publishing, Photoshopping, video editing, etc.), others have education- and career-based management skills. This stands to reason, since many of them had a relatively comfortable childhood or at least their cultural capital is well above average. Two of the camgirls interviewed are even graduates from *grandes écoles*.[5] From this point of view, the French camgirls interviewed display similarities with the middle- and upper-class white American sex workers studied by sociologist Elizabeth Bernstein (Bernstein 2007).

3.3 A Massive Time Investment in a Relatively Low-Paid Business

Many interviewees spoke about the remarkable and unexpected success of their first shows. They mentioned "beginner's luck" in explaining the three-figure sums earned while they were trying out broadcasting. The hypothesis could be put that this success owes very little to chance and is rather the result of the promotional strategies of the website managers, who use social media and blogs affiliated with the platforms to spotlight the new sex models they find promising and who, by means of a performative effect, sometimes become so. Likewise, some platforms' ranking algorithms—veritable "black boxes" about which little is ultimately known—seem to place a premium on new players. These incentives encourage the sex models to invest time in the business, to take it seriously. Yet once the interest in the first broadcasts has passed, it has to be said that disappointment is often considerable. Whereas the failure of subsequent shows is a factor in the withdrawal of many camgirls from the business, it also has the opposite effect among the more motivated girls by prompting an escalation in commitment: in the belief that their low audience figures and poor earnings are due to a lack of commitment on their part, some camgirls decide to increase their time investment—but also their emotional and bodily investment—in the business. It comes as no surprise that sexcamming is the only job worked by virtually all the camgirls interviewed (15 out of 20) and that they generally spend dozens of hours a week on it.

Elizabeth Bernstein, in her study of the apparently improbable engagement of these women in sex labor, explains it as being due to the gendered disparities of postindustrial economic life and the relatively high pay of the sex industry compared to other service sector jobs (Bernstein 2007). From the point of view of pay, however, the case studied by the American sociologist presents a notable difference compared to the case studied here. Although two of the camgirls interviewed state that they earn more than 3000 euros a month, these pay levels remain rare and most of the girls struggle to earn any more than 1000 euros.[6] In addition, these sums correspond to turnover, a not-inconsiderable proportion of which is deducted from those girls who declare their income, as most of them do: the majority of French camgirls have *freelance entrepreneur* status (a scheme designed to simplify unincorporated business establishment and social security contribution formalities) and pay approximately 25% of their earnings in social security contributions. Moreover, as with all entrepreneurial activities, sexcamming incurs outlays: purchasing a good-quality webcam, regularly buying new clothes, having numerous sex toys and accessories to hand, and so forth. Lastly, freelancers do not get paid leave. At the end of the day, considering the services they provide, camgirls' earnings are generally low despite the huge amount of time they put into their work.

To understand the personal investment demanded by sexcamming, we look again at the example of camgirl Ophelia Shibari, who generally spends six to eight hours a day on her work: she logs on in the afternoon after her treatment and ends her camgirl workday at around 10 pm. Her total working week, including the time she spends on the platforms, in chats with customers on Twitter and setting up the room before the broadcast, comes to over 40 hours. Yet she says she earned an average of 800–1200 euros a month in the last quarter, that is, an hourly rate below the minimum legal wage in France. Similarly, the other camgirls interviewed have hourly earnings that rarely exceed 10 euros an hour. Although sexcamming is an "honorable refuge" (Bourdieu 1984: 415) for certain middle-class women with disadvantaged life courses, it is not an easy way to make money: the few women who manage to earn hundreds of euros in a few hours, sometimes called "sex millionaires" by the press, are statistical exceptions who perpetuate the myth of easy money and the *self-made woman*. The camgirls who report earnings of more than 3000 euros a month owe their success primarily to a huge time investment in the business, as shown by the case of Irina Alpha, who says she works up to 70 hours a week.

4 The Monetization of Amateurism

It is interesting in two respects to demonstrate that the time investment is a necessary condition for making a living from sexcamming. It helps demystify the imagined workings of the business and focuses on how camgirls learn to deal with the paradox at the heart of the monetization model. Indeed, the activity's singularity lies in its promise of amateurism perceived as a guarantee of authenticity. The sexcamming economy is hence based on the tricky exercise of conceptually distancing the work from the money. To make their shows pay, the camgirls have to provide the guarantees of amateurism expected by their customers.

4.1 Distancing Sex from Money to Guarantee Authenticity

The generic term of *authenticity*, omnipresent in the world of sexcamming, underpins the workings of many social activities. Some tourism anthropologists, for example, have analyzed the commoditization of cultural forms presented as protected from the excesses of capitalist society even though they are "sold by the pound" (Greenwood 1982). Authenticity also applies to the field of art, and to the assumed disinterested nature of the artist, to the principle of his or her recognition in the field (Bourdieu 1995). It is also a cornerstone of the sociology of emotion, especially Arlie Hochschild's study on flight attendants (Hochschild 1983). The sociologist shows that, to gain customer loyalty, flight attendants learn to express emotions perceived as sincere by the passengers. Particularities of fields and approaches aside, these examples demonstrate the ambiguity between the imperative of authenticity and marketization. In each of the examples, the monetization of the products or services depends on the supply players' capacity to shape reality so that it chimes with the customer's perceived universe: that of an activity shielded from self-interested calculation and the primacy of the market.

In the case of sexcamming, the amateurism criterion is the catalyst for the veracity of the establishment of its recognition as an authentic practice. The Cam4 website hence claims to broadcast sex shows performed by real people ("real people naked and having sex live"), and Chaturbate claims to work with "thousands of live amateurs." By pushing the amateur nature of sexcamming, industry players (platform managers, sex models, business promoters, etc.) endow the shows with particular qualities that differentiate them from other forms of sex trade, starting with classic pornography performed by professional actors. The sexcamming market's symbolic construction requires the negation of the economic nature of the activity (Bourdieu 1995; Jourdain 2010) and signals of non-professionalism in the narrative, which is precisely what the camgirls do on Twitter, their blogs, and the broadcast platforms.

Although there is no unanimously agreed concept of amateurism in the world of sexcamming, the survey makes for an outline of the idealized figure of the amateur camgirl, built mainly on three features. Firstly, the sexcamming amateur is equated with a *passionate commitment*. The amateur is seen as being proud of her taste for sex (*"I love sex"*), staging the pleasure she gets from making the shows (*"It's so good, my darlings!"*) and making the playful side of sexcamming the key motive for her commitment.[7] Secondly, amateurism mirrors a symbolic construction of the practice as a *sideline*. Far from being a full-time job, sexcamming is portrayed as a side job (Weber 1989) on which sex models spend a few hours a week to make ends meet. Thirdly, amateurs pride themselves on the *spontaneity of their performance and persona* on display in their shows. Lack of proficiency in the classic pornographic codes is seen here not as a weakness, but as a quality. In other words, it is a guarantee that the shows produced are original.

Even though the sexcamming economy is based on a classic trade model (sex models are paid to provide a service to meet consumer demand), it circumvents the moral objection to the commodification of the body. The myth of amateurism distances the business from the *forbidden relationship* between sex and economy, thereby forestalling any impressions of sexual exploitation. Yet, in reality, this distance is never complete. The boundaries between sexcamming and the other sex trade forms are porous, as shown by porntube websites entrepreneurs' marketing strategies with their pornographic video broadcast websites based on the YouTube model (Mowlabocus 2008). These websites have gradually diversified from their initial business model of pornographic videos, and many of them now have a dedicated live amateur show broadcasting space directly integrated into their interface. The porosity of the boundaries can also be seen from the content hosted on the porntube websites. Many videos posted on these websites are made by people who do not have the technical resources of the "classic" pornographic industry producers and consequently call themselves amateurs.

4.2 Guarantees of Amateurism

Faced with the image of the money aspect, camgirls seek to give Internet users guarantees of the authenticity of their shows. Among the material signs of amateurism, broadcast location occupies a prime place. Broadcasting from home—as all the respondents do—is vital to amateur branding. Putting the domestic environment on show (bedroom, sitting room, and sometimes bathroom or kitchen) in its most natural state also brings the "girl next door" fantasy into play (Mowlabocus 2008), the neighbor or woman you might pass in the street who chooses to share her private life for fun. Yet it is also worth considering the institutionalization of the amateur brand in the light of the new practices that have fed into the digital spaces in the last two decades. Through this lens, the symbolic positioning of sexcamming appears as part of a broader drive emerging in the early 2000s to blur the boundaries between dilettante and professional practices on the web. Camgirls hence see themselves as "pro-am" (Leadbeater and Miller 2004) and accordingly appropriate the home-based DIY culture, as shown by the interview with Deborah Seeexmaid, a young woman who decided to start sexcamming to pay her rent in the fall of 2016. Like the other camgirls, Deborah produces her shows herself:

> *We're not performers. Well… we are performers, but amateur performers. We're not paid by a company to do it. (…) We're on our own and we do it from home. Porn actors don't shoot their films on their own from their own couch using their own camera. That's not amateur.* (Deborah Seeexmaid, 22 years old)

Typical of the web's alternative work utopias, the camgirl's end-to-end control of the production process here again distances her from classic pornographic cinema with its division of labor and worker subordination. However, the "homemade" distinction does not begin and end with a criticism of the industrial nature of conventional pornography. DIY is also a powerful vehicle for the horizontalization of relations between camgirl and Internet user.

5   Real Sex Trade Professionals?

Guarantees of amateurism are not enough to secure the camgirls a comfortable income. Economic success for the camgirls depends on their ability to differentiate themselves from their rivals and forge close relationships with their customers.

5.1   Producing Singular Shows

In general, novice camgirls start out broadcasting with what they have to hand. However, they quickly realize the importance of producing technically proficient shows, as explained by Padmé Lov, a camgirl for eight months at the time of the interview. A former barmaid, Padmé Lov, found out about sexcamming from a YouTube documentary and has been broadcasting shows since, occasionally with her partner:

> *As soon as I earned the first tokens, I started saving for a new webcam and lighting to attract as many people as I could. (…) On the equipment side, our lighting is good, but we want to buy a green backdrop like some of the pros have. (…) We get our inspiration for the lighting and all that from stuff on YouTube. I've really created a Padmé Lov brand out of my color and set design. 'Cos it's geeky, geeky lighting, and all.* (Padmé Lov, 27 years old)

Although proficiency in technical tools is central to the process of the camgirls becoming more professional, this task is part of a broader online image esthetic-identity construction approach. Camgirls work on singularizing their services to raise their visibility and their own profile (Jourdain 2010; Karpik 2010). They build their brand (Bourdieu and Delsaut 1975) by staging the cultural references they embrace and creating a distinction between theirs and other services on the market:

> *There's this girl that started camming at around the same time as me. She's a suicide girl.[8] (…) She has tattoos. When she started out, she had purple hair. Then it was black and now it's green, I think. It's a really distinctive style. (…) And people like it, so it stays. Having something distinctive counts enormously. You have to find your image and take a line of attack. (…). [Mine], I'm still looking. I know I really like dragonflies. It sounds daft, but it's become a bit of a trademark. When people see a picture of a dragonfly somewhere, they think of me and send me a message. (…) It took me a while to understand that: you have to have a particularity.* (Jade Erotic Dragonfly, 24 years old).

As seen from this account given by Jade Erotic Dragonfly, who had been broadcasting shows for two years at the time of the interview, singularization is a long-winded task. Whether based on erotic skills learned on the job or talents that predate entry to the business, it depends across the board on the ability of the women to understand and meet the clients' expectations. This mainly takes the form of catering to the sexual fantasies of certain viewers, as shown by the interview with Snazzy Ebony, hesitant about some customers' requests:

There are practices I wasn't aware of, like being asked to use certain objects that would never have occurred to me. Like the heel of a shoe: once, I was asked to use the heel of a shoe as a sex toy. (Snazzy Ebony, 30 years old)

So working in sexcamming sometimes requires the camgirls to choose between expanding their sexual scripts (Simon and Gagnon 1986), which they could then make pay, and turning down certain customer requests especially where they are physically risky, distasteful, or seen as degrading. Although some camgirls work in "extreme" practices, sometimes calling for a command of special codes, as with the BDSM (bondage, domination, sadism, masochism) practiced by Oksana Kolero, sexcamming is also based on more conventional sexual scripts. This can be seen from the following for the acrobatic shows performed by Snazzy Ebony, who has installed a pole-dancing pole in her bedroom, and for Kissi Yeeh's erotic storytelling in her pajamas. Whether camgirls merely hint at sex rather than exhibiting it or whether they engage in more esoteric practices (fisting, golden showers, scat, etc.), the success of these shows reveals the complexity of the marketization process and the highly entrepreneurial nature of the business: camgirls, who live as innovators, are quick to try out new practices, inform Internet users that their shows are in the experimental stage, and ask for their opinions afterward.

5.2   Building Intimate Relationships

As with other forms of e-commerce, a screen separates the camgirls from their customers. Although this distancing is not in itself a problem, it does represent a challenge for the camgirls who have to keep up the intensity of their interactions with the Internet users to make sure they keep viewing. This is no mean task since hundreds of viewers might be online at the same time, which restricts the possibilities for interindividual interactions.

Camgirls use different techniques to ensure the longevity of their relationship with customers who could otherwise "take their business elsewhere." Some camgirls, for example, set up polls on their Twitter account, giving Internet users the chance to vote on their future hair color or the theme of the next show. These polls reveal the customers' expectations and are an inexpensive way of getting their input. The relationship is also built on the technological development of connected objects, especially connected sex toys that vibrate "to order," that is, when the customers pay. The success of this technico-economic innovation is based on a particular form of closer interaction: Internet users can remotely touch the camgirls, giving them the impression that they can give the girls pleasure. Where the technologies lend a feel of intimacy to interactions involving hundreds of viewers, the value of the services also depends largely on their personalization. Part of the camgirls' work therefore consists in engaging in customized relations with clients. In this respect, having a social media account like Twitter helps retain loyalty:

> *Well, I'm on Twitter and I try to post photos on a regular basis and answer my private messages. Actually, I don't reply to everyone because, sometimes, I get quite a large number of messages. But as far as my clients are concerned, I do make the effort to answer them and chat with them. And then, sometimes I'll make a commercial gesture. For example, recently, I had a customer who gave me a present. So I offered him a show on Skype and gave him ten minutes for free to thank him for the gift. Sometimes, I also send signed photos. So there you go, I try to show them that it's also a two-way thing between us. I'm grateful, basically.* (Bluealux, 24 years old)

Far from being mere consumers of sexual services, sexcamming customers are therefore also people looking for an intimate connection, who need to talk and to be heard. This explains the non-sexual conversations between Internet users and camgirls at the beginning or end of shows. Some of these chats revolve around shared interests such as video games (most of the camgirls interviewed are keen players), music, and films. Other conversations concern the camgirls more directly, such as when they discuss their ambitions with Internet users, who, in turn, lend an attentive ear. And other chats discuss everyday concerns, as seen from a conversation between camgirl Erinyll and a few Internet users who give her tips at the end of one of her shows on how to polish her parquet flooring scratched by her sofa legs.[9]

This DIY advice may well appear to be trivial, but it shows how clients can get involved in the camgirls' daily lives. The interviews point up more generally the involvement of some Internet users who put their (sometimes professional) skills to use to help camgirls prepare and promote their shows: assistance with Photoshopping photos for a blog, advice on buying broadcasting equipment, and so forth. These helping hands essentially constitute an "altruistic" setup, similar to that which could be found in a real-life couple, and once again help erase the commercial aspect of the relationship. Similarly, when Internet users give presents to camgirls they are "fans" of (mainly on an Amazon wish list where a gift can be ordered without revealing the sex model's address), the gesture shows how the relationship can stray from the market context (Zelizer 2005).

5.3 Relational Ambiguities and Mismanaged Transactions

Contrary to popular belief, the relationship between camgirls and their spectators is not necessarily fake or simulated. The interviews reveal feelings of attachment driven mainly by being in online communities such as those created by multiplayer video games. Some clients share so many moments with the girls in digital spaces other than sexcamming that they end up being seen as *"fellow gamers"* or even *"online friends."*

Yet, although the camgirls are careful to keep their customers close enough to ensure their loyalty, but at a sufficient distance to prevent them from getting too emotionally involved, interactions sometimes take an unexpected turn. Such is the case, for example, when regular viewers start using the language of love in their interactions with the camgirls. The girls then face an internal struggle with a difficult decision to make. On the one hand, this emotional dependence, generally in the form of requesting regularly scheduled private shows and giving presents and cash donations, substantially boosts their income and can sometimes even double it. On the other hand, it is morally hard to accept seeing a fan publicly express his feelings and spend money like water, particularly when the fan's behavior impacts on a person's private life. This was precisely the situation described by one of the best-paid camgirls of our interviewees: one of her regular customers, himself in a steady relationship, spent up to thousands of euros a month on the platform.

Although the camgirls often make the point in the interviews that sexcamming involves consenting, responsible adults, such set phrases barely conceal the emotional strain of the job as reported by Sexypussy, in the business for a year and a half at the time of the interview:

You very quickly run into emotional dependence from some of the viewers. And if you're not equipped for it, if you can't step back, it can be emotionally draining. You have to be able to set limits; set limits with people who are themselves the potential big spenders. So the question becomes: where do I set the limits? Limits are important for your psychological survival. If it's really your job, if you really depend on it, are you going to risk someone no longer coming to your room and spending loads of money on you? Are you going to risk stopping answering him? And if you play a character that has nothing to do with your own personality, can you play her with as much depth and as often as the person wants you to? Personally, that's something I don't do. I don't exactly want to put life and soul into it, you know. (Sexypussy, 26 years old)

The fact that only two interviewees said they allow their customers to say "*I love you*" points to the difficulty of separating private and market spheres and the risks of losing out on the transaction. And for good reason, since it is not just the spectators who suffer from ambiguous feelings. Camgirls themselves sometimes end up getting involved and finding they have feelings for a customer. A number of the interviewees said they had felt attracted to a client at some point in their career:

Basically, I made the mistake of falling into a certain form of intimacy with some. We communicate on Twitter, Snapchat, Skype. It took up a lot, and I mean a lot, of space in my life. So at the end of the day, feelings… Well, you get the picture, yeah…
I'm not sure I understand.
Feelings of friendship got a bit muddled up with the client relationship.
Is it more than friendship sometimes?
It's not love either, you know. I'm really laidback as a person, so people tend to be warm to me. And, at times, it isn't easy. Yes, I see them as friends, but you know… Maybe they don't see it the same way. You just don't know.
Do you mean …

I've already had clients who avoided coming to see me because they too found they had feelings for me. It's not my fault, you know. (Maya Erynys, 40 years old)

These situations often occurred at the start of their career when the girls were single and were not in a steady relationship or were in the midst of a breakup. Sometimes, when the feelings were reciprocated, they say they took the plunge, that is, they met the actual person. Although far from commonplace, these tales point to the potentially performative nature of the myth of amateurism. By the interviewees' accounts, these relationships often turned out to be disappointing if not psychologically damaging, some even seeing them as practically professional misconduct, which they put down to their inexperience. Yet the fact is that these pathways help fuel the image of *the girl next door* and thereby the principle of making an economic return on the activity.

6 Conclusion

Although sexcamming is one of the facets of the development of a new digital sex economy, this booming business is still relatively uncharted territory. By analyzing the drivers for camgirls' engagement in the business and tracing the steps of their professional learning curves, our research offers socioeconomic insights to usefully supplement the studies that consider sexcamming from its political, cultural, and identity angles (Dobson 2008; Senft 2008; Jones 2016; Nayar 2017, etc.). In addition to forming part of the literature on sex work (Weitzer 2009), this chapter contributes to the debates on platform labor (van Doorn 2017) and on the marketization of the domestic universe.

The particular nature of the business is such that working in sexcamming brings intimacy into play: we examine the business entry conditions to show that the first step on the road to entry is the result of a complex convergence of capture devices and a captive audience. Although some camgirls express the pleasure they derive from the job (Jones 2016), the interviews suggest that the main reason for engagement is economic and that making a living from sexcamming demands a considerable investment (physical, temporal, and emotional).

The chapter also looks into the learning processes and systems of use of previously acquired skills on which their business is based. Our case study is interesting in that it shows that it is the negation of the market aspect that guarantees the possibility of marketizing the services on offer. The camgirls' engagement dynamic therefore takes shape in their collective distancing of themselves from classic forms of pornography. As in other cases analyzed in this book, but particularly strikingly here, the commercial aspect is kept at a distance: it is the separation of money and sex that guarantees the authenticity of the service on offer. By broadcasting from home, presenting the activity as a sideline, and, more generally, taking advantage of the gray area between professional and domestic spaces, camgirls take part in spreading a myth of amateurism.

Far from being spontaneous, camgirls' practices and narratives are considered, controlled, and improved over time. The only limits to their individual differentiation strategies are their own inventiveness and their willingness to meet the expectations of Internet users to keep them on board. Although intimate relationships with customers are profitable for the camgirls, they are also often a moral and emotional strain in the long run. Being a hardened professional means learning to keep relations at a good distance, in keeping with the established "feeling rules" (Hochschild 1979). This raises the point of the existence of mismanaged transactions, which become too emotionally involved and can ultimately cost more dearly in psychological terms than they make in monetary terms.

This, together with the question of engagement, begs the question as to the conditions that lead camgirls to leave the world of sexcamming. Do they leave the platforms when new job opportunities crop up? Are these exit logics driven, like the engagement dynamics, by breaks in the life course? Our methodology does not extend to a capacity to investigate the exit phenomena (Ebaugh 1988). However, future research drawing on interviews with former camgirls will surely be able to provide some answers to the question of professional withdrawal from the web platforms.

Appendix

Table 8.1 The interviewees mentioned in the chapter

Pseudonym	Age	Time in sexcamming[a]	Monthly remuneration from sexcamming[b]	Additional paid work[c]
Bluealux	24	6–12 months	≤ €500	Employed on a stud farm
Deborah Seeexmaid	22	1–2 years	≥ €2000	No
Eurydice	27	6–12 months	€1000–€1500	No
Irina Alpha	23	2–5 years	≥ €2000	No
Jade Erotic Dragonfly	24	2–5 years	€500–€1000	No
Kissi Yeeh	29	≤ 6 months	€1500–€2000	No
Maya Crynys	31	2–5 years	€1000–€1500	No
Oksana Kolero	24	≥ 5 years	≥ €2000	No
Ophelia Shibari	45	≤ 6 months	€1000–€1500	No
Padmé Lov	27	6–12 months	€500–€1000	No
SexyPussy	26	6–12 months	€1000–€1500	Waitress (casual work)
Snazzy Ebony	30	6–12 months	€500–€1000	No

[a]The time in sexcamming expresses the time between the date of the first broadcast and the date of the interview

[b]The remuneration data are to be considered with caution. Firstly, income from sexcamming is likely to vary a great deal from one month to the next. Secondly, the figures are estimates based on heterogeneous and sometimes inaccurate information: payments made by the platforms in the last month, annual income calculated as a monthly average, calculation based on the number of hours spent broadcasting over the month, average hourly remuneration estimated by the camgirl, and so on

[c]This criterion denotes all paid non-pornographic work effective at the time of the interview

Notes

1. This work is supported by the French National Research Agency in the framework of the "Investissements d'avenir" program (ANR-15 IDEX-02).
2. The count was made on August 6, 2018. Despite the fact that Ufancyme is a young website with a low volume of hits (858th place in the SimilarWeb ranking of the most visited websites in France), it is a relevant observation

space in which to study sexcamming: many of the camgirls interviewed broadcast on the platform, and a growing number of members of the French-speaking camgirl community seem to be migrating to it.
3. We gratefully acknowledge Clémence Mazard, an intern at the PACTE laboratory, for her valuable help with the launch of the field study in the fall of 2017.
4. As with the state of play in the other digital spaces, a camgirl's pseudonym is an identity marker that positions and differentiates her (Béliard 2009). In order to protect their identity, we have changed the screen names of the sex models quoted, but have tried to keep their spirit (format, sound, cultural references, wordplay, etc.).
5. The *grandes écoles* are top French graduate schools with a highly selective admissions procedure, which are generally reserved for children of the upper classes. See Bourdieu (1997).
6. The earnings analysis is based on the statements of income made during the interviews. Considering the detailed information that most of the camgirls gave us unprompted, we can make the assumption that these statements are truthful. Of the 21 camgirls interviewed, the only two who declined to speak about their earnings are also those with the longest experience in the business (8 years and 13 years, respectively).
7. The passages in quotation marks and italics are excerpts from wording used by camgirls in their work. They may be excerpts from profile pages on the platforms, Twitter accounts, blogs, or chats with Internet users on the platforms.
8. The term *suicide girl* is a reference to the Californian website, SuicideGirls, set up in 2001, which broadcasts photos and videos of naked young women with tattoos and sometimes piercings. *Suicide girls* are part of the Altporn movement, which promotes the do-it-yourself culture in pornography and identifies with alternative cultures (punk and Goth music, skateboarding, etc.) (Attwood 2007).
9. Excerpt from a show broadcast by *Erinyll*, 27 years old, on the Cam4 platform, July 2017.

References

Attwood, F. (2007). No Money Shot? Commerce, Pornography and New Sex Taste Cultures. *Sexualities, 10*(4), 441–456.

Béliard, A.-S. (2009). Pseudos, avatars et bannières: La mise en scène des fans. *Terrains & travaux, 15*, 191–212.

Bernstein, E. (2007). *Temporarily Yours: Intimacy, Authenticity, and the Commerce of Sex.* Chicago: University of Chicago Press.

Bourdieu, P. (1984). *Distinction: A Social Critique of the Judgement of Taste.* Cambridge: Harvard University Press.

Bourdieu, P. (1995). *The Rules of Art. Genesis and Structure of the Literary Field.* Stanford: Stanford University Press.

Bourdieu, P. (1997). *The State Nobility.* Cambridge: Polity Press.

Bourdieu, P., & Delsaut, Y. (1975). Le couturier et sa griffe: Contribution à une théorie de la magie. *Actes de la recherche en sciences sociales, 1*, 7–36.

Bozon, M. (2008). Pratiques et rencontres sexuelles: un répertoire qui s'élargit. In N. Bajos & M. Bozon (Eds.), *Enquête sur la sexualité en France. Pratiques, genre et santé* (pp. 273–295). Paris: La Découverte.

Cruz, E. M., & Sajo, T. J. (2015). Exploring the Cybersex Phenomenon in the Philippines. *The Electronic Journal of Information Systems in Developing Countries, 69*(1), 1–21.

Davies, J. (2013). I Spent a Month Living in a Romanian Sexcam Studio. *Vice.com.* Retrieved February 18, 2019, from https://www.vice.com/en_us/article/mv5e3n/bucharest-webcam-studios-america-outsourcing-sex-trade.

Devereux, G. (1967). *From Anxiety to Method in the Behavioral.* The Hague: Mouton.

Dobson, A. S. (2008). Femininities as Commodities: Cam Girl Culture. In A. Harris (Ed.), *Next Wave Cultures: Feminism, Subcultures, Activism* (pp. 133–148). New York: Routledge.

Duffy, B. (2015). Amateur, Autonomous, and Collaborative: Myths of Aspiring Female Cultural Producers in Web 2.0. *Critical Studies in Media Communication, 32*(1), 48–64.

Ebaugh, H. R. (1988). *Becoming an Ex: The Process of Role Exit.* Chicago: University of Chicago Press.

Greenwood, D. J. (1982). Cultural 'Authenticity'. *Cultural Survival Quarterly, 6*(3), 27–28.

Henry, M. V., & Farvid, P. (2017). 'Always Hot, Always Live': Computer-Mediated Sex Work in the Era of 'Camming'. *Women's Studies Journal, 31*(2), 113–128.

Hochschild, A. R. (1979). Emotion Work, Feeling Rules, and Social Structure. *American Journal of Sociology, 85*(3), 551–575.

Hochschild, A. R. (1983). *The Managed Heart: Commercialization of Human Feeling.* Berkeley: University of California Press.

Hughes, E. C. (1971). Cycles, Turning Points and Careers. In E. Hughes (Ed.), *The Sociological Eye* (pp. 124–131). Chicago: Aldine.

Jones, A. (2015). For Black Models Scroll Down: Webcam Modeling and the Racialization of Erotic Labor. *Sexuality & Culture, 19*(4), 776–799.

Jones, A. (2016). 'I Get Paid to Have Orgasms': Adult Webcam Models' Negotiation of Pleasure and Danger. *Signs: Journal of Women in Culture and Society, 42*(1), 227–256.

Jourdain, A. (2010). La construction sociale de la singularité. Une stratégie entrepreneuriale des artisans d'art. *Revue française de socio-économie, 6*(2), 13–30.

Karpik, L. (2010). *Valuing the Unique: The Economics of Singularities*. Princeton: Princeton University Press.

Knight, B. A. (2000). Watch Me! Webcams and the Public Exposure of Private Lives. *Art Journal, 59*(4), 21–25.

Leadbeater, C., & Miller, P. (2004). *The Pro-Am Revolution: How Enthusiasts are Changing Our Society and Economy*. London: Demos.

Mathews, P. W. (2010). *Asian Cam Models: Digital Virtual Virgin Prostitutes?* Manila: Giraffe Books.

Mauss, M. (1973). Techniques of the Body. *Economy and Society, 2*(1), 70–88.

Mowlabocus, S. (2008). Revisiting Old Haunts Through New Technologies: Public (Homo)Sexual Cultures in Cyberspace. *International Journal of Cultural Studies, 11*(4), 419–439.

Nayar, K. I. (2017). Working It: The Professionalization of Amateurism in Digital Adult Entertainment. *Feminist Media Studies, 17*(3), 473–488.

Riandey, B., & Firdion, J.-M. (1993). Vie personnelle et enquête téléphonique: L'exemple de l'enquête ACSF. *Population, 48*(5), 1257–1280.

Rubin, G. (1984). Thinking Sex: Notes for a Radical Theory of the Politics of Sexuality. In C. Vance (Ed.), *Pleasure and Danger*. Boston and London: Routledge & Kegan Paul.

Sanders, T., Scoular, J., Campbell, R., Pitcher, J., & Cunningham, S. (2017). *Internet Sex Work: Beyond the Gaze*. London: Springer.

Schor, J. B., & Attwood-Charles, W. (2017). The 'Sharing' Economy: Labor, Inequality, and Social Connection on For-Profit Platforms. *Sociology Compass, 11*(8), 1–16.

Senft, T. M. (2008). *Camgirls: Celebrity and Community in the Age of Social Networks*. New York: Peter Lang.

Simon, W., & Gagnon, J. H. (1986). Sexual Scripts: Permanence and Change. *Archives of Sexual Behavior, 15*(2), 97–120.

van Doorn, N. (2017). Platform Labor: On the Gendered and Racialized Exploitation of Low-Income Service Work in the 'On-Demand' Economy. *Information, Communication & Society, 20*(6), 898–914.

van Doorn, N., & Velthuis, O. (2018). A Good Hustle: The Moral Economy of Market Competition in Adult Webcam Modeling. *Journal of Cultural Economy, 11*(3), 177–192.

Weber, F. (1989). *Le Travail à-côté. Etude d'ethnographie ouvrière*. Paris: INRA.

Weitzer, R. (2009). Sociology of Sex Work. *Annual Review of Sociology, 35*, 213–234.

White, M. (2003). Too Close to See: Men, Women, and Webcams. *New Media & Society, 5*(1), 7–28.

Zelizer, V. (2005). *The Purchase of Intimacy*. Princeton: Princeton University Press.

9

Making Money from TV Series: From Viewer to Webmaster with Financial Rewards

Anne-Sophie Béliard

1   Introduction

TV series nowadays have massive followings and enjoy a much improved reputation: American researchers talk about "quality TV" (Feuer 2007), and the French cultural press has created special columns on TV series (Béliard 2015).[1] TV shows are keenly discussed and reviewed on the Internet. Ordinary viewers comment on them, write fanfictions, share subtitles, and rank episodes. New technologies "are enabling average consumers to archive, annotate, appropriate and recirculate media content" (Jenkins 2006). Viewers take part in a "participatory culture": they do not act solely as consumers, but also as contributors and producers working collaboratively.

This development of online activities by viewers concerns "digital working" (Huws 2013). Although fans are driven by the pleasure of sharing their passion for TV series, the economic value of their activities is debatable. Their love of series prompts them to spend time on

---

A.-S. Béliard (✉)
Université Grenoble Alpes, CNRS, Sciences Po Grenoble, PACTE, Grenoble, France
e-mail: anne-sophie.beliard@univ-grenoble-alpes.fr

© The Author(s) 2020
S. Naulin, A. Jourdain (eds.), *The Social Meaning of Extra Money*, Dynamics of Virtual Work, https://doi.org/10.1007/978-3-030-18297-7_9

activities—such as blogging and collaborative databases—which can create value for the series and incomes for them even though such activities are "so new they are not always recognized as work" (Taylor and Luckman 2018: 3). This process raises questions about the relationships between labor and play (Lund 2014) and pleasure and work (Manovich 2001; Bruns 2008), which form the focus of research on "digital labor" (Casilli and Cardon 2015; Scholz 2013). Viewers' online activities could be described as "playbor," a "mix of fun (play) and productive work (labor)" (Citton 2013), since they involve a combination of enjoyment derived from the series and content production (reviewing and ranking). The central issue of this chapter is therefore the tension between "passion" and "money" or "economic value." Since passion is sometimes placed in opposition to economic interest (Bourdieu 1996), this chapter examines the divide between monetization and passionate commitment as two "hostile worlds," to use Zelizer's expression (2011). Why and how do series viewers engage in a process of commodification of passion? Does money change the meaning of passion and, if so, how?

This is an exploration of a relatively uncharted activity: becoming a webmaster of collaborative series websites. Some viewers create and manage websites for series buffs to voice their opinions, such as *BetaSéries*, *trakt.tv*, and *spin-off.fr*. These websites build broad communities and offer a number of services: users can rate seasons and episodes, post comments and reviews, create series files—including cast, production crew, and broadcast date—and produce personal TV schedules and data. They can be described as online databases of series-related information. They include certain participatory methods developed by general and movie databases such as *Allociné*[2] and *IMDb*. Users see these platforms as non-profit economy spaces. Yet these websites have a number of sources of income primarily in the form of advertising, donations, sale of series-related items, and exploitation of user-generated content.

The particularly interesting feature of this case study is that webmasters can monetize both their own activity and the fans' passion (users' free contributions to their website). This particularity ties in with the discussions of "free labor" (Terranova 2000; Fuchs 2008) and "immaterial work" (Lazzarato 1996) which point up the economic exploitation of Internet users and dispossession of their own productive and creative activity (Andrejevic 2013). As Lund explains, "Christian Fuchs and Tiziana Terranova have argued that all of the time and effort devoted to generating 'digital content' on the Internet should be considered a form of immaterial labour, and they emphasize the exploitative character of this unwaged labour" (Lund 2014: 769). In our case, as series viewers discuss their passion online, they produce—and make available for free—an extensive body of information, including private data and personal opinions. The "free labor" provided is at two levels: the webmasters' labor and their potential exploitation of other series buffs' activities on their websites. How does the exploitation of series viewers' free work and passion by other web users generate profits?

This empirical research focuses on male creators of collaborative series websites. Research has shown that the digital platform economy raises gender issues, especially the perpetuation of gender inequalities in digital media industries (Gregg 2008) and the gendered development of an ethos of working for "love" and "passion" (Gill and Pratt 2008). However, this chapter analyzes a male world at the intersection of fan studies and gender studies (Bourdaa and Alessandrin 2017): all the website managers met were men, even though some women were found on the support teams.

The findings cut across a number of questions addressed in this book: How are leisure activities monetized? How does the marketization of recreational activities lead to professionalization? This chapter first explains how taking up webmastering depends on a number of common elements: experience of obstacles as a viewer, a decisive encounter at a defining moment in life, and technical skills. Secondly, it shows that, despite these common features, interviewees are differentiated by their choices of remuneration. The chapter ends with a focus on individual careers and discussion of three ideal-typical professionalization pathways.

Method

Results of this case study are based on a qualitative mixed-methods developed by postdoctoral research at the EMNS—École des Médias et du Numérique de la Sorbonne, Sorbonne School of Media and Digital Studies (2015–2016). The data have been updated for this chapter.

> First, the field survey is based on a one-year "virtual ethnography" (Mason 1999; Hine 2000) of 14 collaborative platforms for French series viewers. The platforms were selected on the basis of three criteria: their collaborative dimension, their interest in series, and their number of visitors.
> Second, semi-directive and in-depth interviews were conducted with ten webmasters regarding their careers, life paths, and practices. The interviewees were city-dwelling, graduate, middle-class men in their 30s, generally in a steady relationship. A couple of factors help explain why the interviewees are male. Webmastering is embedded in the environment of data processing, which is reputedly quite a male world alongside the world of computing (Dagnaud 2018; Collet 2011). In addition, most of the respondents graduated from traditionally male fields of study (engineering college, management school, and computer science).

2 Becoming a Series Website Manager

The interviewees match the figure of "prosumer" (Bruns 2008; Miller 2011; Ritzer et al. 2012) as consumers of series, Internet users, and producers of online content about series. This section focuses on how they become so. It analyzes factors that frame the transition from series viewer to webmaster. Three recurrent elements are found in conjunction.

2.1 A Website to Overcome Obstacles Faced by Series Fans

The interviewees became webmasters on the basis of their own experiences as series viewers. They describe the obstacles they faced as viewers as a key factor in their decision to create a website. The catalyst for the start of their activity was their own experience as viewers. They identify needs and lacks for a better consumption of series. The main trigger was the need for help with choosing the "right" series. One of the main obstacles raised by interviewees is both the wide array of series available and uncertainty about their quality. They became webmasters to provide recommendation devices to reduce uncertainty and facilitate choices:

> *These recommendations, the marks people give series, influence rankings, because you have monthly rankings and annual rankings, so people can consult*

them and from that say to themselves, "I'll start watching this series because so many people on the website have recommended it." (Baptiste, 34 years old)[3]

The way Baptiste describes his website highlights the role of "judging devices" (Karpik 2010) to guide viewers. All interviewees described the start of their activity as a way to help fans choose the "right" series for them from the huge range on offer and to encourage them to express their opinions on the series they watch.

This challenge is related to a second obstacle, the problem of "seriality" (Johnson 2011). Some interviewees highlighted the lack of specific tools to keep track of episodes when they started up their websites:

Alphadrama *was born from an observation of a need, directly inspired by our own experience as viewers. When you watch a series, sometimes you don't really know where you are anymore, you don't know what episode you saw last… It's frustrating. If you follow a number of them at the same time, it's complicated to remember the broadcast dates of new seasons, episodes, etc. In 2008, there wasn't really a French site available for fans to manage their series like that. So that was kind of the origin.* (Jonathan, 28 years old)

This platform does many things, but primarily keeps track of TV shows and movies you watch. (Excerpt from *tracktv* website)

Developing a webmaster activity is a way to address the particular problem of losing track of episodes during a season. Given the time-consuming aspect of series, sites propose devices to rationalize series consumption (broadcast information and calendars):

Alphadrama *is basically first and foremost a monitoring tool. It's really a tool for finding the last episode you watched in the season, picking up your subtitles, etc. In that respect, it's a bit of a rebel website because if you use Alphadrama, it very clearly means you illegally download series.* (Paul, 36 years old)

The third trigger is the viewer's loneliness and need to share his passion. All interviewees use the term "community" to describe their website users. They create websites to help series enthusiasts develop a network of friends with whom they can share information, rates, reviews, and advice.

The decision to start webmastering is determined by the desire to discuss series with other viewers. Stated goals given, in turn, are to "*participate in the community: contribute, react, discuss and make friends*" (*VODkaster*), "*mark episodes you've just watched and discuss them with the community*" (*spin-off.fr*), and "*meet the community*" (*BetaSeries*). This common goal is an extension of a long-standing dynamic. Research highlighted the ability of series to initiate interactions and social ties between viewers before the development of the web (Ang 1985; Brundson 1997; Hills 2002). Webmastering is a new answer to the "imperative need" (Combes 2011) for viewers to talk to each other.

The decision to start a website is therefore rooted in the interviewees' own experiences as viewers. The aim is to get more pleasure out of watching series by facilitating their daily organization and selection as well as social relations with other viewers. Yet this objective also combines with other elements.

2.2   The Importance of Free Time and Collaboration

Life pathways play a major role. Interviewees are between 28 and 46 years old, but they all (with one exception) started their websites when they were younger, in their 20s. Most created them when they were students or at the start of their professional careers when their academic, professional, and social commitments were light enough to enable them to make a significant time investment in webmastering without sacrificing another activity or their love life.

For example, Marc started up his website when he was at journalism school. This coincided with a particular moment in his life when he had free time and little social life. He was single at the time and had a lot of free time to spend watching series and updating his website:

> *When we created the website, I think I was on it all the time, ten hours a day! […] But hey, I'm a geek, I had no social life. I mean, yes, I spent a lot of time on it. I don't know how many hours I spent a day, but, yeah, it took me a long time to get into the social scene. […] I spent a lot of time writing, adding to and expanding the database […] It takes a lot of time, it's boring, but you have to do it. Because there's no point in making an empty website.* (Marc, 33 years old)

Marc's description of this period displays a total passion for series which took up all his time. Yet he does not perceive his investment in the website as a sacrifice, even if it was time-consuming. Note that, unlike other digital activities such as blogging, these interviewees do not tend "to downplay the discipline and investments" (Duffy and Hund 2015: 4) that go into their activity. They all place an emphasis on the time and effort the activity takes, and sometimes even the annoyance of it (*"it's boring"*). However, their narratives regarding the start of their webmaster activity point up the passion-related rewards for their efforts and leave economic stakes to one side. None of them mention an economic need as the reason for becoming a webmaster. Webmastering does not counteract economic insecurity.

This period of life is also a time for meeting and partnering up with people who share the same passion and come on board the series website project. Indeed, each website is now managed by a team of two to twelve people. None of the interviewees created the website on their own:

We started out with three of us, the three founders. I mean, no, we started with a developer, who we hired in the beginning and who is now our technical director. He's in charge of development. (Paul, 36 years old)

Basically, we had three founders. There's my buddy who is currently webmaster, another who's since moved on and me who's a journalist. (Marc, 33 years old)

Creating a series website is not a lonely activity. It is put together by a team of two to three friends who share responsibilities and tasks. For example, Marc was in charge of writing the website's content while his co-founder was responsible for programming and development.

2.3   Possession of Technical Skills

Series websites are therefore built on a division of labor among co-founders. This highlights an important point: webmastering is shaped by individual skills. All the interviewees had complementary technical or academic skills. The interviewees' passion for what they do should not overshadow the "work" side of their activity and the skills it requires:

My buddy, who's webmaster, his profession is web developer. He works in e-commerce. That's really his job. (Marc, 33 years old)

They have all graduated in fields that have given them skills useful to managing series websites such as computer engineering, journalism, film studies, management school, computer science, professional network administration and programming, and management and business creation.

Although today's use of Web 2.0 brings ordinary people to the public stage by removing "the privilege of access to publication that professionals once enjoyed" (Cardon 2010: 9), there are still social inequalities between web users. The interviewees' academic and professional profiles match their leisure activity in terms of management, journalism, and computer programming. Possession or lack of skills reintroduces barriers to entry into the webmaster activity and other new digital occupations such as blogging (Mäkinen 2018) and vlogging (Ashton and Patel 2018).

Common ground drives engagement in a webmaster activity, but the activity is developed taking a player differentiation approach.

3 The "Value" of Passion as a Differentiation Strategy

The main distinguishing feature between series website creators is how they market their passion. They position themselves in relation to one another[4] in terms of the social meaning of passion and money they espouse. This meaning is based on three elements: how they define "their" community by creating original editorial lines; how they monetize their activity; and the strategy of collaboration with dominant players in the TV "world" (Becker 1982).

3.1 Original Editorial Lines to Build Community Loyalty

Series webmasters develop strategies to build a "community," that is, a loyal fan-base of regular users. They share a common concern to differentiate themselves from the professional sphere of journalists and critics. The very idea of community enhances the amateur narrative and practice. The website's success depends on their positioning as intermediaries outside the sphere of professional criticism who take a social and community network approach:

> We realized that the 1.0 take of a journalist talking to an audience was starting to look a little stale. And we also realized between us that the best recommendation you can have is when a friend tells you, "You absolutely have to see this show". It's the strongest tool, it's the strongest driver today for the consumption of a cultural product. We looked on the Web and nobody was doing that, so we said to ourselves, well, we're going to take that approach as our starting point, we're going to forget journalists and create a community of real people. (Paul, 36 years old)

This approach confirms the rise of non-professional narratives against professional prescribers. Its reasoning takes the line that social networks and participative websites can fulfill a function of certification of the quality of cultural and media goods, long guaranteed by publishers (Gensollen 2001). It also underlines the logic of marketizing amateurism found in other digital spaces, such as Brasseur and Finez show in their chapter on camgirls.

This common approach also appears to be a way of distinguishing between interviewees. They position themselves in relation to the general level of community ties and social networking in their activity:

> We only do that, we're only community-based, so it's better than something like Allociné. [...] Allociné *has a problem in that it's got a lot of coexisting content and functions, so the community aspect is obviously not dealt with as well as on our website because that's all we do.* [...] Alphadrama, *to my knowledge, has little or no social dimension. You don't have your friends on* Alphadrama. *Well you can have them, but there is no social networking side as there is with ours.* (Paul, 36 years old)

The social network aspect is a key factor in player differentiation. Some players like Paul work this aspect to the maximum to attract as many users as possible. Other interviewees like Marc bank on a smaller, but cohesive and active, community of dedicated members. This approach is based on a "militant" strategy of promoting lesser known series passed over in silence by their competitors. It is part of an editorial and advocacy project for series that is at odds with the most prominent narratives put across by professionals and other collaborative series websites:

> *Because basically, it's not the successful shows that need help. […] There are great series that are unknown because they're either not in English or they're culturally scorned for many reasons, there are many factors. And I think we brought that out at some point. Yes, back then, I think we had a militant website.* (Marc, 33 years old)

This strategy is based on a strict control of fans' participation. For example, Baptiste strictly controls ratings and reviews with the calculation of a reliability index, which identifies "poor" contributors and encourages users to justify their contributions:

> *Other websites, like* Culture and Reviews, *are really just libraries. We didn't want to create a library. We wanted to create an editorialized social network, which is not the same thing. So we wanted to find systems that don't just make it fun, it's not just, "Oh I love this show so much" when you've only seen ten minutes of it. Our goal isn't just to have a lot of people rating, actually, we don't care. The idea isn't to attract billions of Internet users, the goal is for people to talk about series, exchange ideas, defend their arguments and fight in comments, but in a very civilized way.* (Baptiste, 34 years old)

Editorial strategies therefore take two different approaches: (i) a quantitative approach with respect to an "attention economy" (Simon 1971) whereby the consumer's attention is a rare resource for which economic players compete (Goldhaber 1997; Davenport and Beck 2001), or (ii) a qualitative approach whereby webmasters select their community members to assure themselves of what they see as more qualitative judgments and discussions of series:

> *It's true that the highest-ranking series are the ones with the highest ratings and best quality. There are no "crappy" series at the very top of our ranking. Because we're a quality-based website. […]. I've already seen competing websites include*

> in their top three […] series that we don't consider to be at all relevant for top quality ranking, precisely because there is no such mass effect. […] People didn't need to justify themselves, there was no physical follow-up, so it was not at all qualitative. (Baptiste, 34 years old)

The differentiation strategy is related to the ability to produce an identifiable editorial line by offering different rating, commenting, and networking devices. Editorial lines shape a website's reputation. All interviewees speak in the plural when describing their activity. Indeed, unlike other digital occupations, this activity does not rely on self-representation. Whereas research evidences the promotional nature of bloggers' activities and even a production of the self and of the career (Nathanson 2014), these interviewees do not build their own personal reputation. In fact, their civil identities are not always presented on their website. Their "work" doesn't go "into obtaining and maintaining the production of the self-brand" (Duffy and Hund 2015), but into producing a *collective* identity and reputation for their website and community. This is what interviewees potentially monetize.

3.2 Making a Profit Without Marketizing Fans' Digital Work: Passion and Money, Two "Hostile Worlds"?

Most of the websites studied money without directly exploiting *user-generated content*. The primary source of income is advertising. They generally select advertising agencies for their economic profitability:

> I'm not even sure if you have series- or movie-oriented ads, because I think we had dating website ads for ages […] [My associate] is trying to increase our website's income. He's trying to make more money without necessarily having more advertising, because there are agencies that are more interesting economically speaking. (Marc, 33 years old)

So the websites' advertisements have no connection with the series. The remuneration strategy involves weeding out the least reliable and most "*intrusive*" (Baptiste, 34 years old) advertisements that can put off users. One of the main criteria is to avoid disturbing users so as to preserve the collaborative logic on which the websites are based. The choice of funding is based on the website's status. The smallest and most confidential websites, the ones building a cohesive "fan-base," join advertising agencies. Their incomes remain very low: 1500 euros per year on average, according to Marc.

Some webmasters forego advertising earnings and make a call for donations instead. This funding model takes a "gift" and "counter-gift" line (Mauss 2002 [1925]). Series buffs are asked for a monetary contribution in exchange for the services that the webmasters provide. Rejection of advertising ties in with a more ideological rationale of unwaged immaterial labor. Even though these interviewees have commodified their activity, they set limits: they refuse to be economically dependent on (to "belong to") major structures:

> *As you will have noticed, BetaSeries is a completely free and ad-free website. Neither are we part of a large group. The website is developed and moderated by volunteers in their own time and the servers are currently hosted free of charge.* (Excerpt from the *BetaSéries* website)

This type of funding reflects a kind of romantic idea of a passion as being free from material injunctions. It ties in with a non-economic concept of a passion, which assumes that money debases or distorts a passion. The people who defend this position were the most passionate interviewees and the first to create collaborative series websites in France. Money does not "interest" them (*"We don't do this for money"*), even though they do sometimes reevaluate how they relate to the money based on the time investment their activity demands. This finding reveals a divide between the entrepreneurial logic and the value of passion. This conception of passion echoes the anti-economy of "pure" art identified by Bourdieu (1996), which is in tension with the logic of economic profit on the market. A passion for series goes hand in hand with free exchanges or sharing and community-building. This concept recalls the early Utopian idea of the Internet based on a horizontal, democratic ideal of communication.

These business models generate very little money (from 1500 to 6000 euros per year). They appear to operate in a divide between two "hostile worlds" (Zelizer 2011): the world of passion and the fan community is not exactly what Zelizer calls "intimacy," but the interviewees perceive it as a world separate from economic exploitation and monetary profit. Commodification creates tension between the valuation and devaluation of passion. This ambivalent relationship to money is based on a complex relationship with the world of professional series.

3.3 Exploiting Other Fans' Passion in Order to Earn a Living: Series Viewers as Part of the Series Market

Our interviewees are divided in their attitudes toward dominant economic players in the series field. Some of them develop an "economic angle" to their activity with the economic exploitation of passion. This economic angle is developed by the most visible and visited websites. Their managers can deal with producers and broadcasters because they have a large community of users. Three types of remuneration are involved here.

First, a few webmasters develop an alternative advertising model based on direct collaboration with the series producers. This does not involve working with advertising agencies, but canvassing series distributors to whom the webmasters propose to spread "word-of-mouth" about their products in exchange for their financial participation. These interviewees define themselves as new entrants in the series landscape:

> *You can't canvass advertisers enough. It's the sinews of war! That's what I deal with every day. We approach professionals a lot. Especially since we're a new medium so we need to penetrate the market [...] So there's a lot of work done on this and also on spreading the word, since the mechanics we propose are not the same as other media websites. [...] For months now, we've also had advertisers calling us, but we've been talking to a captive sector, which are basically film distributors, game publishers and series distributors. Ultimately, there's not an incredible number of players. There are four or five series broadcasters in France.* (Gabriel, 36 years old)

In this model, interviewees collaborate with the professional world of series by monetizing fans' passion. This echoes a basic attention economy rationale whereby webmasters sell the attention of their users, the members of their community, to TV industry players:

> *The majority of our turnover today comes from advertising, but with a particular twist because we are not into the traditional processes. Basically, we offer entertainment companies, film distributors, game publishers and series broadcasters mechanisms where we encourage the spread of word-of-mouth about their products. All our actions target the one goal of maximum member interaction with the series and as much member input as possible. Since the more input from people on the series, the more popular the series will be, be it the most awaited series or the series of the moment.* (Gabriel, 36 years old)

Second, a few interviewees are developing the—as-yet nascent—monetization of fans' contributions. They are developing economic alliances with major structures by exploiting and selling *user-generated content* collected on their websites. Such is the case with webmasters who provide audiovisual groups with access, for a fee, to the original content produced by their users. They sell access to their global data and all comments, reviews, and rankings posted by fans. They monetize the recuperation of anonymous data and negotiate their prices directly with their business partners:

> *We've also been monetizing data for some time now. Watch out, there's a scary word. We don't sell anything private. That's in our terms of use, it's in our charter. […] But we do sell general data, so we sell our ratings, our best reviews and the like to VOD platforms. But it's still marginal. […] We have an API used by Canal Sat, filmoTV, nolinefilm and soon other players to easily retrieve average scores, the distribution of scores and the best reviews so they can post them on their own site.* (Paul, 36 years old)

> *We all intuitively discern the value that fans' contributions bring. And TV series have the advantage over films of lasting over time and so it can create a very strong communitarization (My Warner).* (Frédéric, 46 years old)

In this data exploitation model, series buffs' contributions assume economic value. TV channels, broadcasters, and producers pay for access to the anonymous fan-generated content collected by webmasters and use it

9 Making Money from TV Series: From Viewer to Webmaster... 253

on their own interfaces. This strategy takes an approach to the exploitation of personal data, which forms a pillar of economic models today while raising the issue of data protection on the basis of facilitating user expression on digital platforms (Gillespie 2010).

Lastly, webmasters may be paid by audiovisual groups to produce trend analyses on their sample of users. Publication analysis provides information on current successes, expectations, what viewers like and dislike about series, and so forth. These data have a particular value in the audiovisual field for making market trend predictions (Mishne and Glance 2006). They generate information on viewer profiles and desires. In this model, webmasters are remunerated for processing fans' contributions:

> *It's happened a few times. We've conducted assignments for audiovisual groups. They contact us and ask us for a trend analysis based on the data we have. So we've done it a few times, but protecting viewers' identities obviously [...]. They're one-off assignments commissioned by audiovisual companies.* (Jean, 28 years old)

Players are hence hired by channels and producers to develop tools to process and display users' online contributions. However, this model remains small scale. The series websites studied here are still somewhat an innovation in the series landscape. The interviewees reported that professionals are not used to the idea of calling on their services yet. This kind of cooperation calls for both webmasters and channels or producers to enter into a learning process to develop tools to process these collaborative websites' user-generated content. This brings up the issue of public emancipation on the Internet, with its "new interdependencies that force [the cultural industries] to dialogue and interact with amateur productions" (Cardon 2011).

However, the monetization of fan-generated content is harshly criticized by the interviewees who adhere to a non-economic concept of passion and point up strained relations with TV professionals. Some players are reluctant to conclude trade agreements with dominant TV players. They express a certain distrust of the professional series world:

> *Our relations with the channels are somewhat superficial with a general press release, press officer [...] Apart from Canal + with which we've had some*

dealings at times, but still today Canal + is not clear in its dealings with blogs, generally series bloggers. And even France TV is getting involved with some bloggers. I don't think there's a very healthy relationship between bloggers in general and broadcasters. (Gabriel, 35 years old)

Reluctance to monetize content is also based on a fear of the webmasters' work being "hijacked" by major companies and the editorial constraint this might impose. This independence is sometimes referred to as integrity. The most militant interviewees stress the need to separate the financial from the editorial. Independence is valued as a guarantee of quality:

Allociné *have a lot of problems, because they are very popular. They have a lot of problems with comments and even in their dealings with promotion. […] You see, there, they don't separate editorial from advertising, let's call it interdependencies, very clearly. And* Webedia's *buyout didn't help. But at the same time, when they sold to Webedia, I don't think the editorial staff was under any illusions. […] But it's true that when it comes down on your head, it sucks. […] Clearly, if* Culture and Review *could take* Allociné's *place as an independent organization, why not?* (Marc, 33 years old)

Dealings with professionals draw a dividing line between individuals. The more passionate proportion of the interviewees suspect financial dealings with professionals of undermining platform neutrality. They believe that users who have economic dealings with professionals lose their reflexivity. The influence of financiers biases comments and discredits fans' activity. The interviewees establish a symbolic hierarchy between websites working on behalf of producers and advertisers and more financially autonomous platforms that retain their editorial freedom. This dividing line redraws a classic distinction in the sociology of culture between "independent" and mainstream players.

Their contempt for the marketization of passion is related to a critique of commodification as an exploitation of fans' digital work. As "true" fans themselves, some of our interviewees regret the lack of recognition of fans' investment. They manage websites true to the ideal of a crowdsourcing culture. Their practices and commitment echo the imaginary of universal knowledge-sharing and subculture that underpinned the Internet's beginnings (Depoorter 2013; Flichy 2001). They value the sharing economy model (Rifkin 2014). They see monetization as being at odds with the community spirit in which they created their platform. Managing a series website calls for a collective investment. Their activity helps build a "reflexive community" (Marc, 33 years old) on series to which everyone should be able to contribute. This position explains their attitude to money and exhibits a "horizontal" conception of Internet 2.0.

This differentiation paves the way for different professionalization pathways depending on how the webmasters use earnings. Digital activities imply different kinds of monetization, but how can they become a profession?

4 Three Professionalization Pathways: A Graduated Scale of Marketization

This last section analyzes how remuneration choices are driven by individual careers. Recent studies of digital labor analyze "the implications of transforming amateur engagement into professional work" (Taylor and Luckman 2018: 4). In our case, we can identify three different levels of engagement in a professional career built around the webmaster activity. A tripartite typology of the levels is proposed, illustrated by three major series websites in France and based on interviewees' actual professional status, how they use earnings and describe their activity, and the connection with their private life.

4.1 Non-professional Militant "Geeks": Passion Above All Else? The Case of *Crossover*

The first profile is that of an intense attachment to series. *Crossover* is managed by immense fans of series. Its creators, Marc (33, journalist) and Baptiste (34, web designer), have loved and watched series since they were teenagers. Watching and commenting on series is one of their main pastimes. They define themselves as "geeks" with specific, non-mainstream tastes in series.

They describe their activity as an "activist deed" to promote an alternative way of seeing and talking about series. This profile coincides with a strict editorial line based on a small, active fan-base, as previously described, which is incompatible with working with channels or producers. Webmasters need a sufficiently large and representative sample of contributors to be able to deliver trend analysis that can be used by audiovisual groups. This is not the case with those who target niche audiences in a community spirit:

> *It's obviously complicated to draw trends from a website that teaches you about yourself in some way. [...] And we're too small a sample. When I tell you we've got 300, 400 members, can you call it a trend? I don't know. Even if not all of the 300, 400 of us are "hardcore", we're hardcore anyway compared to the public at large, we're geeks. Although there are differences within the group, compared to the population of M6 or TF1 viewers at 8.30 pm, this group is totally alien, it's in a bubble!.* (Marc, 33 years old)

Marc sees this source of income as incompatible with his editorial policy concentrating on a small audience of fans who do not watch mainstream series. In addition to the non-representativeness of their community, this source of income is at odds with this profile's conception of "amateur."

In this profile, militant commitment frames the relationship with monetization. They rely exclusively on sources of income that do not imply exploiting their users' contributions. They do not see managing *Crossover* as a professional occupation. They argue that they do it on an unwaged voluntary basis (*"We're all volunteers," "We do this on a voluntary basis," "We don't get paid"*). In fact, they stress the very low level of income they earn from it:

> *In terms of audience, we get between 6,000 and 10,000 visitors per day; we are almost up to 20,000 pages viewed per day. [...] In economic terms, we earn 1,500 euros a year. Internet hosting costs us 50 euros, more or less. So the money can end up being pretty much nothing. But we don't do it for money either,*

9 Making Money from TV Series: From Viewer to Webmaster…

that's the thing! […] We do it on a voluntary basis! You see, when it earns 1,500 euros, I make 500 euros a year! So… Considering our investment in it, it's not much. And yet, a good part of the money goes to the most regular contributors. We donate, we give some back, around 100 euros per person. It's not a lot but, well… We give 100 euros per person, and we give that to 3 or 4 people in total […] And we get to pay the servers. And it also compensates us a little bit for the time we spend on it. (Marc, 33 years old)

Marc describes webmastering as a voluntary activity, but points out the time and effort involved. It is this mix between "work" and "involvement" that defines the activity as "volunteer work" (Simonet 2010). Commodification provides extra income used to finance the leisure activity. Incomes are almost entirely reinvested in the website. They are used in two ways: to pay hosting fees and to pay the most active users in recompense for their involvement. In this way, the webmasters recognize the value produced by the users. This particular use of income provides an economic reward for their community members' free labor. These players develop a critical vision of merchandization as a form of mercantilism and capitalistic exploitation. They are the most critical of the exploitation of fans' passion by webmasters and professional players.

This use endorses the notion that fans' online participation is "work" that can justify remuneration. Whatever the sums earned, they are described first and foremost as an endorsement of their free work and their commitment to series. Earnings come merely as an added extra compared to their aspirations for the symbolic recognition of their passion. They form a way to keep up the recreational activity without losing money and to display their attachment to series. This case illustrates the fact that it is "possible to marry the economic and leisure understandings of volunteering" (Stebbins 2013: 340–341) as long as the remuneration is low.

This profile displays some money-earning micro-strategies—such as choosing the most profitable advertising agencies—but the predominance of a militant involvement implies an absence of any real monetization policy. They do not set up actual business operating systems or even a formal remuneration system. Only one of the two creators of *Crossover*, the official webmaster, has micro-enterprise status in order to manage earnings:

It's got micro-enterprise status, which is managed by the webmaster. So obviously he's giving me money I'm not supposed to get, which is totally illegal (laugh). *But it's okay, I don't think I'll be turned over to the tax authorities for 500 euros. It's just financial stuff, that's all.* (Marc, 33 years old)

These interviewees see the time they spend on this activity as competing with their "real" working hours and social life. They work mostly as freelancers or self-employed workers. Webmastering is therefore constrained by their schedules and motivation. As their professional and social activities increase, the time spent on the website decreases. Managing a website is no longer a priority as other spheres of social life develop alongside their love for series:

It's just that now I don't have time to do this anymore and I don't think I want it. I've moved on in life [...]. Spending my unpaid time on a website, moderating, managing disputes between members, etc. It's all a bit senseless after a while. And it takes time, more to the point. [...] Now I'm less of a geek! I'm starting to get a life outside of it and all those sorts of things I didn't fucking know about at the time! And then I started working, I moved on. (Marc, 33 years old)

Moderating and managing a website is an expression of these players' passion for series. As the activity remains a leisure activity, they cut back their free investment to the advantage of their professional and private life. Incomes reward their time investment to some extent, but earnings are too low to keep them permanently motivated:

It's true I'd hardly worked on it since 2015, even though I got back to it a bit last summer. And now I've been working on it a lot for the last two weeks. [...] On a daily basis, I can't say exactly how much because there are days when I don't work on it at all and others when I spend a little bit of time checking episodes, looking at the audience. [...] It's a bit complicated when you have a job. (Baptiste, 34 years old)

They do not turn their leisure activity in "love-work" (Cross 2018). It remains a side job with very little income. However, it does provide other forms of reward, especially symbolic recognition of their passion and useful skills for their professional career. Indeed, managing a website has enabled Marc to test and deepen his skills in journalism:

> *My journalism school was* Crossover, *which means that my journalism school didn't teach me much compared to what I learned from* Crossover. (Marc, 33 years old)

The symbolic recompense comes from both professionals and fans. Interviewees explain how some channels like Canal + are *"interested in us."* Some of them have even been invited to events, such as festivals, and to participate in round tables on series. Yet the most important symbolic recompense comes from the members of their community. They describe in the interviews how fans thank them for their "work" (*"We have a lot of people coming back to us saying, 'Thank you for being there to advise us on shows'"*). Even if monetization can be a way to recognize the free labor and value it, this recognition is more symbolic than economic due to the small amount of money involved.

4.2 Semi-professional Series Website Managers: *Alphadrama*'s Start-up Model

This profile defines series buffs who watch ongoing series, especially on streaming, but not with the same militant involvement as the first profile. *Alphadrama* is managed essentially on a voluntary basis by amateurs. However, Jonathan and his team have gradually developed strategies to earn money to both keep their activity going and make it profitable.

These strategies are based on three elements: rejection of advertising, call for donations, and exploitation of fans' contributions. Donations are stimulated by a device on the interface that states the website's monetary needs. Income is reinvested in website management and used to remunerate the team. If donations are non-existent, the activity continues on a voluntary basis. The higher the donation, the more the activity is rewarded:

> *We put a donation gauge at the top of the website, which you can see at all times, as an indicator of the website's current costs and to help develop it. This*

gauge indicates the health status of Alphadrama. *It is reset every quarter. If it reaches 100%, that means the website will continue to grow as it should. If it doesn't reach 100%, the site won't die, but it means it hasn't reached its targets and will continue to rely mainly on volunteers and their free time.* (Jonathan, 28 years old)

This strategy is conducted for the smooth running of the website and remuneration of volunteers. However, *Alphadrama* is not perceived as a leisure activity in the long term. Jonathan explains his wish for the voluntary phase to be temporary. Marketization is not the main goal at website start-up, but the success of series and hence the success of series networks creates windows of opportunity that prompt him to consider professionalization in the field:

For the time being, we still work with volunteers, but in the long run, the ideal would be to be paid regularly for assignments like that, commissioned by the audiovisual groups. We're trying to develop that activity for the future. Yes, ideally, it would be the goal, to earn a living from it. (Jonathan, 28 years old)

Much like the fashion bloggers studied by Duffy and Hund, Jonathan's "passion is no longer just a driver or a byproduct of new media work, but also a means of rationalizing individualized success" (2015: 5). Such is the case with the monetization by means of one-off contracts with audiovisual groups. *Alphadrama*'s webmaster seeks to develop a commodified activity as a permanent source of income and a way of turning his team into professionals.

This trend to convert a leisure activity into a full-time income-earning activity is largely associated with the status of project leader in the case of *Alphadrama*. He likes and watches series. However, the development of digital platforms based on Internet users' participation is his professional activity. He is a professional network administrator and programmer, and a graduate in management and business start-up studies. He heads a company that develops services and websites. He developed *Alphadrama* on the basis of a start-up model in 2008 with entrepreneur status. Managing a *series* website is not his main line of work, but developing websites is. He has created other collaborative platforms alongside

Alphadrama. That explains why his current ambition is to develop the website as a business concern and turn his team of volunteers into employees.

Although *Alphadrama*'s creator hopes his website will become a real source of income, he has not created it solely to make money. The monetization strategy appears to be driven by an opportunity effect: audiovisual production groups came to him with requests, and he seized the opportunity to earn money from his website. Opportunities arise out of the interest that channels and producers show in the website's activity.

4.3 A Strategic Use of Passion: The Business Manager Figure of *Culture and Review*

The third profile is one of complete professionalization. The webmaster activity becomes both the main income for the individuals and their professional activity. At this point, the passion for series becomes secondary to working. Those interviewees develop a strategic approach to passion. *Culture and Review*'s creator explains that he—and his co-founders—identified a "market niche" created by the need for amateurs to have access to rankings, advice, and reviews. They developed the activity as a business. In this case, all the website's team members are employees. Earnings are used to pay the team wages:

> *We have employees. They are all employees. I don't know anyone who works for free* (laughs). *No, it's a real company. Wait… Look! You've got the camera?* [He shows the office on the webcam] *There you go, this is Culture and Review. These are the people here. So, yes, we have employees and all that. We're a real company. We've got about a dozen people, basically. A lot of developers, a few administrative and marketing staff.* (Gabriel, 36 years old)

This profile consists in the website's creator becoming an entrepreneur and hiring employees to keep the business running at a profit. The website's commodification is based on a number of forms of income. It is initially financed by own resources, which gives creators a form of autonomy and freedom:

We funded the project ourselves. So we didn't have the pressure of an investor who might say, 'You have to have these audience figures by the end of the year, this turnover, and so on'. We had the luxury of being able to organize ourselves as we liked. But there's also the flipside: when you gamble your own money, you don't sleep as well at night. You have less margin for error than with other people's money. (Paul, 36 years old)

However, economic profitability becomes the prime concern as soon as the website is launched. The pursuit of financing and monetary profitability has steadily become Paul's main job:

And then, well, my job is to be a salesman and sell all those things. That's my job. […] I mean, I'm the boss so I manage the company every day but the real task is to monetize the site, yes. (Paul, 36 years old)

Monetizing the activity becomes a professional activity. In this case, the exploitation of users' contributions becomes the main income. This strategy is developed by individuals who aim from the outset to earn a living from the activity. Their preparations for the launch of the website are based on the goal of immediate profit:

The problem with a social network is that if you go and there's no one there, you leave. […]. We managed to create a community before we launched the website. It wasn't huge, a few hundred, a few thousand people who followed the project's progress more or less. And then we went through a beta phase with seats that we gradually allotted. We marketed the product. We tried to create a want and a rare quality surrounding people lucky enough to test Culture and Review. *[…] So a little buzz was created around it. […] The site was closed to the public and the community was built up over a number of months, so when the site was fully opened in late 2010/early 2011, it was already up and running. When you went onto the website, there were already notices up, things were already happening.* (Paul, 36 years old)

Paul describes a commercial strategy to promote the website. The way he speaks about his activity underscores his economic approach to monetizing passion. He uses business jargon (*"market niche," "rare," "window of opportunity," "marketed the product"*), which sets his professional attitude apart from the first two profiles in the typology. The task in this profile consists in establishing collaboration with leading TV players and attracting users. His success shows how series websites attract the attention of marketers and companies. This reflects a recognized strategy with respect to blogging: the targeting of bloggers "by digital marketers and consultants as 'key influencers' of consumption" (Adkins and Dever 2016: 14 regarding Taylor's contribution).

This strategy ties in with the individual's professional and educational background. *Culture and Review's* creators are web developers and business school graduates. These interviewees are professional managers for whom a series website is a line of business. Earnings from collaboration with TV companies and marketers become the main source of income and pay 12 employees' wages.

5 Conclusion

This chapter focuses on the implications of monetizing passion and turning it into a source of income. It investigates the leisure activities of male series viewers and shows how they monetize both their own activity and fans' digital labor. Three main findings are presented.

First, there are the social circumstances in which viewers become webmasters. We show that collaborative series websites are not set up by just any series viewers or fans. This underpins the idea that the Internet is not an egalitarian network of symmetrical and fundamentally democratic relations between Internet users. Webmastering is based on a reflexive approach to viewers' obstacles and is developed by viewers when they have free time and meet future associates. They all have specific skills that they can use to invest in the Internet as webmasters.

Second, all the interviewees distance themselves from the professional sphere of series reviews and journalism, but become differentiated when they start to commodify their activity. Their remuneration choices form the point of differentiation. Our interviewees set up websites for pleasure in order to share their passion, but this activity is not just "for fun." It has both material costs (hosting fees) and symbolic costs (time and energy) and can produce some valuable content. We present two alternate strategies of monetizing webmastering and monetizing users' activities. These two strategies overlap with individual political positions on the value of passion. For the most passionate interviewees, passion is deconsecrated by putting a price—and therefore constraints—on tastes and leisure activities. This reveals ambiguous relationships with money and with TV channels, production studios, and commercial companies. Using the fans' contributions to their websites to make trade agreements with TV professionals is seen as exploitation of the fans' free work.

Third, the business models they develop give rise to varying degrees of professionalization. Minimal incomes are used to finance or compensate the costs of the activity (material costs and time investment), but they can become the interviewees' main source of income. We propose a tripartite typology to illustrate how some viewers turn themselves into professional web managers while the most passionate refuse to turn their webmaster activity into "emotional and affective labor" (Gregg 2011; Luckman 2015). This raises the question as to the ideal of horizontal communication on digital platforms by showing how some users can make a profit from other users. However, whatever their profile, webmasters do not describe their activity as a form of social upgrading. They do not see it as a way of acquiring a specific social status. For the most business-oriented people, webmastering is part of their occupation. For "volunteers," it is a way to create a value for and cultivate their passion.

The fact that a few of the interviewees have turned their passion into a profession ultimately takes issue with the statement that what "contemporary workers all appear to have in common is an ambition to follow their own values and, even more, to organize their own lives in their own ways" (Taylor and Luckman 2018: 12). They actually create new digital platform models and even new business models. However, our interviewees belong to a quite privileged category of the population as white, middle-class men. More generally, this research shows that digital activities do not represent free and equal forms of participation and profits for all web users.

Appendix

Table 9.1 The interviewees mentioned in the chapter

Pseudonym	Age	Sex	Main profession	Maturity of online activity
Baptiste	34	M	Web developer	9 years
Frédéric	46	M	Advertising director	4 years
Gabriel	36	M	Marketer	5 years
Jean	29	M	Web developer	8 years
Jonathan	28	M	Network programmer	8 years
Marc	33	M	Journalist	9 years
Paul	36	M	Web manager	5 years

Notes

1. This work is supported by the French National Research Agency in the framework of the "Investissements d'Avenir" program (ANR-15-IDEX-02).
2. This website provides information on cinema and DVD films and their scheduling.
3. All names have been changed to protect the person's identity, with the sole exception of an excerpt from the official Website's presentation.
4. They do not know each other personally, but they know each other's websites.

References

Adkins, L., & Dever, M. (Eds.). (2016). *The Post-Fordist Sexual Contract: Working and Living in Contingency*. Basingstoke: Palgrave Macmillan.

Andrejevic, M. (2013). Estranged Free Labor. In T. Scholz (Ed.), *Digital Labor. The Internet as Playground and Factory* (pp. 149–164). New York: Routledge.

Ang, I. (1985). *Watching Dallas: Soap Opera and the Melodramatic Imagination*. New York: Routledge.

Ashton, D., & Patel, K. (2018). Vlogging Careers: Everyday Expertise, Collaboration and Authenticity. In S. Taylor & S. Luckman (Eds.), *The New Normal of Working Lives: Critical Studies in Contemporary Work and Employment* (pp. 147–168). Basingstoke: Palgrave Macmillan.

Becker, H. S. (1982). *Art Worlds*. Berkeley: University of California Press.

Béliard, A.-S. (2015). When Cultural Criticism Blurs Cultural Hierarchies. *Journalism Practice, 9*(6), 907–923.

Bourdaa, M., & Alessandrin, A. (Eds.). (2017). *Fan Studies/Gender Studies: La Rencontre.* Paris: Téraèdre.

Bourdieu, P. (1996). *Rules of Art: Genesis and Structure of the Literary Field.* Stanford: Stanford University Press.

Brundson, C. (1997). *Screen Tastes: Soap Opera to Satellite Dishes.* London: Routledge.

Bruns, A. (2008). *Blogs, Wikipedia, Second Life, and Beyond: From Production to Produsage.* New York: Peter Lang.

Casilli, A., & Cardon, D. (2015). *Qu'est-ce que le Digital Labor ?* Bry-sur-Marne: INA.

Cardon, D. (2010). *La Démocratie Internet. Promesses et limites.* Paris: Seuil.

Cardon, D. (2011). Réseaux sociaux de l'Internet. *Communications, 88*(1), 141–148.

Citton, Y. (2013). Économie de l'attention et nouvelles exploitations numériques. *Multitudes, 54*(3), 163–175.

Collet, I. (2011). Effet de genre: le paradoxe des études d'informatique. *Tic&société, 5*(1), Retrieved February 18, 2019, from http://journals.openedition.org/ticetsociete/955.

Combes, C. (2011). La consommation des séries à l'épreuve d'Internet. *Réseaux, 165*, 137–163.

Cross, K. (2018). From Visual Discipline to Love-Work: The Feminising of Photographic Expertise in the Age of Social Media. In S. Taylor & S. Luckman (Eds.), *The New Normal of Working Lives: Critical Studies in Contemporary Work and Employment* (pp. 65–86). Basingstoke: Palgrave Macmillan.

Dagnaud, M. (2018). Internet, une passion masculine. *Le Débat, 200*(3), 123–142.

Davenport, T. H., & Beck, J. C. (2001). *The Attention Economy: Understanding the New Currency of Business.* Harvard: Harvard Business Press.

Depoorter, G. (2013). La communauté du logiciel libre. Espace contemporain de reconfiguration des luttes? In B. Frère & M. Jacquemain (Eds.), *Résister au quotidien* (pp. 133–160). Paris: Presses de Sciences Po.

Duffy, B. E., & Hund, E. (2015). "Having It All" on Social Media: Entrepreneurial Femininity and Self-Branding among Fashion Bloggers. *Social Media + Society, 1*(2), 1–11.

Feuer, J. (2007). HBO and the Concept of Quality TV. In J. McCabe & K. Akass (Eds.), *Quality TV: Contemporary American Television and Beyond* (pp. 145–157). New York and London: I.B. Tauris.

Flichy, P. (2001). *L'imaginaire d'Internet*. Paris: La Découverte.
Fuchs, C. (2008). Class and Exploitation on the Internet. In T. Scholz (Ed.), *Digital Labor. The Internet as Playground and Factory* (pp. 211–224). New York: Routledge.
Gensollen, M. (2001). Internet. Marché électronique ou réseaux commerciaux? *Revue Economique, 52*(1), 137–161.
Gill, R., & Pratt, A. (2008). In the Social Factory? Immaterial Labour, Precariousness and Cultural Work. *Theory Culture & Society, 25*(7–8), 1–30.
Gillespie, T. (2010). The Politics of 'Platforms'. *New Media & Society, 12*(3), 347–364.
Goldhaber, M. H. (1997). The Attention Economy and the Net. *First Monday, 2*(4). Retrieved February 18, 2019, from https://firstmonday.org/article/view/519/440.
Gregg, M. (2008). The Normalisation of Flexible Female Labour in the Information Economy. *Feminist Media Studies, 8*, 285–299.
Gregg, M. (2011). *Work's Intimacy*. Cambridge: Polity Press.
Hills, M. (2002). *Fan Cultures*. London: Routledge.
Hine, C. (2000). *Virtual Ethnography*. London: Sage Publications.
Huws, U. (2013). Working Online, Living Offline: Labour in the Internet Age. *Work Organisation Labour and Globalisation, 7*(1), 1–11.
Jenkins, H. (2006). *Fans, Bloggers and Gamers, Exploring Participatory Culture*. New York: University Press.
Johnson, D. (2011). Devaluing and Revaluing Seriality: The Gendered Discourses of Media Franchising. *Media, Culture & Society, 33*(7), 1077–1093.
Karpik, L. (2010). *Valuing the Unique: The Economics of Singularities*. Princeton: Princeton University Press.
Lazzarato, M. (1996). Immaterial Labor. In P. Virno & M. Hardt (Eds.), *Radical Thought in Italy: A Potential Politics* (pp. 133–147). Minneapolis: University of Minnesota Press.
Luckman, S. (2015). *Craft and the Creative Economy*. Hampshire: Palgrave Macmillan.
Lund, A. (2014). Playing, Gaming, Working and Labouring: Framing the Concepts and Relations. *Three C. Communication, Capitalism & Critique. Open Access Journal for a Global Sustainable Information Society, 12*(2), 735–801.
Mäkinen, K. (2018). Negotiating the Intimate and the Professional in Mom Blogging. In S. Taylor & S. Luckman (Eds.), *The New Normal of Working Lives: Critical Studies in Contemporary Work and Employment* (pp. 129–146). Basingstoke: Palgrave Macmillan.

Manovich, L. (2001). *The Language of New Media*. Cambridge: MIT Press.
Mason, B. (1999). Issues in Virtual Ethnography. In K. Buckner (Ed.), *Proceedings of the Esprit i3 Workshop on Ethnographic Studies* (pp. 61–69). Edinburgh: Queen Margaret College.
Mauss, M. (2002). *The Gift: The Form and Reason for Exchange in Archaic Societies*. New York: Routledge.
Mishne, G., & Glance, N. (2006). Leave a Reply: An analysis of Weblog Comments. In *3rd Annual Workshop on the Weblogging Ecosystem: Aggregation, Analysis and Dynamics*. Edinburgh.
Miller, V. (2011). *Understanding Digital Culture*. London: Sage Publications.
Nathanson, E. (2014). Dressed for Economic Distress: Blogging and the "New" Pleasures of Fashion. In D. Negra & Y. Tasker (Eds.), *Gendering the Recession: Media and Culture in an Age of Austerity* (pp. 192–228). Durham: Duke University Press.
Rifkin, J. (2014). *The Zero Marginal Cost Society: The Internet of Things, the Collaborative Commons, and the Eclipse of Capitalism*. New York: Palgrave Macmillan.
Ritzer, G., Dean, P., & Jurgenson, N. (2012). The Coming of Age of the Prosumer. *American Behavioral Scientist, 56*(4), 379–398.
Scholz, T. (Ed.). (2013). *Digital Labor. The Internet as Playground and Factory*. New York: Routledge.
Simon, H. A. (1971). Designing Organizations for an Information-Rich World. In M. Greenberger (Ed.), *Computers, Communication, and the Public Interest* (pp. 37–72). Baltimore: The Johns Hopkins Press.
Simonet, M. (2010). *Le Travail bénévole. Engagement citoyen ou travail gratuit ?* Paris: La Dispute.
Stebbins, R. (2013). Unpaid Work of Love: Defining the Work-Leisure Axis of Volunteering. *Leisure Studies, 32*(3), 339–345.
Taylor, S., & Luckman, S. (Eds.). (2018). *The New Normal of Working Lives: Critical Studies in Contemporary Work and Employment*. Basingstoke: Palgrave Macmillan.
Terranova, T. (2000). Free Labour: Producing Culture for the Digital Economy. *Social Text, 2*(18), 33–58.
Zelizer, V. (2011). *Economic Lives: How Culture Shapes the Economy*. Princeton and Oxford: Princeton University Press.

Having or Blurring It All? Capitalism's Work at the Frontier

Maud Simonet

By studying how our domestic and leisure activities are being commodified and marketized, this book makes a strong empirically based contribution to the study of today's capitalism.

As Anne Jourdain and Sidonie Naulin clearly point out in the introduction, there are, in the literature and beyond, two ways to look at this marketization of our domestic and leisure activity phenomenon. One, based on "our folk understanding of work" (Kaplan Daniels 1987) and where its frontiers lie, analyzes it as a marketization of "non-work" activities. Such an approach therefore tends to raise questions about the extension of the market logic and economic interests into our intimate, personal spheres, and about the contamination or pollution of our private worlds and values. The other approach to this phenomenon is the feminist one. Not buying into the doctrine of the "hostile worlds" and the great divide between economy and intimacy (Zelizer 2005), feminist approaches to domestic activities as "invisible work" and "unpaid labor"

M. Simonet
University Paris Nanterre, Nanterre, France
e-mail: msimonet@parisnanterre.fr

© The Author(s) 2020
S. Naulin, A. Jourdain (eds.), *The Social Meaning of Extra Money*, Dynamics of Virtual Work, https://doi.org/10.1007/978-3-030-18297-7

have pointed out the economic dimension of our mundane everyday life. For Marxist feminists, "our kitchens and our bedrooms" (Cox and Federici 1975), conceptualized as reproduction factories operating with unpaid invisible labor, are the basic structures of capitalism. Hence, from a feminist perspective, the marketization of (women's) everyday life is not a move from "non-work" to work. It's a move from unpaid to paid work. Following that perspective, one could therefore think, as the editors suggest, that marketization paradoxically carries hopes of emancipation. When economic value is placed on its production, the invisible worker might be recognized as a "real" worker.

But the collection of detailed empirical studies this book has gathered clearly demonstrates that this is not a linear nor an inevitable process. The marketization of knitting, crafts, food, or personal belongings, of blogging or sexcamming, does not necessarily lead to the full (economic, social, and legal) visibilization of the person, mostly a woman, who produces and markets these activities, as a worker. *The Social Meaning of Extra Money* does not depict a "professionalization of everyone" phenomenon, nor does it simply describe the commodification of amateurism and housework. What is pointed out and analyzed here is rather the development of a gray zone between unpaid (amateur and domestic) work and paid (professional) work and its different, and even divided, social uses and meanings. Through its multiple but consistent voices, this book is not telling us the story of a frontier that is being crossed but rather the story of a frontier that is being expanded. And it questions who benefits from it and what they benefit from.

Long before platform capitalism, R. Stebbins (1979) once wrote that, when you look close enough, the frontier between leisure and work is more of a continuum, and even more a spectrum, based on multiple criteria (time engagement, peer control, type and amount of remuneration) which differ from one work sphere to another. But he added that for the sake of research, academics felt they needed to step away and put a frontier somewhere. According to him, they usually put it in the wrong place—that is, between amateurs and professionals. If there was a need for a frontier, he said, it should be to separate the casual amateurs from the serious amateurs and the professionals.

The Social Meaning of Extra Money, with its strong empirical grounding, puts that frontier under the microscope. It shows us how wide that frontier is, the different positions that could be inhabited there, and, most importantly, how those positions are distributed along social and gender lines. "Pin money," "savings," and "low income"—the three meanings of extra money illustrated in the book—each relates to a different position along that frontier: a serious hobby, a second job on the side, and an ideal career. As the different contributors point out, all these positions can co-exist within the same activity, but they are never equally distributed. The self-financed hobby and professionalization approach mostly concern middle- and upper-class individuals. The second job on the side is used by the lower classes trying to make ends meet but also to some members of the upper classes in an unstable work situation. All in all, the extra money comes in small amounts, but whatever the activity and the meaning given to it, you are always more likely to make more of it if you are a man and if you already have economic or social capital to invest.

The Social Meaning of Extra Money does not only show us how the frontiers are blurred and expanded, and how this economically benefits "the haves" more than "the have nots." It also amplifies the motto that supports and surrounds it: "Having it all," "getting paid to do what you love," as B. E. Duffy already noted and studied (2017). By combining domestic and professional space-time, leisure, and work, platform marketization promises to reconcile "hostile worlds." But the reality, for most of the workers depicted in the book, is meager economic gains and more invisible unpaid work, in the form of that extra emotional and relational work that is necessary to brand and market your product, and sometimes yourself. This specific romance, as well as the work conditions and remuneration created, reminds us, as N. Fraser has long claimed (since 2009), that there is also a feminine face to neoliberal capitalism and that we should pay more attention to it. Not only do the authors of this book take this advice seriously, but they have taken it into the field.

So why do people accept to stay in the game, stuck on the frontier if it does not pay and does create even more free work? It may be because, as the feminists have long told us, the value of work, whether it's paid, unpaid, or somewhere in the middle, is not just about money. There are moral and social values involved in that valuation too. Women's unpaid labor in the domestic sphere has usually been framed as the ultimate proof of women's value as good spouses, good mothers, ... good women. Workfare on the one side and volunteering on the other side are becoming political proof of our value as active citizens (Krinsky and Simonet 2017; Muehlebach 2012; Rose 2000), while in the "creative industries," and far beyond, unpaid internships are proving our value as a worker-to-be (Hesmondhalgh and Percival 2014; Mensitieri 2018). Unless we realize that someone else is benefiting from the value of our unpaid or low-paid work, we may be willing to keep doing it in the name of love, passion, or citizenship, and sometimes with a good amount of hope that it will pay off in the future (Kuehn and Corrigan 2013; Ross 2009). And even then, when the labor exploitation is made visible, it may not be that easy, for all these reasons, to end it (Simonet 2018). Raising the issue of values and exploitation thus leads us to another question about the profit this extra money is generating. What is the economic meaning, not for the workers but for the employers, of the expansion of the frontier between paid professional and unpaid domestic and amateur work? How exactly do web platforms generate profit from the marketization and commodification of our domestic and leisure activities, and to what extent? That is for sure another story to be told … one we can't help hoping each contributor to this book will soon share with us, in their detailed and subtle ethnographic manner, in a further volume.

References

Cox, N., & Federici, S. (1975). *Counter-Planning form the Kitchen.* Falling Wall Press.
Duffy, B. E. (2017). *(Not) Getting Paid to Do What You Love—Gender, Social Media, and Aspirational Work.* Yale University Press.
Fraser, N. (2009). Feminism, Capitalism, and the Cunning of History. *The New Left Review, 56,* 97–117.
Hesmondhalgh, D., & Percival, N. (2014). Unpaid Work in the UK Television and Film Industries: Resistance and Changing Attitudes. *European Journal of Communication, 29*(2), 188–203.
Kaplan Daniels, A. (1987). Invisible Work. *Social Problems, 34*(5), 403–415.

Krinsky, J., & Simonet, M. (2017). *Who Cleans the Park? Public Work and Urban Governance in New York City*. The University of Chicago Press.

Kuehn, K., & Corrigan, T. F. (2013). Hope Labor: The Role of Employment Prospects in Online Social Production. *The Political Economy of Communication, 1*(1), 9–25.

Mensitieri, G. (2018). *Le plus beau métier du monde—Dans les coulisses de l'industrie de la mode*. La Découverte.

Muehlebach, A. (2012). *The Moral Neoliberal: Welfare and Citizenship in Italy*. The University of Chicago Press.

Rose, N. (2000). Community, Citizenship and the Third Way. *American Behavorial Scientist, 47*(9), 1395–1411.

Ross, A. (2009). *Nice Work if You Can Get It: Life and Labour in Precarious Time*. NYU Press.

Simonet, M. (2018). *Travail Gratuit, la nouvelle exploitation?* Textuel.

Stebbins, R. (1979). *Amateurs: On the Margin Between Work and Leisure*. Sage.

Zelizer, V. (2005). *The Purchase of Intimacy*. Princeton: Princeton University Press.

Index[1]

NUMBERS AND SYMBOLS
2.0, 246

A
Ad, advertising, 1, 10, 40, 48, 62, 76, 78–80, 100, 102, 105, 107, 109, 112, 167, 172, 216, 240, 249–252, 254, 257, 259
Adkins, Lisa, 6–8, 35, 55, 62, 90, 91, 184, 263
Aesthetic, 18, 47, 72, 90, 104
Amateur, amateurism, 99, 211–232, 247, 253, 255, 256, 259, 261, 270, 272
Audience, 10, 12, 15, 46, 50, 53, 54, 62, 76, 86–89, 213, 214, 216–219, 221, 231, 247, 256, 258, 262
Authenticity, 19, 89, 90, 168, 170, 222–224, 232

B
Bankrupt, 152, 156, 162
Benefit/benefits, 11, 12, 14–17, 20, 22, 54, 69, 71, 74, 75, 82, 91, 98, 114, 124, 130–132, 163, 194, 195, 270–272
Blog, 2, 10, 12, 39, 46, 48, 53, 61–91, 212, 216, 220, 223, 229, 234n7, 240, 245, 246, 254, 263, 270
Bourdieu, Pierre, 3, 13, 77, 125, 186, 222, 223, 226, 240, 250

---

[1] Note: Page numbers followed by 'n' refer to notes.

Index

Brand, branding, 1, 17, 19, 37, 38, 40, 47, 76–78, 81, 82, 85, 87–89, 141, 147n7, 168, 169, 224, 226, 271

Business, business model, 5, 11, 14, 16, 18, 24, 36, 39, 43, 49, 62, 69–71, 75, 77, 79–82, 84, 87, 88, 90, 93n5, 99–102, 112, 124, 126, 130–132, 135–137, 141, 144, 145, 164, 168, 187–190, 192, 193, 200, 205n5, 212, 213, 216–224, 226, 227, 230–232, 234n6, 246, 250, 252, 257, 260–264

Buyer, buyers, client, customer, 3, 5, 15–17, 19, 22, 24, 66, 72, 82–85, 87, 90, 98–101, 103–105, 107–111, 113–115, 126, 131, 134, 142, 144, 145, 166–168, 170, 172, 175, 199, 211, 213–217, 221–223, 225–232

C

Career, 13, 15, 35, 49–53, 64, 69–71, 81, 157, 158, 161, 187–189, 191–192, 195–198, 200, 202, 219, 230, 231, 241, 242, 244, 249, 255, 259, 271

Casilli, Antonio, 5, 9, 20, 240

Casual, 6, 162, 270

Collaborative, 98, 99, 203, 240–242, 248, 250, 253, 260, 263

Comment, comments, 15, 19, 40, 43, 45, 46, 55, 83, 86, 88, 89, 192, 239, 240, 248, 249, 252, 254

Commerce, commercial, commercialization, 17, 35, 43, 49, 86, 87, 90, 93n5, 105, 106, 113, 121, 137–140, 153, 154, 165, 169, 174–176, 178, 213, 227–229, 232, 262, 264

Commodification, 1–3, 5–24, 35, 48, 53, 62–64, 66, 71, 72, 77, 79, 81, 82, 86, 87, 91, 151–178, 213, 224, 240, 251, 254, 257, 261, 270, 272

Community, 13, 15, 21, 39, 50, 53, 55, 62, 66, 83, 122, 124–126, 134, 135, 138, 143, 145, 229, 234n2, 240, 243, 246–252, 255–257, 259, 262

Competition, 15, 51, 93n4, 103, 141, 187, 189, 213

Consumption, conspicuous consumption, 33–55, 66, 98, 99, 102, 105, 110, 153, 155, 159, 164, 183, 201, 243, 247, 263

Conviviality, 20, 22, 111, 113

Craft, 5, 9, 10, 14, 34, 39, 46, 52, 53, 62–65, 69–71, 73, 78–81, 84, 86, 89, 90, 192, 193, 270

Creation, 7, 9, 10, 35, 40, 46, 49, 63, 90, 166, 178, 189, 246

Creativity, 7, 15, 34, 53, 68, 77, 82, 89, 142

Culture, 3, 9, 39, 214, 225, 234n8, 239, 248, 254, 261–263

D

Database, 17, 21, 35–37, 39–42, 44–48, 52, 55, 205n1, 240, 244
Dever, Maryanne, 6, 8, 35, 55, 91, 184, 263
Device, 35, 41, 42, 99, 100, 114, 199, 213–219, 231, 242, 243, 249, 259
Digital, 4, 5, 9, 11–13, 16, 20, 21, 23, 34, 35, 37, 54, 62, 88, 91, 97, 98, 100, 106, 107, 203, 214, 215, 220, 224, 229, 231, 234n4, 239, 241, 245–247, 249–251, 253, 254, 260, 263, 264
Digital labor, 9, 17, 20, 88, 240, 255, 263
Do It Yourself (DIY), 19, 33, 38, 39, 48, 52, 61, 67, 80, 86, 90, 185, 225, 228, 234n8
Domestic, domesticity, 1–19, 21–23, 33–36, 42, 45–48, 53–55, 63, 65–67, 72–75, 81, 84, 86, 91, 123, 127, 129, 137, 151–178, 187, 192, 204, 224, 231, 232, 269, 271, 272
Domestic work, 4, 7, 54, 55, 63, 270
Duffy, Brooke Erin, 19, 55, 89, 212, 245, 249, 260, 271

E

Earning, 1, 4, 6, 7, 12–14, 20, 42, 53, 63, 64, 70, 75–80, 82, 84, 91, 93n4, 110, 137, 145, 164, 185, 191, 196–198, 202, 213, 217, 218, 221, 222, 226, 234n6, 250–263
Economy, economic, 2–6, 10, 12–15, 17, 20–24, 33, 35–37, 39–42, 45, 53, 55, 63, 72, 74–82, 86, 93n4, 98, 106, 108, 110–112, 115, 122–125, 128, 130, 134, 135, 138, 145, 151–154, 156–158, 162–165, 183–204
Effort, 21, 47, 167–169, 195, 228, 241, 245, 257
Empower, empowerment, 4, 5, 8, 11, 16, 17, 24, 38, 63, 64, 72, 85, 91, 123, 124, 138, 145, 212
Entrepreneur, entrepreneurship, 4, 6–8, 16, 20, 36, 55, 62, 66, 69, 71, 81, 87, 90, 139, 180n3, 192, 214, 216, 217, 221, 224, 227, 250, 260, 261
Exchange, 20, 22, 37, 39, 40, 45, 46, 83, 84, 86, 100, 104, 105, 107, 132, 134, 137, 173, 248, 250, 251
Exploitation, 5, 9, 123, 224, 240, 241, 251–254, 257, 259, 262, 264, 272
Extra work, 2, 35, 64, 98, 123, 154, 158, 183, 211–232, 240, 269–272

F

Facebook, 5, 9, 39, 46, 72, 88, 122, 143, 144
Family, 8, 14, 16–18, 22, 34, 35, 40, 53, 54, 63–65, 67, 72–74, 81, 82, 89–91, 122–125, 130–133, 135–141, 144, 153–155, 158, 159, 161–166, 174,

177, 184, 185, 187, 189, 191–194, 197, 201, 218, 219
Fan, fans, 14, 15, 18, 24, 229, 239–244, 246, 248–257, 259, 263, 264
Femininity, 4, 7–12, 17, 19, 22, 271
Free, 2, 16, 20, 21, 36, 40, 43, 47–51, 57n5, 62, 68, 77–79, 81, 82, 91, 99–101, 108, 110, 186, 215, 216, 228, 240, 241, 250, 257, 258, 261, 264, 271
Free labor, 9, 20, 91, 240, 241, 257, 259
Free time, 2, 6, 9, 12–14, 19, 22, 23, 65, 66, 112, 183–204, 212, 244–246, 260, 263
Fulfillment, 68, 71, 91, 201, 204, 247
Full-time job, 18, 24, 52, 86, 204, 223
Fun, 19, 20, 35, 212, 217, 218, 224, 240, 248, 263

G

Game, 22, 41, 68, 87, 105, 107, 109–115, 211, 228, 229, 251, 252, 271
Gender, 3, 8, 9, 11, 12, 14, 21, 23, 63, 64, 81, 124, 127, 136–138, 145, 161, 185, 192–193, 212, 214, 215, 221, 241, 271
Gig economy, 12, 13
Gill, Rosalind, 7, 11, 241
Global, globalization, 3, 4, 6, 11, 13, 128, 139, 147n8, 183, 184, 252
Goffman, Erving, 19, 73, 89, 106, 115

H

Handicraft, 12, 21, 34, 39, 45, 53, 61–91
Hiatus, 14, 53, 64–67, 70, 86, 157
Hobby, 14, 20, 23, 34, 36, 50–52, 63, 64, 66, 69, 71, 72, 74, 78, 79, 86, 90, 91, 271
Hochschild, Arlie Russel, 7, 19, 123, 223, 232
Home, 1, 5, 19, 24, 37, 43, 54, 62, 63, 65–68, 71, 91, 100, 101, 105, 107, 113, 114, 121, 125, 127, 129–131, 133–138, 140, 145, 147n9, 156, 158, 168, 169, 175, 176, 178, 187, 191, 192, 195, 201, 203, 212, 218, 219, 224, 225, 232
Hostile worlds, 3, 82, 240, 249–251, 269, 271
Household, 4, 15–17, 23, 53, 68, 73, 85, 125, 130, 131, 135–138, 145, 152–154, 157, 158, 163–165, 167–170, 172–174, 176–178, 183, 184, 201
Huws, Ursula, 5, 6, 8, 12, 69, 239

I

Income, incomes, 1–3, 6, 9, 11, 21, 23, 34, 53, 62, 63, 70, 74–76, 79, 80, 84, 91, 93n4, 125, 129, 130, 137, 153, 164, 186, 189, 196–198, 201, 202, 213, 221, 225, 229, 233, 234n6, 240, 249, 250, 256–264, 271
Independence, 13, 91, 122, 137, 145, 195–200, 218, 254

Inequalities, 5, 11, 13, 18, 21, 64, 81, 98, 212, 241, 246
Information, 35, 38–44, 46, 54, 64, 73, 87, 88, 101, 105, 107, 136, 138, 142, 168, 180n5, 187, 203, 233, 234n6, 240, 241, 243, 253, 265n2
Information and communication technology (ICT), 5, 39, 211
Infrastructure, 35, 39–41, 54
Insecure jobs, 13, 121–145
Insecurity, 7, 13, 128, 129, 145, 218, 245
Instagram, 5, 39, 46, 49, 72, 88
Interaction, 15–17, 19, 22, 35, 40–42, 47, 51, 82–84, 87, 98, 100, 101, 111–115, 157, 184, 194, 215, 216, 227–229, 244, 252
Interest, 20, 36, 38, 41, 42, 44, 54, 65, 68, 70, 74, 83, 99, 104, 109–113, 132, 220, 222, 228, 232, 240, 242, 249, 250, 261, 269
Internet, 4, 8, 10, 35–39, 41, 43, 46, 49, 52, 53, 66, 68, 72, 75–86, 98–100, 122, 143, 144, 203, 211, 213, 216, 217, 224, 225, 227–229, 232, 234n7, 239, 240, 242, 248, 250, 253, 255, 256, 260, 263
Intersectionality, 124, 241
Intimacy, 8, 228, 230, 231, 251, 269
Intimate transaction, 16, 34, 46, 82
Invisibility, 7–9, 54, 203
Item, items, 1, 2, 10, 19, 22, 51, 61, 63, 71, 72, 79, 81, 82, 86, 91, 97–115, 121, 147n2, 187, 240

J
Jarrett, Kylie, 8, 9, 86

K
Karpik, Lucien, 168, 226, 243
Knowledge, 18, 39, 53, 54, 72, 103, 104, 107, 124, 135, 138, 187, 201, 247, 255
Kopytoff, Igor, 3, 168

L
Labor, labour, 5, 7–14, 16, 17, 19, 20, 22, 55, 63, 88, 90, 91, 125, 152, 161, 162, 174, 176, 183, 185, 194, 197, 221, 225, 231, 240, 241, 245, 250, 255, 257, 259, 263, 264, 269, 270, 272
Labor market, labour market, 4, 6, 91, 123, 124, 128, 152, 156–158, 186, 195
Learning, 18, 22, 38, 39, 53, 99–101, 108–111, 115, 194, 220, 231, 232, 253
Legitimacy, 16, 23, 50, 72, 174
Leisure, 1–6, 8–22, 24, 33–55, 61–91, 100, 185–187, 192–195, 202, 241, 246, 257, 258, 260, 263, 264, 269–272
Local, 19, 34, 48, 55, 84, 126, 127, 145, 158, 169, 202, 203
Lower class, 2, 6, 7, 11, 13, 22, 23, 122, 271
Luckman, Susan, 7, 8, 19, 34, 36, 63, 71, 89, 91, 192, 240, 264
Lund, Arwid, 20, 87, 240, 241

M

Man, men, male, 8, 10–14, 17, 23, 24, 33, 43, 64, 70, 75, 81, 123–125, 127, 128, 132, 133, 137, 141, 147n12, 154, 159, 161, 174–178, 184–188, 191–193, 195, 196, 200, 202, 204, 213–215, 217, 241, 242, 263, 264, 271

Market, 2–6, 10, 15, 17, 19–21, 34–43, 45, 47, 49, 50, 55, 62, 82–84, 87, 88, 90, 97–101, 103–105, 108–111, 113, 114, 126, 129, 134, 139, 142, 143, 147n7, 152–154, 156, 159, 161, 163–168, 173–176, 178, 186, 197, 202, 211, 212, 214, 216, 223, 226, 229, 230, 232, 246, 250–255, 269–271

Marketing, 19, 69, 75, 87, 89, 102–105, 147n9, 153, 161, 175, 176, 178, 224

Marketization, 1–24, 61–91, 124, 152, 154, 167–169, 173, 174, 185, 199, 200, 213, 223, 227, 231, 241, 254, 255, 260, 269–272

Meaning, 2, 3, 11, 12, 20, 21, 37, 54, 91, 97, 99, 154, 172, 212, 240, 246, 270–272

Media, 4, 7, 9, 11, 12, 34, 36, 39, 42, 46, 62, 80, 84, 85, 88, 100, 220, 228

Middle class, middle-class, 1, 4, 8, 63, 68, 84, 89, 183–204, 222, 242, 264

Monetize, monetization, 9, 10, 12, 13, 213, 222–225, 240, 246, 249, 252–257, 259–263

Money, extra money, 1–4, 6, 7, 11–14, 17–21, 24, 33, 34, 53, 61–91, 98, 110, 127, 129, 130, 132–134, 136, 144, 145, 164, 184–186, 197, 202, 213, 218, 222–224, 229, 230, 232, 239–264, 271, 272

Moral, 3, 18, 34, 73, 74, 214, 224, 232, 272

Motherhood, 63, 66, 71, 84

Mumpreneur, 14, 71, 84, 90

Myth, 71, 212, 222, 224, 231, 232

N

Network, 4, 5, 34, 35, 37–42, 46, 53–55, 72, 122, 125, 128, 130, 134–139, 141–144, 157, 170, 171, 201, 215, 243, 246–248, 260, 262, 263

Non-economic benefits, non-economic profits, 14–17, 20, 22, 75, 81–86, 98, 111

Non-professional, 2, 22, 50, 89, 97–101, 112–113, 138, 151, 223, 247, 255–259

O

Opportunity, 4, 7, 67, 68, 79, 91, 99, 100, 110, 140, 260, 261

P

Partner, partnership, 1, 14, 48, 50, 67, 73–75, 80, 81, 84, 85, 88, 91, 184, 202, 218

Passion, 7, 14, 15, 19, 24, 63, 66, 69, 73, 77, 83, 89, 90, 203,

239–241, 243, 245, 246, 249–255, 260–264, 272
Photo, 40, 45–47, 49, 50, 52, 57n5, 74, 86, 177, 216, 217, 228, 234n8
Picture, 17, 19, 39, 50, 73, 78, 83, 84, 87, 88, 90, 91, 104, 226, 230
Pin money, 2, 11–14, 20–22, 62, 75, 79, 271
Platform, digital platform, web platform, 1, 4, 5, 9, 11–13, 15, 16, 20–22, 35–41, 47, 50, 61, 62, 71, 72, 76, 78, 80, 82, 86, 88, 90, 91, 97–104, 122, 139, 143, 144, 193, 203, 211, 212, 214, 216, 217, 220, 221, 223, 229, 231–233, 234n2, 234n7, 234n9, 240–243, 252–255, 260, 264, 270–272
Play, 20, 41, 64, 68, 74, 87, 99, 100, 108, 110–115, 124, 136, 171, 199, 224, 230, 231, 234n4, 240, 244
Playbor, 20, 240
Pleasure, 15, 20–22, 63, 68, 78, 91, 223, 228, 231, 239, 240, 244, 263
Post-Fordism, 4, 7
Practice, 2, 15, 21, 22, 34–37, 39, 41–44, 46–48, 51, 53–55, 68, 98, 101, 102, 106, 108–115, 122, 125, 127–129, 132, 144, 152, 154, 155, 172, 174, 187, 192–194, 200–204, 219, 223–225, 227, 232, 242, 247, 254
Precarity, precariousness, 178, 186
Presentation, 72, 89, 265n3

Prestige, 134, 195, 203
Price, pricing, 2–4, 15, 17, 34, 37, 38, 50–52, 73, 77, 87, 103, 105, 108, 110, 112, 114, 134, 139, 141–143, 161, 164, 168, 173, 175, 177, 252, 264
Product, 2, 4, 5, 7, 16, 17, 19, 20, 22, 46, 62, 76–78, 80, 82, 85, 86, 88, 90, 98, 100–110, 112, 114, 115, 122, 126, 127, 134, 139, 141, 143, 144, 147n4, 152, 163, 169–171, 193, 223, 247, 251, 252, 262, 271
Production, conspicuous production, 3, 5, 9, 16, 19, 21, 33–55, 68, 70, 90, 147n9, 152–164, 168–173, 175–178, 180n2, 180n3, 219, 225, 240, 253, 264
Professional, 2, 7, 9, 12–15, 18, 20, 23, 24, 35, 36, 41, 43, 47, 49–53, 55, 64, 67, 69, 70, 72, 73, 77, 78, 80, 81, 84, 88, 90, 91, 93n4, 93n5, 98–100, 104, 105, 107, 112, 125, 145, 151, 157, 158, 161, 174, 180n5, 186, 187, 190, 193–195, 197, 205n5, 212, 219, 223, 225–232, 244, 246–248, 251, 253, 254, 256–260, 262–264, 270–272
Professionalization, 14, 24, 88, 241, 255, 260, 261, 264, 270, 271
Profit, 2, 7, 51, 75–82, 125, 127, 184, 200, 202, 213, 241, 249–251, 262, 264

Profitability, 12, 23, 127, 140, 162–165, 192–193, 195, 249, 262
Promise, 14, 80, 138, 213, 214, 216, 222, 271
Promotion, 106, 114, 169, 195, 197, 198, 215, 217, 254
Public, 10, 16, 21, 35, 36, 38, 52, 54, 62, 66, 89, 115, 125, 129, 137, 216, 246, 253, 256, 262
Publication, 61, 62, 86, 246, 253

Q

Quality, 3, 19, 23, 36, 38, 45, 50, 55, 104, 168–173, 224, 239, 242, 247–249, 254, 262

R

Rank, ranking, 16, 38, 44, 77, 80, 84, 88, 187, 220, 233n2, 239, 240, 242, 248, 249, 252, 261
Rate, rating, 44, 57n3, 132, 215, 216, 222, 240, 248, 249
Recognition, 4, 8, 15, 20–22, 66, 72, 84, 91, 145, 174, 176–178, 223, 254, 257–259
Relations, 3, 55, 79, 101, 127, 132, 138, 175, 178, 184, 228, 232, 253, 263
Reputation, 17, 51, 53, 54, 88, 122, 145, 239, 249
Resource, 17, 21, 22, 34, 38–40, 64, 65, 70, 72, 73, 80, 86, 123, 124, 127, 128, 135, 136, 141, 152, 163, 190, 192, 196, 224, 248, 261
Review, 36, 44, 240, 243, 248, 252, 254, 261–263
Reward, 14–16, 20, 21, 40, 47, 51, 52, 57n5, 85, 174–176, 239–264
Risk, 6, 69, 108, 144, 193, 212, 216, 230
Role, 4–5, 8, 12, 16–18, 35, 37, 39–41, 43, 46, 47, 52, 55, 62, 64, 99–101, 108, 111–113, 115, 126, 137, 145, 152, 171, 174, 177, 178, 192, 199, 202, 243, 244
Rule, 104, 106, 108, 123, 178
Rural, 5, 127, 128, 147n9, 151–178, 203, 204

S

Sale, 42, 48, 55, 70, 73, 75, 76, 80, 91, 97–102, 104, 105, 112, 115, 126, 134, 144, 154, 159, 161, 162, 167, 168, 173, 175, 176, 190, 193, 217, 240
Savings, 2, 11–14, 20, 22, 147n6, 226, 271
Scholz, Trebor, 5, 9, 20, 88, 240
Second-hand, 22, 97–115, 139
Self, 24, 89, 98, 249
Self-employment, 5, 71, 196, 198
Seller, sellers, 18, 20–22, 42, 52, 62, 64, 66, 68, 69, 71–82, 84–91, 93n4, 98–102, 106–115, 142
Service, 4, 5, 7, 12, 15, 17, 36, 40, 48, 61, 62, 81, 86, 100, 108, 125, 126, 128, 134, 142, 156,

Index

183, 195, 196, 199, 205n5, 214, 221, 223, 224, 226, 228, 232, 240, 250, 253, 260
Sharing economy, 5, 217, 255
Shop, 1, 40, 48, 50, 62, 64, 66, 67, 69, 72, 73, 76, 79, 80, 82, 84–90, 139, 140, 145, 155, 165–169, 194
Side job, sideline activity, 2, 13, 14, 20, 22, 23, 80, 185, 196, 204, 223, 258
Simonet, Maud, 7, 9, 257, 272
Singularization, 3, 167–171, 226
Skill, skills, 5, 7, 15–19, 21, 22, 24, 34, 39, 48, 49, 53, 54, 65, 68, 72, 73, 75, 78, 80, 81, 86–88, 90, 97–115, 124, 128, 145, 174–176, 178, 186, 190, 194, 201–203, 213, 219, 220, 226, 229, 232, 241, 245–246, 259, 263
Social class, 3, 11, 12, 21, 23
Socialization, 15, 52–54, 82–84, 107, 140, 144
Social mobility, 123, 158, 162
Social reproduction, 9, 90
Stable job, 162, 197
Stage, staging, 19, 47, 73, 90, 101, 130, 175, 213, 219, 223, 226, 227, 246
Standardization, 42, 47
Status, 2, 9, 13, 16, 23, 41, 47, 52, 53, 101, 107, 108, 110, 114, 135, 145, 158, 174, 180n3, 184–187, 192, 195, 196, 198, 201, 203, 204, 221, 250, 255, 257, 258, 260, 264
Stebbins, Robert, 9, 86, 257, 270

Subsistence, 14, 157, 163, 164, 169, 170
Success, 18, 35, 63, 80, 81, 85, 89, 100, 111–113, 126, 127, 189, 192, 213, 220, 222, 225, 227, 228, 247, 253, 260, 263
Symbol, 39, 178

T

Taylor, Stephanie, 7, 34, 62, 63, 91, 192, 240, 263, 264
Technical, 34, 37–39, 42, 45, 54, 98, 111, 114, 173, 198, 201, 202, 204, 224, 226, 241, 245–246
Terranova, Tiziana, 9, 20, 91, 240, 241
Trade, trader, 16–18, 22, 43, 50, 66, 77, 93n5, 121–145, 154, 161, 170–172, 176–178, 183, 212, 223–231, 253, 264
Transaction, 5, 10, 15, 20, 34, 35, 41, 46, 62, 76, 83, 84, 99–101, 105–107, 110, 111, 113, 114, 161, 173, 229–232
Transnationalism, 18, 22, 121–147
Trust, 99–101, 104, 115, 125, 130, 214
Twitter, 5, 72, 88, 214–216, 221, 223, 227, 228, 230

U

Unemployment, 6, 7, 13, 14, 23, 69, 130, 132
Upper class, upper-class, 2, 11–13, 22, 23, 63, 75, 185, 186, 201, 220, 234n5, 271

V

Value, valuation, 4, 6, 7, 9–11, 14–16, 19, 20, 24, 33–55, 89, 90, 98, 100, 103, 105, 110–112, 136, 151–178, 216, 228, 239, 240, 246, 250–253, 255, 257, 259, 264, 269–272

Volunteer, volunteers, 50, 52, 250, 256, 260, 261, 264

W

Wage, 7, 8, 14, 53, 69, 74, 80, 128–130, 132, 136, 158, 222, 261, 263

Weber, Florence, 9, 33, 42, 45, 46, 52, 124, 184, 198, 204, 223

Website, websites, 12, 14, 18, 24, 35, 37, 39, 40, 43, 48, 55, 77, 84, 99, 100, 103, 104, 107–112, 114, 193, 195, 213, 214, 216, 217, 220, 223, 224, 233n2, 234n8, 240–264, 265n2–4

Woman, women, female, 8, 11, 13, 14, 17, 21, 24, 39, 54, 55, 63, 66, 71, 72, 81, 86, 91, 121, 123, 126–129, 132–134, 137, 141, 147n4, 174, 175, 177, 180n6, 186, 215, 218, 219, 222, 224, 225, 270

Work-life balance, 4, 14, 43, 54

Y

YouTube, 39, 50, 224, 226

Z

Zelizer, Viviana, 2, 3, 13, 16, 34, 46, 78, 82, 136, 178, 229, 240, 251, 269

Lightning Source UK Ltd.
Milton Keynes UK
UKHW051452090919
349113UK00009B/4/P